William S. Phillips's painting of
Hanna Reitsch test flying a prototype of
a rocket-propelled plane, the Me 163B.

Seconds after takeoff, Hanna Reitsch pulled
the lever that should have released the launching
trolley, but did not. Her instructions in such
case were to bail out. She successfully landed.

The detail from the above painting that
appears on the cover of this edition is used by
courtesy of The Greenwich Workshop.

# THE DEVIL'S SLED

The Me 163B hit a ploughed field just short of the runway at 150 mph, bounced violently twice, lost a wheel, and came to a standstill after a 180 degree turn. Hanna's first thought was that as she was not hanging in her straps she was at least the right way up, although she was convinced that the aircraft had somersaulted, and that she was alive. Luckily there was none of the lethal rocket mixture on board: had there been, she would have been killed instantly.

She automatically opened the cockpit roof and undid her shoulder straps. Cautiously, she ran her hand over her body to check for injuries: there were none. Then she noticed a trickle of blood from her head. She traced its source to her nose, or rather, a cleft where her nose had been.

When she turned her head, everything went dark, so she kept as still as possible. Carefully, without moving her head, she fished her pencil and notebook from her pocket and tried to describe what had happened. Then she tied her handkerchief round her face to spare the rescue party the shock of seeing how badly injured she was, and also perhaps as a brave gesture of vanity. Only then did she allow herself to pass out. "What a woman!" Späte later commented.

## THE BANTAM AIR & SPACE SERIES

To Fly Like the Eagles . . .

It took some 1800 years for mankind to win mastery of a challenging and life-threatening environment—the sea. In just under 70 years we have won mastery of an even more hostile environment—the air. In doing so, we have realized a dream as old as man—to be able to fly.

The Bantam Air & Space series consists of books that focus on the skills of piloting—from the days when the Wright brothers made history at Kitty Hawk to the era of barnstorming daredevils of the sky, through the explosion of technology, design, and flyers that occurred in World War II, and finally to the cool daring of men who first broke the sound barrier, walked the Moon and have lived and worked in space stations—always at high risk, always proving the continued need for their presence and skill.

The Air & Space series will be published once a month as mass market books with special illustrations, and with varying lengths and prices. Aviation enthusiasts would be wise to buy each book as it comes out if they are to collect the complete Library.

# FLYING FOR THE FATHERLAND

## The Century's Greatest Pilot

## Judy Lomax

FALCON ™

BANTAM BOOKS
NEW YORK · TORONTO · LONDON · SYDNEY · AUCKLAND

*This edition contains the complete text
of the original hardcover edition.*
NOT ONE WORD HAS BEEN OMITTED.

FLYING FOR THE FATHERLAND

*A Bantam Falcon Book / published by arrangement with
John Murray (Publishers) Ltd.*

*PRINTING HISTORY*
*John Murray (Publishers) Ltd. edition published 1988*
*Bantam edition / July 1991*

PRINTED IN THE UNITED STATES OF AMERICA

OPM   0  9  8  7  6  5  4  3  2  1

# Contents

*Acknowledgements*                                          vii

1   **A Patriotic Childhood**                                1
2   **Winged Student**                                      13
3   **Spreading Wings**                                     28
4   **Flight Captain Reitsch**                              46
5   **From Peace to War**                                   63
6   **Flying for the Future**                               75
7   **High and Low**                                        89
8   **Desperate Measures**                                 104
9   **Descent into Hell**                                  119
10  **The Prisoner**                                       136
11  **Suspicion and Persecution**                          154
12  **At Home and Abroad**                                 170
13  **Flying for Nkrumah**                                 184
14  **Success but No Escape**                              200
15  **Death of a Patriot**                                 216

## Appendices

1 Extracts from a letter by Hanna
  Reitsch to her brother Kurt                228

2 Extracts from 'The Last Days in
  Hitler's Air Raid Shelter' Interrogation
  Summary                                   233

3 Extracts from Trevor-Roper's Introduction
  to *The Last Days of Hitler*              256

Bibliography                                258

Chronology                                  263

Index                                       268

# Acknowledgements

Without the co-operation of people who knew Hanna Reitsch, I could not have attempted to write her life story. I am particularly grateful for the help of her brother Kurt and his wife Helma, who have given me hospitality both in Hanna's flat in Frankfurt and in their own home, and to Ernst Paulsen and Helmut Heuberger for their unfailingly helpful advice.

I have interviewed glider pilots and test pilots, diplomats and journalists, people who knew Hanna at school, during the Second World War, in prison, and in Germany, Austria, England, India, Ghana and the United States. Gradually the circle widened as one person led me to another. People who did not know me, as well as those I was able to meet, have given me documents, letters, tapes, and photographs, and have answered innumerable questions patiently and painstakingly.

At home, the librarians at Newbury Library have coped cheerfully with my insatiable requests for books, many of them published long ago and never translated into English. My family and friends have also given me their support without complaining, and my husband in particular has made many valuable suggestions.

I am grateful to the publishers of Hanna Reitsch's autobiographical books for permission to quote from both the German and English editions. In many cases, however, I have used my own translations. Thanks are due to Erica Powell for allowing me to use an unpublished typescript on which she and Hanna Reitsch worked.

Wherever direct speech is given, I have used the spoken or written words of my sources, translated where necessary. When conversations and incidents were related to me from memory, I have endeavoured to check their accuracy, as I have also tried to do with written accounts.

I hope that all those who have helped me during my research will forgive me for simply including them in an alphabetical list of acknowledgements (* denotes personal interview):

*Individuals*: Horst Amberg; Col. Neil Armstrong; Waltraud Bals*; John Barker; Professor Rudolf von Baumgarten; Marie-Josephe de Beauregard; Elly Beinhorn*; Marianne Berg; Inge Berger; Nancy Bird Walton; Barney Blackley; I. D. Blackwood; Ingrid Blecher; Thilo Bode*; Gretl Böss*; Tom Bower; Clifford Boxsey; Jack Brackenbury; Wing-Commander Reginald Brie; Captain Eric Brown*; Käthe Bruhn; Lt-Col. H. W. Bushey; Colin Butters; Dr Nora Campbell; Ninin Moreno Cassini*; Ary Ceelen; Rick Chapman; Elfrieda Chudoba; John Coker; John Coleman; Lord Dacre of Glanton (formerly Hugh Trevor-Roper); Helmut Dette*; Hans Deutsch*; Robin Dispain*; Edgar Dittmar*; Rudi Dollinger*; Elisabeth Dornbusch; Robert Dreschler; Brian Drewitt; W. F. von Engelhardt; T. M. Fairmiloe; Charlotte Faust; Dr Herbert Fleissner; Michael Fleissner; Dr Forstmeier; Susanne Först; Herr Forwig; Carl Francke*; Scott Fraser; Peter Fruehoff; Otto Fuchs*; Generalleutnant Adolf Galland; Erwin Glasenapp*; Peter Gray; Capt. Delphine Gray Fiske*; Hubert Greim; Frank Handscomb; Bill Harrison; Rika Harwood*; Sylvia Henseler-Trinkaus; Hajo Hermann; Gertrud Heuberger*; Helmut and Adelheid Heuberger*; Barron Hilton; Clara (Lala) Hirth; Gisela and Armin Holzrichter*; Jean Ross Howard*; Hanna Hubner-Kunath*; David Irving; Hans Jacobs*; John Jeffreys; Brian Johnson*; Brigitte Keller; Bruce Kendall; David Killingray; Gisela von Koppenfels; Dedo Graf Schwerin von Krosigk; Barbar Kuchler; Dr Joachim Küttner*; Heiner Lange; Sidney Liat; Byron Lichtenberg; Täwe Löhr*; William Mahoney; Maria Mayer; Basil Meads; June Milne; Rajeet Mitter; R. G. Moulton; Timothy Mulligan; Wolfgang Muthesius; Heinz Nowarra; Claudia Oakes; Michael Oakey; Dr Georg Pasewaldt*; Bde-Gen. Ernst and Dr Carola Paulsen*; Father Karl Pehl*; Heinz Peters*; Gertrud Piehl; Vera von Pirscher; Erica Powell*; Hilda Rautenberg; Philip Reed; Dr Walter Reichhold; Kurt and Wilhelma Reitsch*; Jim Reynolds; Michael Riddell*; Peter and Helen Riedel*; Otto Rietdorf*; Lawrence Robertson; Michael Rubinstein; Dagma Rüter; Landa Ruprecht (*née* Klaus)*; W. Sachsenberg; Hanna Schantl*; Elisabeth Scheel; Karl Schieferstein*; Dr Lotte Schiffler*; Cläre Schiller; Hans Schütz; Sheila Scott*; Richard Searle; Dr Hedi Seebacher; Meera Shankar; Biddy Shout; Sergei Sikorsky; Daniel Simon; Peter Skinner; John Slattery; Shirley Souza; Wolfgang Späte*; Cheryl Spalding; Otto Spätz*; Maggy von Spaun*; Berthold Schenk Graf von Stauffenberg; Lisa Steimmig; Georg Steltzer*; Walter and

Erica Stender*; B. J. Stephens; M. Stiegler; Dr Anne Stolle; Karl and Suzanne Striedeck; Irene Teutloff*; Bernard Thomas; Hannes Trautloft; James Tucker*; Lex Tudhope*; Mark Tully; Joh. A. Freiherr von la Valette*; Karl Vey*; Eugen Wagner; Dr Berndt von Waldow; Wing-Commander K. H. Wallis; Robert F. Walsh, Jr.; Anna Walter*; Dr. Ruth Wasner; Fred Weinholtz*; Ann Welch*; Vivian White; Chris Wills*; Ron Wilson; Frank Winter; Hans Wolf*; Robert Wolfe; Ron Wood*; Wing-Commander Gerry Woods; Colonel Robert Work; Mano Ziegler*.

*Organisations* Alte Adler (West Germany); Austrian Women Pilots' Association; Berlin Document Center (Mission of the USA); British Women Pilots' Association; Derbyshire & Lancashire Gliding Club; Deutscher Aero Club; Deutsches Museum, Munich; Fédération d'Aviation Internationale; Fédération des Pilotes Européennes; German Bundesarchiv, Koblenz and Freiberg; German Embassy, London; German Women Pilots' Association; Helicopter Foundation International; Historical Aviation Service; Imperial War Museum; Landmannschaft Schlesien (West Germany); National Air & Space Museum, Smithsonian Institution, Washington, DC; National Archives (USA), Washington, DC; Newbury Library; RAF Air Historical Branch, Personnel Management Centre; RAF Museum, Hendon; Royal Aircraft Establishment, Farnborough; Twirly Birds; US Army Community and Family Support Center (Retired and Veterans Affairs Division); US Army Freedom of Information/Privacy Office; Wasserkuppe Pilots' Association; Whirly-Girls.

Denn
was auch immerauf
Erden beitcht,
beitcht durch Ehre
und Treue.
Wer heute die alte
Dtlicht verrät,
verrät auch morgen
die neue.

Adatbert Stifter


*For whatever survives on earth, survives through honour and truth.*
*He who today betrays the old duty tomorrow betrays the new.*
(Author's translation of quotation used by Hanna Reitsch on printed cards)

# FLYING FOR THE
# FATHERLAND

# A Patriotic Childhood

Hanna Reitsch was a child in one world war, and a heroine of Nazi Germany in the next. During her childhood in the eastern German province of Silesia, she absorbed the patriotic and religious beliefs of her parents. To these she added as a young woman an obsession with flying which, with her love for her Fatherland, became her lifelong inspiration and placed her on a public pedestal as a test pilot in the Third Reich.

She was born on a wet, windy night at the end of March 1912. Her character, even as a small child, showed all the contrasts of stormy weather: she was at the same time a compulsive extrovert and a self-conscious introvert. Her infectious laugh and sudden tears came equally readily, and she seemed to have inherited both her father's puritanical Prussian thoroughness, and her mother's Tyrolean exuberance.

Her mother, the eldest daughter of a widowed Austrian aristocrat, had convinced herself that she would die during the birth. It was always accepted in the family that this created an unusually and perhaps an unnaturally strong bond between herself and Hanna. Emy Reitsch was not normally a worrier; she talked effusively, with a basic common sense which drew family and friends alike to her for comfort and encouragement. Small and delicately built, she dressed simply, almost puritanically. Hanna adored her.

Neither Kurt, who was two years older than Hanna, nor Heidi, who was four years younger, caused Emy any serious concern: it was Hanna whom she considered the most sensitive of her three children, and whom she felt she had con-

1

stantly to protect against real or imagined dangers, and Hanna who needed to be calmed and guided.

Hanna also loved her father, but from a respectful distance. Doctor Willy Reitsch, an eye specialist, spoke only when he had something to say. He was thought to resemble Beethoven, with heavy eyebrows and a dark brooding expression, until he smiled: then he seemed more approachable. His outlook on life was serious, based on traditional Prussian concepts of honour and duty, and his appearance was always immaculate. Strict and expecting high standards of behaviour, he found it easier to deal with his son's misdemeanours than with the naughtiness and high spirits of his daughters. Kurt could be beaten, a ritual in which, while he was still small enough, his father would lay him across his knee and apply the full force of his hand.

On the one occasion when her father raised his hand to Hanna in anger, she ran away from home. She was seven years old, and had belched loudly and proudly, an accomplishment which she had just been taught by Kurt. It was long after dark when she returned home, frightened out of the woods by trees which seemed in the gloaming to have turned into menacing villains.

Both her parents were deeply religious and intensely patriotic, making no distinction between their respective Prussian and Austrian origins; their shared German-speaking background was more important than artificial territorial boundaries, and both felt themselves to be Germans in the broader cultural sense. Hanna learnt from an early age to believe in God and Germany, and to love her home in Silesia.

Doctor Reitsch and his wife had settled soon after their marriage in Hirschberg, a picturesque old Silesian town in a peaceful valley of fields, farms, and sun-dappled villages surrounded by wooded hills and snow-capped mountains. To the south lay Austria, to the east Russia; in 1918 Czechoslovakia became the southern neighbour and Poland the eastern. Although Silesia had for a short time, more than six centuries earlier, fallen under Polish rule, it had for several hundred years been under Austrian or German domination. In the nineteenth century it was firmly and patriotically a part of Germany, with strong Austrian traditions. The mountains reminded Emy, who never lost her soft Austrian accent, of the Tyrol.

One or other of the children often accompanied their father, a respected member of the community and of the local Masonic lodge, on home visits to his patients, or went with their mother on Lady Bountiful tours to distribute presents of food to those considered to be in need.

Hanna joined happily in the rough-and-tumble of her brother and his friends, dressed as often as not in practical lederhosen. After Heidi was born, she was fiercely protective, but still preferred the company of boys. Heidi, who was quieter, more even-tempered, and less physically adventurous, was considered the prettier of the two girls. Both were blue-eyed and blonde, but Hanna's features were sharper, her expression more intense, and the set of her jaw more determined.

When she was four, according to a much-told family story, Hanna made her first attempt to fly, and had to be restrained from leaping with arms spread as wings from the first-floor balcony. Later she took to climbing trees, and when she was eleven fractured her skull after falling from her perch on a high branch.

Their life was frugal and peaceful. The girls' dresses were lengthened and passed down until they could no longer be made to fit. Pleasures were made rather than bought, and among the most eagerly anticipated were family walks on fine summer weekends: then the children were sent to bed early on Saturday evening and woken at half past one in the morning to dress in the dark, before taking a tram through the valley to the foot of the nearby mountain range.

The sense of adventure made the three-hour uphill walk as dawn gradually broke over the mountains seem easy, although Heidi occasionally flagged. Then Hanna kept her going by telling her stories, old familiar tales and new ones drawn from her endlessly fertile imagination—her cousin Gertrud, who was nearer Heidi's age, never forgot sitting under a tree while Hanna kept a group of children enthralled with her story-telling ability.

Even after such an early and strenuous start to the day, there was always a family service at home before Sunday lunch. Grace was said before every meal. The existence and presence of God was accepted unquestioningly by the children. Willy Reitsch was a Protestant, but hated to parade his feelings in public and so rarely went to church. Emy, a devout Catholic, had agreed to bring the children up in her husband's faith, but made secret early morning visits to her church, often taking Hanna with her. The grandeur and solemnity, and the pervasive smell of incense and burning candles, made a deep impression on the child.

Music was as natural a part of their life as religion. Indeed, it was through their mutual love of music that Willy and Emy Reitsch had met. Willy was an accomplished amateur cellist. Although he was not otherwise a sociable man, he liked to invite other music-lovers to his home to play and to listen to string trios and quartets. The connecting doors between his consulting-room and the living-room were then thrown open to make more space, and Emy acted as hostess to both listeners and performers. Her parents' musical gatherings were among Hanna's earliest and happiest memories.

Almost before she could talk, Hanna could sing in tune, in a clear, high voice. One of her mother's favourite three-part Austrian yodelling songs was a prelude to every meal. Kurt played the violin, and Hanna and Heidi the piano, although they often found their father's perfectionism discouraging when they were practising.

Hanna was six when the First World War ended, leaving the family unharmed and life in Hirschberg outwardly as quiet and uneventful as before. Although Willy Reitsch explained to his children that patriotism was equally valid and important to people of every nation, it was felt particularly strongly in Silesia. By the Treaty of Versailles the eastern territory of Upper Silesia became part of Poland, and in the rest of the province the terms imposed on Germany by the Allies were bitterly resented.

Emy and Willy Reitsch shared the general feeling of injustice, and the fear that Communism might spread. Militant Communist uprisings in their own country following the Russian Revolution, and the experiences related by refugees from Baltic areas previously partly occupied by Germans, as well as by returning prisoners of war, strengthened the conviction that Communism was an evil which must at all costs be resisted.

Hanna absorbed her parents' patriotic outlook. She loved the town and surrounding countryside of Hirschberg as much as the spacious first-floor flat which had always been her home. In pride of place in her bedroom was a framed photograph of Emy Reitsch; posters and pastel drawings of the mountains partially covered one wall.

Heavy, dark wooden furniture, art books, pictures, and piles of music gave the flat an atmosphere of genteel and cultured solidity. It had a distinctive smell, neither pleasant nor unpleasant—a combination of aromas drifting from the kitchen, where simple but plentiful food was prepared on a huge range, from the consulting-room, where ether and other substances were stored in a row of carefully labelled jars, from the polish used on the parquet floors, and from a heating stove which stood in one corner of the living-room.

The dining-table was the family focal point. Mealtimes were cheerfully prolonged gatherings at which each member of the family related the experiences of the previous few hours. Hanna and Emy talked most. It was over the dinner-table that Hanna shared her enthusiasms, and voiced her grievances when she felt that she had been unfairly treated at school. This was usually when her 'honour' was at stake: then she would plunge from her normal exuberance into a depth of depression in which she sometimes convinced herself that she could no longer bear to live. She had inherited her sense of honour from her father; but it was sometimes difficult to tell exactly what she meant by it. Emy, who was protectively aware of her daughter's sensitivity to criticism, was usually ready to rush into school to sort out any difficulties; her husband was less sympathetic.

Hanna was, as a friend at the girls' school she attended in Hirschberg put it, 'difficult to overlook'. Outwardly she had such an air of self-confidence that few people outside her family were aware of how unhappy she sometimes felt. She could rarely stop talking for long, and laughed loudly, suddenly, and—or so it seemed to those who found her laugh irritating rather than infectious—unnecessarily often. The school class reports frequently commented that 'Hanna Reitsch laughs without reason.' She enjoyed being the centre of attention. If she considered a lesson to be boring it was often because she had not had enough opportunities to speak—'and that', she admitted, 'is terrible for me.'

Hanna was aware that she talked too much and was inclined to exaggerate, a tendency which she made strenuous but unsuccessful attempts to curb. 'Hanna always talked in superlatives,' one of her schoolfriends told me. 'Everything was larger than life when she talked—but that was just her way of expressing herself. There was no malice in her, although she could sometimes seem bossy or overpowering.' Her natural ability to talk was useful when she was required to give a class lecture, but the rest of her school work was rarely better than average.

When there was a disruption in the class, Hanna could usually be found at the bottom of it, well aware of the weaknesses of individual teachers and of how to play on them. She saw nothing wrong in minor deceptions, provided they hurt no one, such as using her excellent sight to catch a glimpse of some other girl's work, or copying a crib for a Latin translation. In spite of her highly developed sense of honour, Hanna never considered such subterfuges to be cheating. It was rather an expression of friendship both to give and to accept whatever help was available.

Although she was friendly and sociable, Hanna also enjoyed solitary walks and bicycle rides. Her destination during her last few years at school was often to some vantage point from which she could watch the activities of a gliding club on the Galgenberg: her parents never knew how often she cycled the few miles from Hirschberg to lie on the grass gazing enviously at the easy soaring flight of the birds and the attempts of the gliders to emulate them.

Walking, cycling, tree-climbing, and shooting with an airgun, as well as skiing and skating, were a natural part of life in Hirschberg, though Emy Reitsch discouraged other sports in case they caused injury or unfeminine muscles. Running in the streets, as many of the other girls did, was forbidden because it was unladylike.

It was in music, rather than in sport or study, that Hanna excelled. Her clear, high, soprano voice, and her ability and willingness to show off, made her a favourite of the music teacher, her father's friend Otto Johl. Among the sopranos in his 'Little Choir' Hanna's was the dominant voice, and on school open evenings she was often called upon to sing a solo, or a duet with the star of the contraltos.

Her social life was unsophisticated. Although many of her classmates had boyfriends, and Kurt's friend Gustav-Adolf admired her adoringly from a distance, she showed no romantic interest in the opposite sex. She was not allowed out alone in the evenings, and could only go to the local cinema if the film was considered suitable. Visits to her schoolfriends, who came from socially acceptable families in the area, took much the same form as the tea parties of their mothers.

From time to time there were receptions and dances, usually given by army officers and their wives: open sandwiches and wine were served and everyone, young and old, fat and thin, joined enthusiastically in old-fashioned waltzes and polonaises. Cavalry officers, many of them sporting Iron Crosses from the First World War, provided occasional daytime entertainment on horseback at steeplechases and mock hunts.

Sometimes a military band played in Hirschberg, stirring the patriotic feelings which Hanna and her friends shared with their parents. But the schoolgirls of Hirschberg were not interested in politics. Their school study of history stopped with the 1848 revolutions in Germany, Austria, and France, and discussions on current affairs were not part of the curriculum. According to two British students, who stayed with the Reitsch family, Frau Reitsch would occasionally launch into a tirade against the government, in which she indiscriminately blamed other nations for anything she thought was wrong in Germany: sometimes the culprits were the French, sometimes the Russians, sometimes the British, occasionally the Jews, but most often the Italians—as a Tyrolean, Emy Reitsch was aware of problems and tensions with Italy in the southern Tyrol. The message from Willy and Emy Reitsch was however more often one of international tolerance.

Frau Reitsch extended a warm welcome to the two British students, who spent Christmas 1928 as guests of the family in Hirschberg. James Tucker, who bore his inevitable nickname of 'Tommy' with fortitude, was struck by the depth of the

Reitsch family's religious fervour; but Nora Campbell, a puritanical Scottish Presbyterian, considered the dolls dressed in Tyrolean costumes which represented the holy family in a crib under the Christmas tree to be little better than pagan idols.

It was a Christmas to be remembered, a Christmas of clear skies and crisp snow, skiing and skating, concerts in the town and musical evenings at home, visits and visitors, church in both the Protestant and the Catholic churches, and ceremonial present-opening round a candle-lit tree on Christmas Eve. In the evening of Christmas Day, they were joined by the von Bibersteins and the von Müllenheims, family friends whose aristocratic names Nora and Tommy found secretly amusing.

At nine o'clock, Frau Reitsch clapped her hands and made an announcement: 'You will all take the last tram to Himmelreich and climb to Spindler-Baude and spend the night on the mountain.' They felt and looked like polar explorers as they climbed in the clear, cold light of a full moon. The snow was frozen on the trees so that it did not fall off however hard the branches were shaken. Hanna enthused inexhaustibly, demanding agreement from the others that the light on the snow, and the snow on the trees, were beautiful, glorious, heavenly; that a particular tree looked like a king with a crown; that it was like being in fairyland.

For Willy and Emy Reitsch it was a Christmas tinged with sadness, the last one for which it could be guaranteed that the family would be together. Kurt left home to join the navy in the New Year. Hanna was already working for her school leaving examination, the Abitur. It was the door to the future, enabling her to start studying towards becoming a doctor. When she passed it in 1931, her parents were delighted, and presented her with a gold watch. She refused the gift: it was not at all what she had been waiting for.

Instead she was determined to keep her father to a bargain which had been her chief motivation during her last few years at school: he had promised that she could have a course of lessons at the gliding school at Grunau, a few miles from Hirschberg, provided she did well in the Abitur and did not mention flying again until she had had her results. Dr Reitsch had imagined that her strange wish was merely a passing childish whim, particularly when she kept her side of the deal: Hanna was normally so little given to reticence that he had taken her silence to mean that she had forgotten about wanting to fly.

Hanna's obsession with the idea of flying was, however, so great that she had exercised a self-control of which no one had considered her capable. Keeping quiet about something which she longed to talk about was the most difficult thing she had ever done. She had been helped by a book which she had come across in the school library, a slim volume translated from sixteenth-century Spanish with the unexciting title *The Spiritual Exercises of Saint Ignatius Loyola*. The prescribed prayers and meditations, which involved considerable soul-searching and depended on a firm belief in the tenets of Christianity, were to be repeated three times a day. Hanna found no difficulty in thinking about herself and God first thing in the morning and last thing at night, although remembering to do so at midday was not always so easy.

Quite why she wanted to fly, she could never explain: she talked vaguely about the love she shared with her mother for the mountains, about birds, about physical and psychological freedom, and about being nearer to God. After seeing a film about the start of the flying doctor service in Australia, she decided that she would combine flying with medicine by becoming a flying medical missionary.

Although Dr Reitsch was reluctant, his sense of honour gave him no option but to keep his promise. He had encouraged his daughter's interest in medicine by describing the intricate mechanism of the eye, and had demonstrated operations on pigs' and sheep's eyes which he had brought home from the local butcher. Hanna's mother assumed that both medicine and flying would be interludes before marriage, but stoically accepted Hanna's right to make her own decisions.

When Hanna left the girls' school in Hirschberg, with the intention of studying medicine, she was an idealistic and ambitious nineteen-year-old. Her promised flying lessons would, or so she persuaded herself and her parents, eventually enable her to take her skill as a qualified doctor to those most in need of her care in some dimly imagined and vaguely exotic, but deprived, part of the world. Once the cloud of secrecy was lifted, she could chatter gaily about her intention of becoming a flying doctor in Africa. The ambitions of her schoolfriends were more mundane: marriage, domesticity, and motherhood, or, for the more emancipated, teaching.

Before allowing her either to learn to fly or to embark on her medical studies, Hanna's parents insisted that she should make up for her lack of interest in domestic matters: cooking, washing, ironing, and cleaning had always been entrusted to a maid, or rather a series of maids. She was enrolled for a year's course as a boarder in Rendsburg at the Koloniale Frauenschule (Koloschule), an establishment where young ladies were prepared for life and work in the colonies. Although by 1931 there had been no German colonies for well over a decade, there were still strong ties with African territories which had been removed by the Treaty of Versailles.

The Koloschule, which overlooked the Kiel Canal, was opened in 1926. It served as a reasonably priced all-round finishing school, although the emphasis was on team-work and on practical rather than decorative and social skills. It was all supposed to be good character training, with the bonus that there was a plentiful supply of young men not far away at the naval training school.

Only the Koloschule girls were allowed to swim in the canal, a privilege which was however less appreciated than were the frequent opportunities to wave at the German navy. Whenever a naval ship approached, it hooted an advance warning and slowed down as it passed under the windows of the imposing purpose-built schoolhouse. By then, the girls had all run from the kitchen, the laundry, the fruit and vegetable garden, the hen run, and the pigsty, and were lining the bank. Hanna gained considerable kudos among her fellow pupils from having a brother in the navy, although on the one occasion when she and some of her friends were invited to spend a few hours at sea on his ship it was cold and rough.

For the first time in her life, Hanna was separated for more than a few days from her mother, on whom she was still unusually emotionally dependent: she later claimed that she would, she was sure, have died if anything had happened to Emy before she was nineteen. She shared a bedroom with a girl who became her closest friend and confidante in a tower overlooking the canal. In the evenings, Hanna and Gisela sat together at a window on the spiral stairs of the tower: they called it their Orion window, and considered it their private and secret place. They were there at Hallowe'en, and made a pact that wherever they were and whatever they were doing, at eight o'clock every All Souls' Eve for the rest of their lives they would think about each other. Neither of them ever forgot the tryst.

The girls were divided into four groups. Hanna's and Gisela's group was always the noisiest: they sang while they were polishing, they sang when it was their turn to work in the garden or to make cheese, and they sang when work had stopped in the evenings. When they were not singing, they were usually talking and laughing. Almost the only time when they did not sing was during pig duty. The pigs were no problem when they were still small enough to be endearing; but the bigger they grew, the fiercer and the more frightening they became. Unfortunately for Hanna, her pig duty was the week before they were to be slaughtered, and so they were at their biggest and most ferocious.

Meals were prepared by the pupils, using as far as was possible home produce. Work outside, to which few of the girls had previously been accustomed, started early, and gave them all hearty appetites. The highlight of the day was the second breakfast, at which all the previous day's left-overs were set out. It was a free-for-all scramble for the best bits, and it was not long before Hanna had put on a considerable amount of weight. As she was so short, this did little for her appearance, and the bows with which her clothing was adorned gradually flattened as she became fatter.

The skills that Hanna was supposed to have acquired at the Koloschule were rarely used later. She never again mended her own shoes, made another pair of boy's trousers, baked her own bread, or bottled and made wine from freshly picked fruit. On her one attempt to demonstrate her culinary expertise at home, she cooked more than enough to feed the entire school, and her family were so sick of rice by the end of the week that any further half-hearted offers to cook were refused.

There were tears when the time came to leave Rendsburg. First Hanna cried, and then Gisela, and then Hanna again, and soon everyone was vowing eternal friendship. Hanna had by then had her first taste of flying, during the school holidays, but still expected to become a doctor.

# 2

# Winged Student

It was during her first holiday from the Koloschule that Hanna's ambition to enrol on a course at Grunau was at last realised. Gliding was a peculiarly German sport, developed in the years after the First World War as a way of circumventing the ban on powered flying imposed by the Treaty of Versailles. It was predominantly a male activity, although women were not barred, and Hanna was the only girl on the course.

'This looks easy,' she thought on the first day when it was her turn to climb into the pilot's seat and fasten her harness. The other pupils were the ground team, and were ordered first to walk and then to run forwards, keeping the bungee attached to a ring in the nose of the glider taut. As it started to move forwards, Hanna concentrated on what the instructor had said about using the ailerons and foot pedals to hold it steady. Then it was released: ignoring the order to stay on the ground, she gave way to the temptation to see what would happen if she pulled the stick back a little.

After a series of kangaroo jumps the glider came to an ungainly halt. Hanna's attempt to laugh as if nothing had happened was interrupted by the anger of the instructor, Pit van Husen. As a punishment for her disobedience and lack of discipline, she was grounded for three days: she was not even to sit in a glider.

It was not a good beginning, but she put a brave face on her humiliation and frustration while the others progressed to their first free flight. She told herself over and over again that in gliding the one unbreakable law was strict discipline, and that disobeying an order could involve both the pilot and others in unjustifiable danger.

When she arrived home every evening, she avoided her parents, explaining that she was tired and locking herself in her room. During the daytime she joined in the team-work on the ground and concentrated even harder than before, watching what the others did and listening to the instructor's comments so that she could learn from their mistakes. In her determination to keep up with their progress, she pretended that her bed was a glider, using a walking-stick as a rudder.

Her nocturnal exercises paid off: when her three-day punishment was over, she had not after all dropped behind, and was the first to complete the thirty-second A test successfully. To prove that it was not a fluke, she did it again. A gratifying roar of approval went up from the onlookers. She no longer minded that as the only girl on the course she came in for considerable teasing from the men about her size—she was only just over five foot, and weighed only a little over six stone.

The director of the school, Wolf Hirth, who was almost a god to the younger pilots, was intrigued: first he had been told that this chit of a girl was a positive menace to flying, then that less than a week later, when she had missed much of the practical experience, she had passed her first test with apparent ease. He decided it was time to make a personal assessment, and was impressed. Hanna was given his particular attention throughout the remaining days of the course, during which she successfully completed her B test. It was the start of a lifelong friendship with Wolf Hirth and his wife Lala, as well as with a fellow pupil called Wernher von Braun. While they sat together on the grass between lessons, von Braun told her about his dream of a rocket that would fly to the moon.

During her last few months at the Koloschule, Hanna told Gisela again and again every detail of her introduction to flying. She stood on a table so that she could be seen while she re-enacted her experiences for the entire school. If her parents had hoped that she would be satisfied with one gliding course, they were to be disappointed: she was obsessed, and extracted a promise of another before she started her medical studies so that she could take her C test.

Again she was the only girl on the course, although this time she was treated with greater respect as the protégée of Wolf Hirth. Her enthusiasm was however once again to get the better of her self-discipline: on her test flight she was revelling so much in the sensation that she was at last flying as freely as a bird that she forgot that she was supposed to be in the air for only ten minutes. When she at last looked at her watch, she realised to her dismay that she was already several minutes overdue. So that the glider would not have to be hauled back before the next flight, she decided to land on the starting-place. It was a manoeuvre requiring a skill and control which Wolf Hirth, who was watching anxiously as she made a perfect approach and landing, did not expect from someone so inexperienced. 'From the flying point of view,' he told her, 'the performance was perfect.' Hanna glowed with pride, although she had also again been reprimanded for disobedience.

As a mark of his trust in her ability, Wolf Hirth allowed Hanna to fly a new glider which normally only he and the instructors were allowed to touch. She had permission to stay in the air for as long as she liked. A strong west wind over the ridge ensured perfect gliding conditions, and she sang as she made full use of the weather conditions to soar to her heart's content. Every now and then, the less privileged pupils, among them a young journalist called Wolfgang Späte, looked up to see if she was still in sight.

When she landed, after five and a half hours, Hanna was astonished to find that she had broken a world record. Records were constantly being made and broken in the early days of gliding: it was only ten years since it had been considered an achievement to stay in the air for nearly a quarter of an hour.

For the first time, the name of Hanna Reitsch was heard on the radio. Wolf Hirth and the Grunau school also received considerable publicity. Since the first post-war gliding camp in 1920, Hirth had been working hard to catch up with his elder brother's pre-war reputation as a pilot. In spite of the disadvantages of needing glasses and of having lost a leg in a motor-cycling accident, he had achieved his childhood ambition of becoming as famous as his brother. By the time Hanna became his protégée, he was one of Germany's leading glider pilots and designers.

Hanna set off for Berlin for her first term as a medical student with only one thought: she must continue to fly. Her studies took a poor second place. She spent much of her time at a flying school at Staaken on the outskirts of the city, working towards a licence to fly powered sports aircraft and hanging round the workshops. Powered flight presented her with no problems, but she found it neither as challenging nor as stimulating as gliding: it lacked the poetic appeal and closeness to God and the elements of flying without an engine.

'Powered flying is certainly an unforgettable experience, but gliding is incomparable,' she explained. 'Powered flight is a magnificent triumph over nature—but gliding is a victory of the soul in which one gradually becomes one with nature.'

Several other women flew from Staaken, but it was only with one, Elly Beinhorn, that she struck up more than a passing acquaintance. Elly, who was five years older, had just returned from flying round the world: she had had a pilot's licence for three years and had already become a household name for her solo long-distance flights. Her pleasure in flying was, however, different from Hanna's: for Elly, it was principally a way of enjoying new experiences, and she made it pay by writing about her travels.

Hanna also struck up a friendship with a fellow pupil, the actor and broadcaster Matthias Wiemann, and a brief acquaintance with a gang of workmen who allowed her to drive their tractor. When they started arguing among themselves about politics, the divisions she discovered upset her. Her political interests were limited, and there had never been any dissension on the subject in her family. She felt that it was enough to be patriotic: it did not occur to her that this could be expressed in a variety of ways, nor that politicians could be devious. Because she was open and honest, she assumed that other people were equally honourable, and could not in any case imagine that politics could have anything to do with flying, or have any direct bearing on her own life.

Hanna wrote to her mother, with whom she exchanged frequent letters, that unless she could bring herself to go about Berlin without continually thinking of flying, she would never again be able to learn how to stand with both feet on the ground. At the same time, when she was in the air she felt somehow closer to God. Her mother wrote her homilies about humility whenever a flying success threatened to go to her head. Hanna often resented these at the time, confident that she had deserved any praise which came her way; but then she would search earnestly for any sign that her mother might be right, and be grateful for Emy's determination to keep her feet, metaphorically at least, on the ground.

Wolf Hirth, whom Hanna called her 'flying father', also urged her to keep her flying in perspective. The career opportunities for male pilots were limited enough; for women, there were, in his opinion, none. At home in the holidays, Hanna nevertheless spent most of her time either at Grunau, or at the Hirths' home. In the evenings, she spent hours going through the typescript of a book Hirth was writing about the art of soaring flight.

It was a mutually beneficial exercise: through Hanna, Wolf could assess the clarity of his explanations, and she in turn absorbed the theory of soaring in thermals and air waves. Hirth had discovered the technique of soaring in cloudless thermals; he had deliberately flown in search of thunderstorms and into a strange elliptical cloud with an even stranger name, the Moazagotl. This appeared in southerly winds above Hirschberg, a phenomenon first noted by and so called after a farmer, Gottlieb Moetz. After Wolf Hirth and the son of a local teacher, Hans Deutschmann, had flown simultaneously into the Moazagotl in March 1933, Hirth's report on their experiences was greeted with excitement. Gliding had until then relied chiefly on the air currents created by hill slopes.

Hanna longed to put her new theoretical knowledge to the test. The opportunity presented itself, out of a clear sky, in May 1933. She had returned to Hirschberg from Kiel, where after her first term in Berlin she was continuing her medical studies with increased dedication—there were no opportunities for gliding on the flat north German plains, where there were neither ridges to give lift nor airfields from which a glider could be towed. Wearing a light summer dress and sandals, she was invited by Wolf Hirth to join him and Lala,

*Grunau Baby*

who were on their way to do some filming at Grunau. She could fly a new training glider, a Grunau Baby: it would, Hirth suggested, be useful practice if she were to fly blind, using only her instruments.

There was no indication as he towed her to 1200 ft that she would find herself for the first time really 'flying blind', although the prospect would not have alarmed her: she was confident that in any situation she would be able to react immediately and correctly to the readings on her instruments. Knowing that one day she would have to rely on them, she had trained herself to take whatever action would be necessary to keep control: using a set of nine flash cards showing every combination of readings she had tested herself until she was sure that she would instinctively have the right reaction in any emergency.

As soon as Hirth cast her off, Hanna began disappointingly to lose height. At 250 ft she looked for somewhere to land, just as the glider began to quiver and her instruments told her that she was climbing. She circled, dropped again, and then found herself rising in a stronger air current. Still circling, in under three minutes she was taken up 1500 ft, following Hirth's instructions so implicitly that when she at last glanced at the sky she was astonished to see above her a menacing black cloud.

When she was sucked upwards towards it, she was at first exhilarated, certain that she could come to no harm so long as she concentrated on her instruments. At 3600 ft the world was blotted out by a thick veil as she was drawn up at 20 ft a second. She had a moment's anxiety that she might be in danger of landing on the top of the Schneekoppe, at 5200 ft the highest peak of the Riesengebirge, until she realised that she was already well above it.

Her confidence turned to fear as she found herself climbing faster and faster through what she later termed 'a frenzied staccato, an ear-splitting hellish tattoo' of rain and hail. 'There's nothing to worry about,' she told herself repeatedly as she struggled to keep the instruments reading as they should. She even managed to convince herself that it was true—up to 9500 ft—but all too briefly. Soon she was being thrown about so violently that it was almost impossible to keep control. Then to her horror the reassuring instruments seemed to be sticking and she realised that she was experiencing a new danger: icing. She could no longer tell what was the right position for the control column as a high-pitched whistle warned her that she must avoid stalling.

Mere fear gave way to terror. She punched a hole in the ice-covered windscreen, pulling frantically at the stick as the pain in her head and the scream of the wind in the ailerons told her that she was diving. Later she said that the glider went into a vertical dive and that as she heaved at the controls she performed a series of involuntary loops before continuing her screaming headlong dive. Her light clothing was no protection from the cold, and the rain soaked her through the hole in the windscreen. Hoping that the glider would still have some stability if she left it to its own devices, she relinquished the stick.

The storm had reached a crescendo which threw her helplessly to and fro in the cockpit and dragged her again upwards. As she wondered how long it would be before the glider broke up, she tried to think what Wolf Hirth would do.

'Everyone knows fear sometimes,' he had told her. 'If you're alone, talk to yourself and keep talking.'

'Hanna,' she screamed aloud, 'you should be ashamed of yourself! You're a coward! You wanted to fly in a thundercloud—well, now get on with it!'

The sound of her own voice was reassuring. Even if she could not control the aircraft, at least she was once again in control of herself. She had lost all sense of time. Then at last there was light. She was out of the storm, but the sky was beneath her and the earth above. Mechanically she seized the controls and as she reversed the position of earth and sky she saw high above her the towering pillar of the storm cloud as it drew slowly away.

She was grateful to be alive as she landed, a few miles from Grunau in front of an inn on a 4500 ft-high mountain ridge—greatly to the astonishment of the skiers who were relaxing after their afternoon exertions. A girl in a sodden summer dress, her hair dripping, and an aircraft which looked as if its wings were liberally strewn with bullet holes where the hail had inflicted considerable damage, were not everyday sights in a peaceful ski resort, especially in the neutral zone between Germany and Czechoslovakia, where it was forbidden to land.

Wolf Hirth was equally relieved that she was all right, and angry that she had not only risked her life and his glider, but had also crossed the border. He came to her rescue in a powered aircraft, accompanied by Schneider, the designer of the Grunau Baby. They dropped a bungee tow-rope, then circled overhead while Hanna organised her take-off with a team of volunteers from the hotel. She was aware that without an unusual amount of luck she could have suffered serious injury or even death, have destroyed the new glider, have lost her licence, and deserved at the very least to be grounded.

Instead, she was treated as a public heroine: she had created an unintentional altitude record, which was reported in the national press as well as on the radio throughout Germany. Hanna basked happily in her glory until her mother warned her again against the sin of false pride. She was at first offended, and then admitted to herself—of not to anyone else—that she was indeed guilty of the charge and should, on this occasion more than any other so far, make a serious attempt at humility and gratitude to God for her good fortune.

She was, however, eager to share her adventure with anyone who would listen, and found an appreciative audience when she was invited, as an old girl who had become a celebrity, to talk at the Koloschule in Rendsburg. Although she admitted that her instructor had had good reason for being angry with her, the message which came over most clearly was that she had achieved something spectacular. When she described any flying experience, Hanna drew her listeners into feeling that they were almost there with her: her voice dropped to a dramatic whisper, then rose in a crescendo of enthusiasm, while she demonstrated air currents with her hands, and her arms became the wings of the glider which she was struggling to control.

The attention of some of the pupils nevertheless wandered from time to time to several huge bowls of grapes, and they wondered who was going to eat them, and when. Suddenly Hanna broke off her story: 'Oh, what lovely grapes! Can we eat them?' she exclaimed, as she grabbed a bunch and started to shove them into her mouth. The great adventuress had stepped off her pedestal, and the grapes were passed round the assembled company.

Her story-telling was as vivid privately as it was in public, and often attracted an uninvited audience. Not long after her storm-cloud record, she was reliving it for Austrian relatives, the Heubergers, over lunch at an inn in the Tyrol. Gradually conversation at the other tables ceased as everyone in the room listened, spellbound: it was not, as her cousin Gertrud explained, that Hanna was talking particularly loudly, but because she was such a compelling talker.

When Wolf Hirth invited Hanna to become an instructor at a new gliding school on the Hornberg in Swabia during the summer term following her spectacular record, her parents gave their consent. They were beginning to wonder if she would ever qualify as a doctor, but realised that it was pointless to oppose her. Hitler had by then been voted into power; Hanna, like her parents, welcomed a strongly nationalist leader who would protect Germany from Communism and provide jobs for the unemployed. But she was too absorbed in her own affairs to give the matter any serious thought.

She based her teaching on her own experience and inexperience: she was too young, and too recent a pilot, to feel that she could adopt the position of a superior, but young enough to join in as an equal with her pupils and to explain by her own example. Her cheerful enthusiasm and open friendliness made her popular both among the men she had learnt from and with, and among the boys and men she instructed—there were no girls on any of the courses she taught.

At the end of a C course in which she felt that her teaching method had proved itself, her confidence received a severe blow: the last pupil to take his test crashed, for no apparent reason, and was killed. When she went to break the news to his mother, she found that he had told both his family and some of his companions at the flying school about a dream: it had correctly foretold the events leading to his fatal crash.

No blame was attached to Hanna, but she felt that she was under a cloud. She set out immediately after the funeral to participate for the first time in the Rhön soaring contests at the Wasserkuppe, 3000 ft above sea-level in the Rhön mountains. The Wasserkuppe ('Water Hill') was considered the birth-place of gliding. Annual gliding meetings had been held there since 1920, when Oskar Ursinus, editor of a magazine called *Flugsport*, had invited like-minded enthusiasts to gather. Twenty-four people had turned up for the first summer camp, some ex-wartime pilots and others, like Wolf Hirth and fourteen-year-old Peter Riedel, complete beginners.

Hanna did not distinguish herself in the 1933 Rhön competitions. She was flying the Grunau Baby, and had enlisted her pupils at Hornberg as a launching team. They hoped as much as she did that she would succeed or at least that there would be some indication that their heroine was as good as the more experienced competitors. Instead, after each launch she flopped ignominiously down the slope of the hill to the valley bed, and each time, while she bit back her tears, her team had to retrieve the glider and she would try again. The laughter of some of the onlookers was humiliating, although she had to admit that if she had been in their shoes she too might have found it funny. She was determined to learn as much as possible from watching the other pilots, and her disappointment at her own performance in no way diminished her outward cheerfulness.

In the meantime, the others were finding the lift which constantly evaded her. Heini Dittmar, who was also competing for the first time, proved both his ability and the flying capabilities of the Condor which he had built himself. Wolf Hirth, in a new glider called the Moazagotl after the cloud, was sometimes ahead of and sometimes behind his chief rival, Peter Riedel. Many had faster, more competitive gliders than Hanna, and she used this as a partial excuse for her failure: but Paul Steinig, an instructor who was also flying a Grunau Baby, managed a flight of 60 miles.

Peter Riedel finished as overall winner. Hanna's humiliation was complete when she was awarded a booby prize of a mincer and a set of kitchen scales, which she interpreted as a hint that girls should stay where they belonged. The only thing that could be said in her favour, as far as her flying went, was that she had never given up trying, and in the final address to the prize-winners there was a reference to her persistence in the face of bad luck.

Hanna's dogged determination had impressed Professor Walter Georgii, a tall and gangling meteorologist who was at the head of Germany's gliding research efforts. He invited Hanna to join an expedition to South America, at her own expense. Three places for which he had managed to raise business sponsorship had already been filled, by Wolf Hirth, Peter Riedel, and Heini Dittmar. Georgii was convinced that Hanna's personality, her enthusiasm, and her ability to attract favourable press attention would make her an asset both as an ambassadress and as an extra pilot.

Astonished and flattered by the invitation, Hanna accepted unhesitatingly. There was, however, a problem. She did not feel she could ask her parents to contribute to the cost of yet another term of flying instead of study. She raised the 3000 marks she needed for the expedition by accepting an offer from a film company, UFA, to double in flying sequences for the heroine of a film called *Rivalen der Luft*. Heini Dittmar flew for the hero. They lived during the two months of filming in tents at Rositten, on the Baltic coast; Hanna was able in her spare time to fly for as long as she liked over the dunes and the sea. She and Dittmar were inevitably together except when they were in the air.

The heroine was small and energetic, and bore a certain similarity to Hanna, as indeed did a thunderstorm sequence to her own adventure. The similarities did not in the least offend her, although her parents were alarmed by her venture into the world of entertainment.

'I loved my part,' she commented. 'I'd never have been allowed to have so many crashes anywhere else!'

On the long sea voyage to South America, Hanna firmly rejected Heini Dittmar's tentative advances. She complained to Peter Riedel that Heini was being a bit of a nuisance. Peter was by then deeply involved in a passionate shipboard affair. Although Hanna sympathised and did her best to ensure that the young lovers could spend time together unobtrusively, she had no wish for romance herself. Her ideas about love and marriage were puritanical, and she was determined to explore the possibilities of flying to the full before limiting her horizons to domesticity.

The friendship which grew on the expedition between Hanna and Riedel was that of a brother and sister. He found her cheerful, helpful, modest, an excellent companion, and 'a flight-crazy young girl'. She had, however, in spite of her femininity, an aura of untouchability, and he felt that her good humour hid an iron will and an intense but unpolitical patriotism. But he could never explain why one day when they were walking together in Rio and he suddenly exclaimed, 'Hanna, you are like Joan of Arc', she did not laugh, as he thought she would, but flashed a questioning look at him; then, as if she knew what he meant, she talked about something else.

In Rio, the frustration of a three-week wait for their gliders to be released by the Brazilian customs, while each day they were told it would all happen 'tomorrow', was hard to bear. While they waited, they explored and were fêted. Their principal object, however, was not to engender goodwill between nations, which they both created and received in good mea-

sure, but to further their knowledge of thermal flying, for
which the South American climate was particularly suited.
When at last the gliders were released, Hanna was deputed to
give daily aerobatic displays with the Grunau Baby while the
others attempted long-distance flights with the Condor, the
Moazagotl, and the Fafnir.

After a month in Rio, they moved on to São Paulo, where
Hanna made a spectacular landing in the Grunau Baby on a
football pitch in the middle of a game. It was only at the last
minute that players and spectators scattered: they had not
realised that the low approaching aircraft had no engine.
Hanna, the girl who had fallen out of the sky, created a
sensation in the local press.

By the time the team left Brazil, enough interest had been
created by their activities for several gliding clubs to spring
up, and for existing flying clubs to clamour for the privilege
of being their hosts. They were most in demand among the
sizeable German settlement, which lavished on them flowers,
speeches, gifts, and receptions. Peter Riedel noted a remark
made by a leading member of the German community: 'We
are so pleased about the improvement in relations between
Poland and Germany. We get on very well here with the
Polish community. This far from Europe, the things we have
in common seem far more important than the things which
divide us.' In 1934, when Hitler had been in power for a
year, few people anticipated war.

From Brazil they went on to Argentina, where Wolf Hirth
broke a world record with seventy-six consecutive loops during an aerobatic display. Hanna proudly became the first
woman to receive a Silver C Soaring Medal, after a three-
hour flight over almost endless pampas where herds of horses
and cattle were the only signs of life. Peter Riedel set up a
new long-distance soaring record which was, to his intense
annoyance, wrongly attributed in the German gliding press to
Wolf Hirth.

A few days before the end of the trip, Hanna was accompanied on a goodwill flight by a handsome young Spanish pilot.
She was so inspired by the beauty of the flight that she
clutched her companion's hand and squeezed it—she would
have made the same spontaneous gesture whoever had been

sitting beside her. It was misinterpreted, however, and when she found both her hands clasped with reciprocating Latin passion she felt 'a strange vibration' and was suddenly intensely conscious of being a woman. This, she thought, must be love.

Later that evening, she took fright: 'I found myself on the threshold of something most of me believed I needed, but which a small nagging spoil-sport in my subconscious warned me I might later regret, for it was a threshold that once passed could never be backed out of.' She thought, as so often in a crisis, of her mother, who had brought her up to regard marriage as such a sacred and blessed event in a woman's life that she should not even accept a kiss on the lips from anyone except her husband-to-be. Hanna, near to tears and longing to throw herself into the arms of her potential lover, escaped before it was too late with the excuse of a hastily invented fiancé. She threw herself on her bed and sobbed, and in the morning wrote a hopeful and inviting letter of apology for her behaviour. It was not answered, and when she left South America by ship she was convinced that she was nursing a broken heart.

All regrets about the dashing Spaniard were banished when, a few days out at sea, Georgii invited her to join the Gliding Research Institute at Darmstadt. 'You can't leave us now,' he said, 'you belong to us, in Darmstadt, at the Institute.' Although Hanna was expected, by her parents if by no one else, to return to university in the summer term, she could no longer envisage a life in which anything could be as important to her as flying. She accepted Georgii's invitation without hesitation and abandoned the idea of becoming a doctor.

Hanna was delighted with the whole South American adventure. The good relations which had been established with their hosts were, she felt, even more important than their own flying successes or the scientific results of the expedition: 'We had', she claimed, 'built a bridge of understanding, and that was the most valuable achievement of all.'

As the ship steamed slowly up the Elbe early in May, three Klemm aircraft circled overhead. In Hamburg, there was a reception committee of military officers, government officials, and gliding friends. In her delight at seeing her mother and sister, Hanna did not share Peter Riedel's misgivings about the changes he saw in Germany: 'The effect on me of the well-meant semi-military reception was like waking from a wonderful dream to a blue-grey reality,' Riedel wrote later. 'I was beset by doubts about much which had previously seemed right but which I now questioned, without finding any answers.'

There were speeches on board and speeches ashore, a formal dinner of honour at the luxurious Hotel Vier Jahreszeiten in Hamburg with yet more speeches, and an equally formal reception laid on by the mayor. Although the foreign press had virtually ignored the expedition, because of Germany's increasing unpopularity abroad, at home it was given all the recognition that its participants could have hoped for.

Their only disappointment was that the four vultures which they had brought back to Darmstadt failed to co-operate in the plan to use them to find thermals. The birds knew when they were on to a good thing: when their cage was opened, after they had been lavishly fed in it for several weeks, they refused to fly away. Eventually three were given to a zoo, and the fourth was rumoured to have been seen walking out of Darmstadt towards Heidelberg.

# 3

# Spreading Wings

Flying professionally was even better than flying for fun.
From the time she joined Georgii's team at Darmstadt, Hanna
was able to combine work and pleasure. The Deutsche
Forschungsanstalt für Segelflug (DFS) was considered the top
research establishment for motorless flight not only in Germany, but throughout the world. Hanna shared a wide range
of flying duties with Heini Dittmar. Within a few weeks, she
had added a women's long-distance soaring record to her
collection, with a flight of over a hundred miles.

She would have flown for nothing, and considered such
practical questions as a salary and insurance unimportant.
When she was asked by a colleague whether Schneider had
covered her fully against all risks for flying his Motor Baby at
Tempelhof in 1934, she was so angry that she refused to
speak to him for the rest of the day. 'I don't want insurance,'
she told him. Her fellow glider pilots envied but did not
begrudge her good fortune. 'Hey, Hanna, how about marrying me?' one of them teased her. 'Now that you're rich!'

When Hanna had been with the DFS for a few months, she
was included in a German team sent to Finland to stimulate
interest in gliding among Finnish youth. The expedition was
headed by Count Ysenburg, the Berlin head of the Deutsche
Luftsport Verband set up by the government to co-ordinate,
and control, flying as a sport. The other representatives of
German gliding were an instructor from Berlin, an Akaflieger
(a member of a civilian flying group operating from a university), and Dr Joachim Küttner, an aviation research scientist.
Küttner was unaware that he was half-Jewish, and it was not

until he was later officially investigated that he discovered that a grandparent on each side of his family was a Jew.

Hanna had already proved herself an excellent ambassadress. She took pride in demonstrating wherever and whenever possible the superiority of German gliding. At the same time it was in a spirit of missionary zeal that she set out to take gliding to those who might, with a little persuasion and tuition, be able to benefit.

Oblivious of any political pressure, Hanna put her enthusiasm across with her customary unfettered spontaneity. She was interested in every aspect of Finnish life, was particularly impressed by their saunas, and appreciated the hospitality with which the Germans were invariably treated. There was no shortage of willing pupils, both military and civilian. They had never seen anything to equal her aerobatic displays, nor heard anything like her flying stories. They called her 'die Hanna'—'the Hanna'—and the Scheherazade of gliding.

The team felt a glow of pride in a job well done when their visit was widely reported in the Finnish press and was followed by a spate of appreciative letters. Another German team was invited to assist in a scheme to set up a gliding school in every village throughout the country: the Finns were to become a nation of flyers.

Hanna's participation in the 1934 Finland expedition pleased the new Reich Air Ministry, and she was offered a decoration as a reward. As she claimed to attach no value to such honours, she asked instead for permission to enrol at the Civil Airways Training School in Stettin. Her powered flying experience had so far been limited to small sports planes: at Stettin she would be able to acquire licences for bigger and more powerful aircraft.

It was an unusual request: the school normally took only male trainees and was run on strict semi-military lines. For a woman to go there would, as Hanna was well aware, cause a sensation. She was nevertheless allowed to join the men. As this met with Air Ministry approval the commanding officer at Stettin, Colonel Pasewaldt, had no option but to accept her.

He had never had a woman under his command before, but did his best to smooth the way. Nevertheless she found herself the butt of ribald jokes and the recipient of extra drill practice. Obeying the order 'Chest in!' presented her with particular difficulty: as she admitted, her physique, combined with her inability to follow the commands that were familiar to the men, 'was disturbing the splendours of the masculine silhouette'. It was, however, not long before her flying ability, combined with her friendliness and eagerness to learn, overcame the initial resentment and she was treated as 'one of the boys'.

Hanna was one of 150 pupils at various stages of their training. Their day started with early morning exercises at 6 a.m. and proceeded according to a strict timetable. Flying and theoretical instruction began at 7.30 a.m. and continued throughout the morning and afternoon. The evenings were free except for those on night-flying: the others gathered in the clubhouse. Discipline was strict. Hanna was treated in exactly the same way as her fellow pupils, although separate accommodation was provided for her since it would hardly have been considered suitable to have a woman sharing the men's barracks.

Her fur-lined flying suit and boots were so many sizes too large that she looked almost as broad as she was tall. In any cockpit she had to sit on a pile of cushions, which were always slipping and needing readjusting. She practised the correct manner of addressing an officer, lowering her voice to a husky bass and attempting a military staccato, and laughed as heartily as the men who treated her as a standing joke.

Hanna was at Stettin for nearly a year. Commander Pasewaldt found her 'a totally uncomplicated person' and attributed her popularity to her ability as a pilot and her unfailing good humour: 'She had no particularly feminine charms and wiles, a very fine instinct for flying, and no sense of danger. When she flew, it was like anyone else going for a walk—she had mastered the medium.' For her part, she felt that the presence of a woman who was as sincerely devoted to flying as any of them had 'acted as a kind of leaven, particularly as the discipline was unimpaired'.

By the time Hanna left Stettin, all pretence that the aircraft which the Heinkel, Focke-Wulf, and Junkers factories had been working on for nearly two years were peacefully destined for Lufthansa had been abandoned. Lufthansa, the national airline formed by Erhard Milch in 1926 with government backing, had always provided cover for military training at its civilian flying schools. Its undercover military role had been stepped up when Milch became Secretary of State for Air in 1933.

Plans for the resumption of military flying had started immediately after the First World War. Although the Germans were not allowed an air force, they were permitted to keep a Defence Ministry. From 1924, civil aviation was effectively under military control. The Army Command had made sure that there were enough flying enthusiasts and experts in key positions for a Luftwaffe to be formed instantly. Between 1928 and 1931, a military flying training centre was secretly converting regular officers into potential air force pilots at Lipetsk in Russia.

More openly, but no more obviously, the Defence Ministry had since 1920 been encouraging gliding as a way of circumventing the Treaty of Versailles restrictions and ensuring a ready supply of enthusiastic young pilots who could later easily be absorbed into an air force. When it was suggested at the Wasserkuppe that gliding could have a military use, the idea was dismissed: little did the gliding enthusiasts know that this was because pilots were at the time being trained in Russia, nor that the military potential of the sport had already been taken into account.

Hitler appointed as his Air Minister Hermann Goering, one of his earliest supporters and closest friends. Goering had played little part in the secret rebuilding of the air force: in the 1920s he was abroad, principally in Sweden, where he was treated first for severe depression and then, as a result of the drugs used to combat this, for morphine addiction. During his active flying days in the First World War, he had been slim. By the time he added his position as Air Minister to various other political roles entrusted to him by Hitler, he was gross and flabby, although he seemed at least for the time being to have regained his often unstable mental health. Aviation had to share his time with his duties as President for the Reichstag, Minister of the Interior for Prussia, Minister of Hunting, winer and diner of foreign dignitaries, head of the

Gestapo, and part-owner of a Ruhr newspaper in which he could air his political opinions.

The Luftwaffe officially came into being in March 1935, and was greeted enthusiastically as a signal that the repression of the Treaty of Versailles had finally been thrown aside. There were elaborate ceremonial parades in front of, and aerial displays above, Hitler, Goering, and Milch: nearly 2000 Luftwaffe aircraft and 20,000 officers and men were revealed. Civilians who lived near airfields were astonished to find that overnight the hangars had been taken over by military guards giving stiff salutes, and that rows of aircraft sporting the swastika had appeared. Peacetime conscription was introduced, and even Hanna was aware that the international atmosphere was 'extremely tense'.

Although she did not join the National Socialist party, Hanna considered the concepts of nationalism and socialism individually admirable and indeed essential. She could see no reason why a party combining them should not be equally acceptable. Like most people in Germany in the early 1930s, she felt that Hitler was the answer to their prayers: he brought hope and work to the unemployed, a promise of prosperity where there had been poverty and despair, and a vision of a peaceful and powerful Germany which was irresistible to a people which felt itself to be discriminated against and hemmed in. Rearmament was welcomed as a means to jobs and peace.

It was now more important than ever for Germans abroad to create a good impression in order to offset the growing unease in other countries. It was with this in mind that a German team was sent to Lisbon to participate in an international air display during a week-long festival in May 1935. Hanna was one of the pilots chosen to spread goodwill. While the rest travelled by sea, taking their gliders in crates, she took four days to fly the tow-plane, a small sports Klemm, down through Switzerland, France, and Spain to Portugal. It was her first long-distance flight, and she had with her a young Akaflieger, a student from the technical high school at Darmstadt.

The journey was fraught with problems which almost from the start threatened rather than improved international relations. Bad weather forced her to make an unscheduled landing at a French military airfield at Lyons, where the swastika was greeted with what she termed 'considerable agitation'. When the aircraft was searched for such prohibited articles as photographic equipment, a camera belonging to her companion was found. They were both promptly locked up and interrogated. A crowd gathered to see the two German spies. It was only after the intervention of an irritated German consul that they were allowed to leave.

When she arrived in Lisbon, Hanna immediately embarked on a tour of the city with some Portuguese friends. She was still dressed for flying, and immediately attracted a crowd. Two soldiers in medieval costume accused her of the indecorous crime of wearing pyjamas in the street, arrested her, and shut her in a narrow, bare cell to await trial. Her friends advised her not to spoil the fun: Hanna was however inclined at first to take her second arrest in a few days seriously. When she was peered at through the grille by an endless stream of curious holiday-makers who made comments which she could not understand, her sense of humour was sorely strained.

The mock trial, before a white-bearded judge in a crowded marquee, reassured her: her skill and fame as a flyer were extolled; her virtues were said to outweigh the undoubted seriousness of her crime; and the German people were praised for their courage and energy in rising again after their defeat in war. 'Can it be wondered that I felt proud and happy?' she asked as she later described the 'brilliant and charming comedy': 'As I left the tent, my hand was almost numbed with the congratulations pressed upon me, but I hardly felt it in my gratitude to this charming and friendly people.'

When she returned to Darmstadt, her original rather vague position involving general duties had been elevated to that of chief test pilot to Hans Jacobs. Jacobs, a tall, slim, dark-haired man with drooping eyes and a quiet but decisive manner, was responsible for the design of many of the most successful German gliders. Hanna's first full tests were conducted on the Kranich. During its construction, she visited the workshop every day so that when the time came for the first flight in an untried aircraft she would already feel familiar with it.

Then came the painstakingly detailed trials as she took it higher and higher, faster and faster, day after day, each time discussing her observations afterwards, suggesting modifications, and then retesting it when these had been carried out. No aircraft would be put into production until the test pilot, the designer, and the men in the workshop were satisfied that between them they had done their best to discover and cure every potential or actual weakness. Even then, there were usually improvements to be made later in the light of technical developments or as a result of the experience of other pilots. It was work requiring an ability to concentrate, a certain amount of instinct, and considerable technical knowledge. Hanna's concentration and instinct were remarkable, but the criticism was sometimes levelled against her by her male colleagues that her technical background was inadequate. Hans Jacobs was, however, satisfied with her overall performance as a test pilot.

Hanna's initial flights with another of Jacobs's designs, the See Adler (Sea Eagle), were less successful. The Sea Eagle

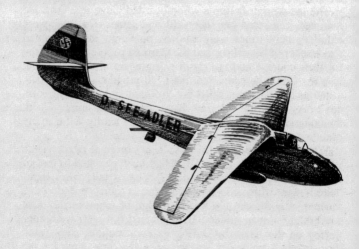

*Sea Eagle*

was an amphibian glider which had to be towed across the water before it could take off. At the first attempt, on a lake near Munich, the boat towing it failed to reach the take-off speed. The next effort, behind a speedboat, was even more disastrous: both Hanna and the glider were dragged under the water by the weight of the tow-rope. A shorter rope with balsa-wood floats was used next, and the Sea Eagle at last left the water. Even better results were achieved with a tow from a Dornier flying-boat. The Sea Eagle proved so seaworthy that in a rising wind it could be landed on the water and would ride out the waves even when it was impossible for a small boat to tow it back to the shore. It was eventually decided, however, that the uses to which a glider which could only take off and land on water could be put would not justify the high costs of production.

The Sea Eagle was nevertheless used to try out a catapult launching device intended to cut down the distance needed for take-off by heavily laden transport aircraft. It had already been tried on land, and Hanna had to establish whether it could work on water. The catapult, a flywheel with a steel rope led over a cone-shaped drum, was set up on a scaffold on shore. As the cable was taken up by the drum Hanna and the Sea Eagle were snatched towards the scaffolding: she had to judge the moment when she should drop the tow precisely, and then turn rapidly and land again on the water. The feeling as she approached the construction on shore at speed was, as she put it, 'distinctly unpleasant'.

In the autumn of 1935, soon after the tests on the Sea Eagle, Hanna made a second visit to Finland. It was as successful as the first. She received an effusive letter of appreciation for her efforts in both Finland and Portugal from Wolfgang von Gronau on behalf of the German Aero Club: it was largely through her efforts, he told her, that the standing of German gliding, and with it of German aviation in general, had received 'such a strong boost abroad'. Her activities in Finland had, he wrote, 'had an extraordinarily worthwhile effect on the various aspects of German-Finnish relations':

Your unstinting personal commitment, your untiring work as a teacher of Finnish glider pilots, and your friendly co-operation with the Finns, have proved a living example of the spirit of the new Germany, not only to individual Finns, but also to the Finnish people as a whole; that spirit, which they saw in your work, has created a deep impression. You have thus had an admirable political effect.

It is one of the most pleasant of duties to express, dear Hanna Reitsch, the sincere thanks and recognition of the Aero Club of Germany, and to include my personal thanks, particularly as I know that the quiet satisfaction of having done your duty means more to you than any outside recognition. You will always be able to cherish the memory that you have worked in such difficult times towards the enhancement and strengthening of Germany's reputation abroad.

With best wishes and Heil Hitler!

Hanna did indeed enjoy the knowledge that she was, at all times and to the best of her ability, doing what she considered to be her duty. She had, however, no objection to receiving recognition for her achievements, although she still considered that using her flying ability and her personality to improve her country's image was outside and above politics. Nevertheless being proud of being German was inevitably seen, in the sense expressed in von Gronau's letter, as being political. However much she might protest to the contrary, and although her closest friends agreed that she was always politically almost unbelievably naïve, Hanna had already unintentionally placed herself on a political stage on which she felt she did not belong.

Her mother continued to worry about her, and wrote to her every day, often in verse. Her message was always the same: trust in God, and thank Him for your good fortune. Hanna was grateful for the peace of mind which she gained from her daily homily. Emy's conviction that Hanna was in God's hands, and that nothing would happen to her unless He had willed it, masked her own constant fear that sooner or later her daughter's end would be His will. But she considered the spiritual danger of vanity and overweening pride to be even greater than the physical danger of flying. Hanna did her best to heed her mother's warnings, but could not always claim to be entirely free of personal ambition and self-congratulation.

Neither Hanna nor her mother would have considered that Emy's letters, written at night when the household had gone to bed, were in any way an expression of a political standpoint. Emy Reitsch shared with her daughter 'the happiness . . . of knowing that every test . . . is in the cause of Germany and the saving of human lives'. In her desire to save the lives of future pilots by ensuring the safety of the aircraft they would have to fly, Hanna did not take into account the implication that these might equally be used to destroy lives. Her work was initially only with gliders, although the developments that she tested were later often put to military use.

During 1935, Messerschmitt fighters, Junkers, Dornier and Heinkel bombers, and Stuka dive-bombers were being developed rapidly. At the beginning of the year, between 180 and 200 aircraft were built each month: from July, monthly production was increased to 300. However much Hitler protested that he and Germany wanted peace, no one could deny that the aim was to make these aircraft as effective in attack as in defence should the need arise.

One of Hanna's most satisfying tasks, both professionally and personally, was the long and demanding series of dive-brake tests which she conducted in 1936 for Hans Jacobs. When these were completed, she felt that she had contributed to the safety of future generations of civil and military pilots, had proved her ability in public, and had even helped to make aviation history.

There had in the previous year been a number of fatal gliding accidents. Such strain had been put on aircraft that they had broken up, usually while inexperienced pilots were attempting blind flying in cloud: this was, as Hanna realised, what might easily have happened to her on her celebrated storm-cloud flight. Jacobs dismissed the suggestion that the answer was to build stronger gliders: strengthening a glider would make it heavier, and therefore potentially faster, and would merely mean that the problem would occur at a higher speed.

Instead he fitted self-operating dive-brakes on the upper

and lower surface of each wing: one was set to open with the air flow, the other against it. The use of spoilers to control air speed and stability was an untried concept: when Hanna made the first flights to test its efficacy on a Sperber glider, both she and Hans Jacobs were fully aware that she might be putting herself in danger. On the first trial, she was released a 13,000 ft and tried the brakes at a moderate speed. Her own description gives a clear idea of the initial problems which she had to describe so that Jacobs could work out how to solve them:

> with the brakes still open, I dive, slowly increasing speed—5 mph faster—10 mph, and now the strong turbulence set up by the brakes that are open into the wind starts to buffet the ailerons and the elevator so that the whole plane begins to shudder. I press myself against the side of the plane and listen, every sense alert to try to determine the source and cause of the vibration. Then I close the brakes for a moment while I note down briefly what I have heard, felt, and seen. Then, increasing the speed, I open the brakes again and, as expected, the vibration is now so strong that the control column is torn out of my hands. Clearly the dive brakes are unsatisfactory in their present form, so I land and discuss with Hans Jacobs what I have observed. To reduce the disturbance which they make in the slipstream, we decide to dampen the brakes with a series of holes and slots.

The painstaking attempts to perfect the system continued day after day, week after week, as usual accompanied by daily letters from Emy Reitsch. Eventually, Hanna had to make the final and most alarming test, the vertical dive. Watched by Hans Jacobs, Professor Georgii, and the assembled pilots and engineers of the Glider Research Institute, she climbed to 9000 ft. For a moment, she was tempted to postpone the dive by another day: perhaps the glider would not, after all, withstand the strain.

'I don't have to do it,' she thought. 'I could make some excuse to land and go up again tomorrow. It's my life I have to answer for.'

Then she imagined her mother in front of her: 'She feels, I know, more strongly than anything else except her love for me, that however much she may worry I must live the life allotted to me.'

Inspired by the maternal vision, but tense in every nerve, she put the Sperber into a vertical dive, 'through 7000—8000 —9000 ft, while the machine, all the while as steady as a board, never once exceeds the speed of 125 mph'.

Her excitement was shared by everyone waiting anxiously on the ground, and later by Udet, his friend and colleague Ritter von Greim, and other Luftwaffe generals to whom the dive brakes were equally successfully demonstrated. On that occasion, instead of levelling out at 600 ft, as on the first demonstration, Hanna continued to dive until she was only 300 ft above the heads of the onlookers: by then, Jacobs was beginning to feel extremely nervous—it was his work that was being put to the test. He need not have worried: Hanna knew what she was doing, but could not resist the temptation to show off perhaps a little more than necessary. Once again, her audience was impressed, and she was invited to repeat the performance in the spring of 1937 for the chief German aviation designers.

When she was not test-flying at Darmstadt, Hanna continued to play her part as an aerial ambassadress whenever called upon to do so. Her public appearances, whether at home or abroad, were sure of a favourable reception. The more attention could be diverted from the political and military aspirations of the Third Reich, the better for its leaders. There was plenty of scope for propaganda in Germany in 1936: for three years, plans had been under way to make the Berlin Olympics the greatest international showpiece for modern Germany.

National news from the start of Hitler's regime reported only what seemed good for Germany and the Führer. The best way to ensure this was to own the newspapers. It was not long before the entire press, as well as radio, was under direct or indirect government control, overseen by Hitler's Minister of Propaganda and Public Enlightenment, Dr Joseph Goebbels. Nothing was to be published or broadcast which might weaken the strength of the Third Reich, offend the honour and dignity of Germany, or mislead the public; in other words, all news must be favourable to Hitler and the Nazi party. This created an apparent uniformity of opinion in the country.

The vitriolic anti-Semitic verbal attacks of the Nazi leaders were infectious. It is impossible to assess how many people were genuinely affected, and how many merely paid lip-service to the racial attitudes advocated by their leaders. As one of the first edicts of the Nazi state was that no Jew could be a journalist, there was no counter-propaganda platform. By 1936, Jews had been deprived by law of the right to German citizenship; they could neither marry nor conduct extramarital affairs with German citizens; and they had been banned from all professions except the law, medicine, and private business— in none of which they were welcome. Shops, hotels, even entire towns, displayed signs proclaiming that Jews would not be admitted.

It was, however, tacitly admitted that other nations might not understand the official Nazi attitude to the Jews: a week or so before the start of the Winter Olympics at Garmisch, near Munich, all the local anti-Semitic signs were removed, as they were in the summer for the main sporting festivities in Berlin.

The winter games started the year well for Germany's image abroad. The visiting foreigners were impressed by the scenery, the weather, the games, the lavish and efficient organisation, and the courtesy of their hosts. Part of the daily entertainment was an aerial display given by Ernst Udet, Peter Riedel, and Hanna Reitsch above the open-air ice rink.

Udet, a First World War flying ace and an inveterate showman, had just been made a senior Luftwaffe colonel, after considerable persuasion had been exerted by Goering: his salary had gone down from 200,000 to 13,000 marks a year, and he had had to sell his flying circus, his two private aircraft, and his sports car. His heart was not in administrative work, for which he had neither the ability nor the knowledge, and he took every opportunity to escape from his desk to demonstrate his outstanding and fearless talent in the air.

The Winter Olympics finished on 18 February. Three weeks later, German troops moved into the demilitarised zone of the

Rhineland, which had been occupied by the French under the terms of the Treaty of Versailles from the end of the war until 1930. Hitler's military occupation of the Rhineland was a bloodless victory, accompanied by dramatic promises of future peace, and was greeted in Germany, if nowhere else, with wild enthusiasm. A general election was held at the end of March, before there was time for the euphoria to subside: according to the official figures, there was 99 per cent turnout, of whom 98.8 per cent confirmed Hitler's dictatorship: few people would have dared to vote against him, but the majority would probably have voted for him voluntarily.

Germany nevertheless still needed as many boosts abroad as possible in the following months. Hanna was sent in May with Peter Riedel to Sweden, with two gliders belonging to Lufthansa. She was only there long enough to give several acrobatic displays, and then left Riedel with Ernst Jachtmann and Joachim Küttner to continue the good work. Anti-Semitism had not yet made itself felt when it came to representing German gliding abroad: Küttner had come from Finland, where he had stayed to establish a gliding school after the 1935 German expedition. He was, and remained, one of Hanna's closest friends: in spite of her support for the nationalist and 'socialist' ideals of the Nazis, she never succumbed to the pressure to discriminate against people on racial grounds, and even managed to remain oblivious of the discrimination so openly exercised against the Jews. With her blue eyes and blonde hair, she had of course perfect Aryan colouring.

There were fewer visitors to the Berlin Olympics in August than had been hoped. They were described in England by Commander Stephen King-Hall as the most memorable event of the year in the realm of sport, although his praise was barbed:

> The occasion was regarded—quite rightly—by the rulers of the Third Reich as affording a gigantic opportunity for advertising the energy, efficiency, and high standard of physical fitness obtained under the national discipline of the new-born Germany.
>
> There is no doubt that the elaboration, the efficiency, and the pageantry of the games reached heights never

before equalled and unlikely to be surpassed. This is the kind of thing that Nazi Germany does supremely well. For three years all the relevant resources of Germany had been laid under charge to make this Olympiad the most wonderful sports gathering the world had ever seen, and the results were marvellous. Nothing had been forgotten, even to flocks of thousands of peace doves which rose at the appropriate moment into the air before the vast crowds, the 5000 competitors, and the officials of 52 nations gathered in the colossal stadium. The fate of these doves is not known . . . Perhaps they have flown south over the Alps in search of olive leaves in Italy.

Among the foreigners who entered enthusiastically into the spirit of the event was an impressionable English schoolboy called Eric Brown. Eric's father was one of a group of First World War British fighter pilots invited to Berlin by Udet, whose habit of entertaining members of the foreign flying fraternity in Germany was unpopular with those at home who resented his sudden rise to prominence. They had a point: it was not long since Udet had been turned down as an instructor at Rechlin, the chief Luftwaffe testing centre, because he was considered to be something of a joke, a mere stuntman and a flying clown. As a figurehead and a propagandist for the Luftwaffe, he was however an excellent choice. Eric Brown immediately fell under Udet's spell, and was even further impressed when the newly appointed colonel introduced him to 'the great German aviatrix, Hanna Reitsch'.

During the first week of the Olympics, Hanna was one of a German gliding team which gave formation and acrobatic displays above the stadium and the airfields of Tempelhof and Staaken. Five other nations—Bulgaria, Yugoslavia, Austria, Switzerland, and Hungary—were represented in what was supposed to be an international aerobatic gliding competition. The magazine *Luftsport* reported that 'Everyone worth mentioning, Bräutigam, Hofmann, Huth, Krekel and the never-failing Hanna Reitsch romped around the sky . . .' All those mentioned were German. Another German woman, Melitta Schiller, who had scientific and technical as well as flying qualifications, performed aerobatics in a Heinkel He 70 Blitz on the Olympic flying day, when German military air power was paraded in the skies above Berlin.

The 1936 Rhön contest had been postponed until the second half of August because of the Olympic Games. When Hanna arrived at the Wasserkuppe, she discovered that she was officially barred from competing by a new sentence in the regulations: 'Women are not permitted to enter the competition.' Until then, nothing had actively been done to prevent women from taking part, although their participation had never been encouraged.

Hanna was furious, and set about getting her own way with terrier-like persistence by enlisting the support of Udet, whom she of course already knew both as a Luftwaffe leader and as a fellow gliding enthusiast, and Goering, whom she met for the first time several years later. When Hanna Reitsch was determined, the only way to escape was to give in. She competed in a Rhönsperber Junior, with more success than she had had with the Grunau Baby. Out of sixty-one competitors, she finished the contest in fifth place overall, two behind

*Rhönsperber Junior*

Peter Riedel and one above Wolfgang Späte, and achieved the longest flight, of over 600 miles.

The ban on women was part of the policy of encouraging young men to fly so that they could later become military pilots. There was no point in wasting government money on training women, as they were not allowed to fly in combat. Almost imperceptibly, gliding as a sport was brought under government control. First a voluntary light-blue uniform was introduced; at the 1933 Rhön competition there were few uniforms, but the proportion of men in light blue increased year by year. Then came drilling and marching. This seemed a small price to pay for the privilege of subsidised flying, whether as a member of the Hitler Youth, with a flying club, or as a cadet with the Nazi flying corps. Discipline was strict, but then discipline was in any case a prime requirement for glider pilots.

The steps towards militarisation were so gradual that they were accepted unquestioningly by the majority, and seemed ominous only to a small and unrepresentative minority. The Heil Hitler salute had already become a standard form of official greeting throughout the country. Glider pilots were for the most part young and idealistic, and if they thought about politics at all those who flew at clubs, as well as Hanna's colleagues at the DFS, approved of the new regime.

While Hanna was entertaining the crowds over Berlin and fighting for her right to compete at the Wasserkuppe, German military air power was being tested for the first time, in Spain. The Spanish Civil War had a romantic appeal, but whereas it attracted individual leftwing idealists from Britain and France, Germany hastened to the aid of Franco's struggle for supremacy of the Right. Hitler had just agreed to a non-intervention pact prohibiting the sale of arms to Spain by France, Russia, Germany, Italy and Portugal. The first German volunteers travelled ostensibly as civilians, on *Kraft durch Freude*—'Strength through Joy'—cruises from Hamburg. *Kraft durch Freude* was one of many Nazi slogans chosen for their innocuous public appeal.

In spite of the unease which afflicted so much of Europe during the mid-1930s, they were the happiest years of Hanna's life: indeed they were perhaps her only really happy years. She had outgrown the tempestuous conflicts of emotion which had so often assailed her during her youth. Her passion for flying had become a way of life, and even a means of earning her living, and she felt that she knew where she was going.

# 4

# Flight Captain Reitsch

In the spring of 1937, Hanna became a Flugkapitän, or Flight Captain. It was a civilian title normally reserved for the most eminent, and of course male, Lufthansa pilots. She had earned it through the work that she had undertaken during the previous year, and in particular for the tests on dive brakes for Hans Jacobs. Officially, she satisfied none of the minimum requirements for the rank: she should have had a commercial licence for at least six years, have worked as a test, research, or experimental pilot for a full three years, and have clocked up at least 2000 flying hours on powered aircraft. Udet had, however, decided to make her an exception, the first honorary flight captain in Germany.

She was inordinately proud of the distinction conferred on her, and never let anyone forget it. Her claim to despise honours, made only two years earlier, was apparently forgotten, as was the humility advocated by her mother. Hanna always wanted to share her delight in herself with other people, and assumed that they would feel an equal pleasure with and for her. It was both an endearing and an infuriating trait, and one that on occasion turned friends against her: male pilots did not like to feel inferior.

Considerable publicity was given to her promotion, and to the claim that she was the first female flight captain in Germany. As far as she knew, this was true; a Berliner who had captained a Zeppelin airship in 1913 had been forgotten. Although she was not entitled to wear a captain's uniform, or indeed any uniform, she designed an official-looking outfit for herself, and wore it proudly on ceremonial occasions.

Whenever she saw any of her friends or relatives, she embarked on a lively and enthusiastic account of her latest exploit in the air, or told them with pride how she was now a Flugkapitän. Her vivid and entertaining stories brought a touch of glamour and excitement into the routine of their own lives, and they did not object. Many people have told me that she was an equally good listener, but that after a few minutes she dominated almost any conversation. She was, however, so busy with her work at the DFS, as well as with competitions and expeditions, that she had little time for old friendships, and was rarely at home in Hirschberg. Her parents occasionally visited her—her mother more often than her father, whose medical and musical interests continued to absorb him.

Even at her sister's wedding, in March 1937, Hanna outtalked the rest of the family. Heidi had grown up into a cheerful, attractive, and warm-hearted young woman. She was still prettier than Hanna, as well as gentler, with a natural and easy-going manner and none of her older sister's ambition and instinct for self-dramatisation. Kurt's schoolfriend Gustav-Adolf Macholz had transferred his affection to the younger of the Reitsch girls: Hanna was as delighted as anyone else about the marriage.

It was generally agreed among those who knew them both that he would in any case have been no match for Hanna. Her cousin Gertrud Heuberger considered him 'very nice, but a bit dim', a judgement not shared by Kurt; but the Heuberger family prized intellectual ability above the qualities which Macholz showed as an honest and handsome young army officer. By the time Gustav-Adolf's leave was over and he had to abandon Heidi to the care of his parents-in-law, she was expecting their first child, and was looking forward to the time when they would be able to make a home of their own.

Kurt had been transferred to destroyers in 1936, and in 1937 went twice to Spain with the torpedo-boat *Seeadler*. A few days before the pocket battleship *Deutschland* was bombed in Ibiza, several light bombs narrowly missed his ship: like the *Deutschland,* it was part of a non-combatant international patrol. He knew nothing of the outrage felt throughout the rest of the world when a few days earlier German aircraft had been used in the destruction of the small Basque town of Guernica. As usual, the Nazi press reported only what it was told to report: Guernica was not mentioned. German aircraft and pilots had by then been actively supporting Franco's struggle for the supremacy of the Right in Spain for a year.

While Kurt's life was in danger in Spain, Hanna was on a gliding expedition in the Alps. The International Study Commission for Motorless Flight was meeting in Salzburg under the chairmanship of Professor Georgii. Glider pilots from Germany, Austria, Switzerland, France, and Czechoslovakia were competing. For once, there was another woman competitor, with the Austrian team. Hanna outshone her in a Sperber Junior specially built for her by Hans Jacobs. It was so tailor-made that when she was in her seat she could hardly move: no one else could fit into the tiny cockpit.

She was one of six German glider pilots who crossed the Alps at the end of May, flying from Salzburg to land over a hundred miles away and several cold and anxious hours later in Italy. Hanna's delight was echoed in the newspaper headlines: 'German pilots' triumphant success . . .' Although Heini Dittmar had flown over the highest peaks the previous year, he had landed twenty miles short of a full Alpine crossing. With no radio contact and no engine, flying over the Alps was a hazardous undertaking. Each pilot was issued before leaving with emergency rations, Very lights, and parachutes, none of which was standard equipment for normal cross-country flights.

Hanna alternated between elation at the beauty of the peaks and valleys beneath her, and near despair. Sometimes, and indeed even at the start, she encountered only down draughts, until at last she was able to gain height under a cloud or in the lift from a steep slope. Then, with a mountain chain called the Sea of Stone ahead of her, she was again drawn down relentlessly. She had never felt closer to death:

> Now I am completely surrounded by mountains, and feel myself gripped by fear. If this is the end of my flight . . .
> Still my bird is aiming at the Sea of Stone . . . The steep bleached and weatherbeaten walls of rock and the jagged peaks look nearer and nearer. But above me a few

strands of cloud are gathering, a small ray of hope. Can I reach them before my Sperber is smashed to pieces on the rock?

It is eerie to see the mountain towering higher and higher ahead! No chance below me of landing safely! The pale shadow of my Sperber Junior is already coming up to meet me over the stony ground. My fear is growing and choking me. Then suddenly, only thirty yards away, I see two jackdaws circling near the mountainside. I fly close to them, so close that I am afraid that I shall brush the mountain. And now I too am lifted . . .

She was saved by the birds, and flew on, sometimes as high as 13,000 ft, shivering in thin white trousers, her hands numb without gloves, so cold that she could scarcely appreciate the beauty of the glaciers. Even her brain felt frozen by the time she landed, on an Italian parade-ground: the soldiers gave her glider a triumphal shoulder ride to the barracks.

Hanna felt that she had a special relationship with the Sperber Junior after it had carried her across the Alps, and crept into its hangar in Darmstadt every morning to talk to it and stroke its sides.

It was however not with the Sperber, but with another new Hans Jacobs design, a Reiher, that Hanna entered the first International Gliding Contest at the Wasserkuppe just over a month later. The Reiher still needed considerable modification, and although Hanna managed a flight to Hamburg, created a women's long-distance record, and shared a prize of 1000 marks for the longest distance with Heini Dittmar and a member of the Polish team, she had difficulty in holding it level. The Germans showed their supremacy in the sport which they had invented and developed. Hanna finished in sixth place, three places behind her arch-rival Wolfgang Späte: Heini Dittmar came first, for which he won the Hitler Prize.

Neither effort nor expense was spared to impress the foreign participants, for whom food and lodging were provided free of charge in a well-run camp. Spectators were charged one mark a day, and as many as 4500 people turned up each day to watch. A full-time force of some 150 men policed the ground and looked after the gliders. The foreigners—from

Britain, Poland, Czechoslovakia, Austria, and Yugoslavia—commented favourably on the efficiency of the Rhön organisation. They were even more impressed by the enthusiasm and friendliness of the back-up teams who rushed unasked to help: the British nicknamed them 'the Wasserkuppe slaves'.

Gliding in Britain was a newer and more haphazard sport than in Germany, and the Germans were surprised to discover that anyone who had passed the C test could fly cross-country 'without the police saying anything about it'. Later in August, sixteen young Germans joined nine aspiring British pilots on a gliding course in England run by an organisation called the Anglo-German Fellowship. With Wolf Hirth and Eva Schmidt, another blonde, blue-eyed pilot, Hanna spent a couple of days at Dunstable while the course was in progress: the object of their visit was to promote interest in and sales of Hirth's two-seater Minimoa. From Dunstable, they went to the British National Gliding Competition at Camphill in Derbyshire.

It was Hanna's first visit to England. A shadow was cast over it before she arrived at Camphill. British and German glider pilots shared an idealistic and obsessive interest in flying and agreed that political differences were irrelevant. Not everyone in Derbyshire shared this view. There was criticism in the local press when it was announced that some of Germany's top glider pilots were to be there, as well as the twenty-five youths who had been at Dunstable.

The day before they were to leave, Wolf Hirth's Klemm was put out of action. The Camphill airfield had been formed from a dozen small fields; the dividing stone walls had been laboriously taken down by flying-club members. When Eva Schmidt came in to land after refuelling the Klemm, she ran across one of the remaining wall roots. The aircraft was immediately wheeled down to the club workshop, where the young Germans from the Anglo-German Fellowship worked to repair it at high speed throughout the night. No one else was allowed near it. *The Manchester Guardian* called Hanna Captain Anna Reitsch and published a photograph of the Klemm's tail, complete with swastika, sticking out of the workshop door.

Hanna made little impression in England, but attracted the

*Fieseler Storch*

appreciative attention of a British pilot called Reginald Brie at an international air show at Zurich that summer. He had never seen a high-performance glider before, and admired a display in what he described as 'a very elegant-looking soaring plane, with long tapering wings': 'The landing was especially skilful—I never thought it would pull up in time: when it came in on its last swoop, I was certain it would overshoot. When a rather diminutive, attractive, fair-haired girl stepped out of the cockpit, I was most surprised.'

The attractive, diminutive girl was of course Hanna, the only woman pilot present among the representatives of several countries. The emphasis was on military flying, with daily formation flights and demonstrations by half a dozen European air forces. Udet, Milch and Goering were all there, and the Germans were clearly out to impress with their latest aircraft, including Dornier bombers. Udet flew a Fieseler Storch, so called because its tall, thin landing-gear was reminiscent of a stork. Flying was still, in spite of political tensions, very much an international camaraderie. Brie was disappointed that the flying meeting organised by the Swiss received very little attention in the British press; so, no doubt, were the German representatives, who were using every opportunity to publicise their Luftwaffe's superiority.

Although there was no more committed Nazi than Goering, Udet held himself as aloof as possible from the political aspects of the Luftwaffe. On occasion, he even went so far as to express openly critical views, although only in private, and preferably abroad. In Zurich he showed a Swiss pamphlet to several glider pilots, including Heini Dittmar's older brother Edgar. 'It described events quite differently from the way they were presented in Germany, where propaganda had been given out which everyone was meant to believe—just as in Russia today,' Edgar Dittmar told me fifty years later, 'but there in the document Udet showed us we saw everything, not as it had been presented to us and as we were meant to believe it, but as it really was. It was dangerous—if one of us glider pilots had said a word in Germany, it would have cost Udet his head.' Udet had already told Dittmar that before long there would be war. 'Of course, I didn't believe in the seriousness of the situation,' Dittmar admitted, 'but the rest of the world saw it differently.'

'Germany was rearming,' Hanna wrote in the first of her autobiographical books many years later. 'We saw it. The world saw it. But we saw it with different eyes from the rest of the world.' No one except the Germans appreciated their particular brand of patriotism and of hope for the future. Hanna was far from alone in not suspecting 'the tragedy that was being prepared'. She wanted peace, and was certain that 'The German people wanted peace, even if the rest of the world will no longer admit it.'

It was, however, to be as she put it a peace 'which allowed us to live', and which accepted Hitler's concept of Lebensraum: it apparently did not worry Hanna and her fellow patriots that this inevitably threatened the 'living space' of neighbouring nations. Nazi Germany offered an answer to the prayers of, as Hanna described it, 'a nation which had a confined living space squeezed between other nations, and which, after years of poverty and uncertainty, was at last seeing bread and making progress, and knew that in the world the weak will always be threatened: because it believed that it too had a right to protect itself, it saw in its growing military strength an increase in its power and in its ability to maintain peace'.

'What nation in the world would not have felt a justifiable pride?' asked Hanna, who called Stukas, bombers, and fighters 'guardians at the portals of peace'. It was, therefore, not surprising that when, in September 1937, Udet invited her to join the élite band of military test pilots at Rechlin, near Berlin, she accepted the secondment with alacrity.

She carried out her duties at Rechlin with pride, knowing that she had reached the summit of aviation, and with a constant sense of satisfaction that her caution and thoroughness would protect the lives of those who flew after her. They in turn would protect the country which she saw beneath her as she flew and which meant so much to her: 'a country of fields and meadows, of hills and mountains, of woods and water. There might be others on earth more splendid, but this was the only one for me, because it was my homeland. Was it not worth flying for?'

Her first task at the military testing centre was to test dive brakes on Stukas. Udet, who had been made head of the Luftwaffe's technical department, was obsessed with the idea of dive-bombers. He had been enticed by Goering into the Luftwaffe with the promise of two Curtiss Hell Divers: their dive-bombing ability had excited him when he was in the United States in his flying-circus days, although then he had thought of using them for stunts rather than as military aircraft.

The Stuka was not an easy plane to fly for someone as small as Hanna: it was large, heavy, and high off the ground. Both physical strength and courage were needed to dive it from high altitudes. Dive-bombing tests were also made by Melitta Schiller, who at the end of 1937 became the second woman Flugkapitän. Hanna ignored, and was even on occasions heard to belittle, Melitta's achievements. As they were at the time the only two professional female test pilots in Germany, and probably in the world, they might have been expected to support each other. Instead, according to the accounts of people who knew them both, they were bitter rivals. Hanna refused to have anything to do with Melitta, who was several years older, or to acknowledge her as an equal. Her attitude can only be explained as professional jealousy, although she would not have admitted to such an ignoble sentiment and expected to be treated on equal terms by her male colleagues.

Hanna took her orders directly from Udet, as did her immediate boss, Karl Franke. Franke had every possible flying qualification as well as an engineering diploma. He claimed that he knew only two 'truly gifted natural pilots': Udet and Hanna. In Franke's opinion, 'There was actually nobody, neither male nor female, who could compete with Hanna as far as flying was concerned . . . She was at that time the most gifted pilot in Germany, maybe even in the world.'

She nevertheless turned down his invitation to take over the controls of a Dornier bomber in which they flew together to Augsburg: 'Franco, I can't—I've never flown such a big aircraft.' While Franke was at a meeting, she taught herself to fly it mentally, sitting in the cockpit to familiarise herself with the controls and thinking over her observations from the outward flight. When he returned she told him confidently: 'Now I can fly it.' She then piloted him expertly back to Rechlin. Through her combination of concentration and instinct, Hanna needed less conversion time than most of the men on any unfamiliar aircraft. They saw this as favouritism, and were often resentful.

No women, and very few men, had ever flown a helicopter. When Professor Focke asked Franke to 'train' a revolutionary new aircraft, the FW 61, he invited Hanna to fly him to Bremen in her favourite bomber, a Dornier 17. The FW 61, designed by Gerd Achgelis and built at the Focke-Wulf factory, has gone down in German aviation history as the world's first viable helicopter: with its two vertically mounted three-bladed rotors, held clear of a wingless biplane fuselage on outriggers, it looked more like a giant mechanical mosquito supported on a tricycle than a serious flying machine.

For Franke's introductory flight, it was tethered to the runway so that it could rise only a few feet above the ground: no one knew quite how it would behave. He soon discovered that fast control movements were essential to keep it balanced as it hovered at the end of its tether in the reflection from the air cushion: it was such a difficult and uncomfortable ride that after fifteen minutes he had had more than enough.

There was no pitch lever, so ascent and descent could only be controlled by engine power and throttle. On his second take-off, to which he agreed only reluctantly, Franke gave too much power: as there was no give in the anchor ropes, the helicopter broke loose. Once it was free to rise above its own turbulence, it became much easier and pleasanter to handle. When Franke landed, after half an hour, Hanna was so excited that she hugged him—her friends were used to her emotional outbursts. 'You must never fly it tethered again,' she said.

Although she had not dared to suggest it, Hanna accepted with alacrity when she was asked if she would like to fly the helicopter. She had of course been watching carefully, and followed her observations with a detailed discussion before climbing into the cockpit. Deliberately emptying her mind of the flying habits which had become second nature, she first looked down to see the position of the undercarriage wheels in relation to the white painted circle from which she was to take off. Then she opened the throttle slowly, revving the engine in short bursts until 'the miracle happened and the helicopter began to rise vertically from the ground'.

At 300 ft, she throttled back until she was hovering motionless in mid-air. The experience was exhilarating: 'I thought of the lark, the light little bird which hovered above the fields. Man had wrested from it the most wonderful secret . . . how to rise vertically towards the sun . . . and hang motionless between heaven and earth.' Within a few minutes, Hanna felt that she had mastered the unfamiliar technique. Then, using the throttle and controls, she moved backwards, sideways, and forwards again to position herself directly over the white circle on the ground, before dropping almost vertically to land on the spot from which she had taken off. It was an impressive performance.

A few weeks later, she was called upon to repeat it for Charles Lindbergh, who was equally impressed and called the helicopter the most striking aeronautical development he had ever seen. Hanna was proud of the part she had played in persuading one of the greatest living aviation pioneers that Germany had an exciting new aircraft, and proud of the series of world records which she created on a flight in four stages from Bremen to Staaken—although as so few people had flown helicopters, it would have been difficult not to achieve a number of firsts.

Udet was equally excited by and sceptical of the claims made for the Focke-Achgelis helicopter. When Hanna demonstrated it for an audience of army and air force generals, Udet put it to the test in a competition with the Fieseler Storch, the new liaison and reconnaissance aircraft which he had given its first public airing at the Zurich air show. Visibility was down to fifty yards: the spectators were relieved, and scarcely less surprised, when Udet succeeded in clearing the invisible control tower in the Storch.

Then it was Hanna's turn. She rose, hovered, bobbed the helicopter in a curtsey, and flew a few yards in every direction, low enough over the heads of the assembled generals for her display to be clearly seen despite the fog, and finally dropped vertically to land lightly in front of them. This was enough to convince Udet and his colleagues. Hanna was awarded a military flying medal, although she was still technically a civilian on loan to the military testing centre.

Apart from Lindbergh, whose warnings about the strength of the Luftwaffe and enthusiasm for anything German were becoming an international joke, the representatives of aviation outside Germany refused to take the helicopter as seriously as Udet had hoped. So much propaganda was emanating from Nazi Germany that stories of a wonder-aircraft which could rise vertically and hover at the pilot's will were dismissed as yet another attempt to impress with less than a half truth.

Even if there was such an aircraft, many people agreed with Reginald Brie, who had sold several Cierva autogiros to Germany and had trained German pilots to fly them: although he later changed his opinion, he explained to me that at the time he thought that 'The only thing the autogiro could not do was hover in still air, which seemed a bit silly anyway as people wanted to get from one place to another.' The autogiro was simpler, cheaper to build and, in Brie's view, generally more useful than the helicopter, with its superfluous ability to stay in one place.

Apart from the suspicion that the helicopter was not the wonder-aircraft the Germans claimed it to be, few people outside Germany were in any mood to praise the country's technological achievements, or to believe that Hitler's aims were as peaceful as he tried to make out. It seemed increasingly as if the people who had so vociferously voted him into power were living on an island of self-congratulation in which even the words of the Nazi marching song, 'Today Germany hears us, and tomorrow the whole world', failed to act as a warning.

Six million people who before Hitler's rule had been unemployed had work: they believed in the present after the hardship of the past, and were reluctant to see the future as anything but bright. The contention of the Nazi leaders that fellow Germans in foreign-held territory should be allowed to share Hitler's promised land was welcomed. The ideal of German unity was mixed up with the prospect of prosperity, rearmament with motorways and cars for the people: the Volkswagen was as much a symbol as the Stuka or the swastika.

Udet, who was at heart still a showman, had the bright idea of forcing the helicopter on the attention of the world at the 1938 Berlin Motor Show, the one annual national occasion on which favourable international press coverage could be assured: the German car and motor-cycle industry was highly regarded, and had proved itself with a series of Mercedes-Benz and Auto-Union racing successes. For once, political differences would be laid aside when as usual Berlin became for three weeks the world's motoring showplace and meeting-point.

Goering accepted Udet's scheme of presenting the helicopter to the public during the variety review to be held every evening. Hanna was to fly it on the first night, to guarantee maximum publicity: the Focke-Wulf test pilot, Karl Bode, who was to take over on subsequent evenings, was less glamorous, although he had considerably more experience with the helicopter. As the venue for the performance was the Deutschlandhalle, a covered stadium with a huge tiered seat-ing capacity, the stunt was obviously a hazardous undertaking. Hanna was confident of her own ability, but aware of the danger: 'If it was technically unsafe, then the risk to thousands of spectators' lives ought not to be taken at all. The technical aspect was however not my responsibility, but the designer's.'

As the opening night approached, Udet became increasingly nervous: the responsibility for the propaganda success of the demonstration was his. On two occasions, he even tried to back out of it, or at least to withdraw Hanna: if anything were to go wrong, a public disaster involving Germany's flying heroine would destroy his own reputation and probably his career. Hanna's brother and several of her friends tried to persuade him to replace her. Her parents gave only their reluctant consent—even at the age of twenty-six, Hanna felt it necessary to gain their approval. She herself would have refused to take part if she had felt able to disobey an order: she resented being used as a stunt artiste in a variety show, and was afraid that her colleagues would ridicule her.

Once Udet had persuaded Goering to agree, and Goering had in turn gained approval from Hitler, there was however no going back. Although neither Goering nor Hitler knew Hanna personally at the time, they considered her as great an asset to Nazi propaganda as the helicopter itself.

Eric Brown, who was staying with Udet during the final stages of preparation for the opening night, commented that Udet's flat resembled the waiting-room at Charing Cross Station. Among the constant stream of visitors, Brown, by then a student, identified Milch, Molders, and Jeschonnek. Hanna was a frequent guest. In the evenings she, Udet, and Eric Brown sat together talking about flying and drinking wine: Hanna talked but did not drink.

Politics were never discussed. The young Englishman suspected that this was because of his presence, but it is unlikely that Hanna and Udet talked in private about anything except flying. They liked and respected each other, and were mutually useful: as Udet's protégée, Hanna's career seemed guaranteeed, while he recognised both her ability as a pilot and her publicity value for military aviation.

The helicopter was assembled before the start of rehearsals

inside the stadium. An African village was constructed as a background to the theme of Germany's lost colonies: their loss was still resented and nostalgia leant a glamour to their memory. Everywhere Hanna went, she was haunted by the exaggerated promises of garish posters: 'Deutschlandhalle—Kisuaheli! Through the tropics at 200 miles an hour! Dancing Girls, Fakirs, Clowns, Blackamoors!' She felt ill at ease among the strange assortment of entertainers who were all equally unlikely inhabitants of any colony.

Hanna and Karl Bode adopted different approaches to the problem of flying in an enclosed space. He played for safety by flying low; she flew high for maximum effect—it would, she felt, be more exciting if the helicopter were to be seen above even the highest tiers of seats, rather than below half the spectators. It was unfortunate for Bode that there should have been an audience of Luftwaffe generals when one of the rotor blades broke while he was flying during a rehearsal. Although no one was injured, the visual effect of danger was exacerbated by the way the helicopter rocked in the turbulence near the ground.

In the evening after the accident, Hanna telephoned Elly Beinhorn, who had witnessed the first part of the rehearsal: 'Did you see the accident?' Hanna asked her. 'Thank God you weren't there: it was dreadful—there were splinters from the rotor blades flying around and the flamingos were all creating.'

Goering was less worried about upsetting the flamingos than about spoiling the propaganda effect of the display with an accident: he insisted that Bode should be withdrawn from the programme in favour of Hanna. Neither pilot was pleased. Bode had good reason to be annoyed: a technical fault could not be blamed on him, and he would have had most of the work and none of the glory. Hanna had reluctantly to endure the spotlights night after night. She managed to convince herself that she was sacrificing her self-esteem for the greater good and glory of Germany: the honour of being chosen to show the world her country's latest aeronautical achievement outweighed the indignity, of being associated with the vulgarity of circus and music hall entertainment.

On the opening night, she watched the early part of the

entertainment with Udet, who in spite of the official ban on smoking was lighting one cigarette after another to calm his nerves. The only part of her performance that was worrying her was the Heil Hitler salute with which she had to finish. She had practised it for hours, while Udet sat in an armchair comfortably puffing at a cigar, before he had professed himself satisfied.

Dancing and singing chorus girls in skimpy costumes, somersaulting clowns, circus acrobats, so-called African natives billed as 'Blackamoors', 'Fakirs', and even exotically elegant flamingos cavorted in turn round the village of jungle huts in the arena of the vast stadium. At the end of the main part of the review, the hall was plunged into darkness for a few seconds.

'Ladies and gentlemen, you are reminded to hold on to your hats and any other loose items.' The announcement was made into a tensely expectant silence over the loudspeaker.

As it gradually became light again, giant spotlights picked out a tent: it opened slowly to reveal a strange silver machine which had certainly never been seen in any German colonial jungle. The lights focused on the lettering of Deutschland painted on its wingless fuselage as mechanics in spotless white overalls pushed it into the centre of the 240 ft by 120 ft arena.

Hanna was almost overcome by an urge to laugh hysterically as she rose above the spectators: thousands of people were gazing up at her, all obediently sitting with their hands on their heads so that their hats would not be whirled off in the helicopter's draught. It was only because she was encountering an unexpected technical problem that she was able to regain her composure: so much oxygen was being used by the vast audience that the engine was lacking in power. For later performances, all the doors were opened wide to allow a constant supply of fresh air: this may explain why several eyewitnesses later insisted that Hanna actually flew through the barn doors at the entrance of the stadium.

Forty thousand people saw Hanna's flight in the Deutschlandhalle during the show's three-week run. It was her most widely publicised pre-war flying achievement. The helicopter at last received recognition in international aviation circles, although to those with less interest in flying the meticulous displays were something of an anticlimax after the circus acts and chorus girls. Hanna had neither sought to become a variety artiste, nor did she enjoy the experience. Professionally, it enhanced her reputation, but at the same time it damaged her relationship with her colleagues: her intrusion into a male world had been accepted reluctantly, but her cheerfulness and unassuming attitude had in the past usually smoothed over any tensions.

Now, her growing fame and her close association with senior members of the Luftwaffe were increasingly resented, especially as she had never learnt to curb the enthusiasm with which she talked about her own achievements. She wanted to be treated as an equal, and resented it when she was treated as a woman. Wolfgang Späte admitted to me that he had attempted, unsuccessfully, to use masculine charm to get round her in a disagreement over who should fly the Reiher 111, a new glider at the DFS where, after her attachment to Rechlin ended, they were colleagues. He was convinced that if

*FW 61*

he had said the word, Hanna would have married him, and that she would have been a wonderful wife for the right man. Hanna still had no intention of marrying.

When she came up against what she considered to be obstructive attitudes caused by male prejudice, she turned for support to her superiors. Udet in particular was prepared to give it, and to single her out for tasks in the public eye where her femininity was an asset. This merely exacerbated the problem, as she then seemed to be behaving as if she was rather more than equal. Her role as Nazi Germany's flying heroine, unsought but not at the time unwelcome, was to cause her problems for the rest of her life.

# 5

# From Peace
# to War

Within a month of Hanna's last performance in the Deutschlandhalle, Germany had absorbed Austria in the Anschluss.
Hanna had always felt that the Austrian side of her family
was as German as she was: their official inclusion in what
was rapidly becoming Greater Germany reaffirmed their common heritage.

Since the end of the First World War, the Anschluss had
been the wish of many Austrians, including Hanna's uncle
Richard Heuberger, a blind history professor. He had lost his
sight in the First World War, but had not allowed this to
curtail his energy or curb his interest. Although he had strong
reservations about Hitler, the choice seemed to be between
two evils: Austria too, under Dollfuss and Schuschnigg, was
a dictatorship. Helmut, the youngest of the professor's three
children, was an enthusiastic member of the Hitler Youth,
although the National Socialst party had been banned after an
abortive Anschluss attempt in 1934: he joined the crowds which
shouted 'Heil Hitler!' in the streets to welcome the Germans in
February 1938 after the bloodless overnight German victory.

The Anschluss was approved in Austria in April by a
plebiscite majority of 99 per cent. There was, not surprisingly, equally little dissent in Germany. Other European countries, as well as a more significant minority of Austrians than
the official result of the poll suggests, considered that Hitler
had unlawfully swallowed Austria to satisfy his territorial
appetite: it was seen as the action of a dictator denying a
people its democratic rights, and it was assumed that the vote
was rigged or the voters coerced.

In August, Hanna went to the United States for the first time. She was so unaware of the international attitude towards German rearmament and anti-Semitic discrimination that it came as a shock when she met occasional criticism of her country. Udet, in approving her visit, was aware that she would play a useful ambassadorial role in combating the spread of such feelings.

Peter Riedel, who had recently become assistant air attaché in Washington, had suggested that 'it would give American soaring a boost' if Hanna Reitsch were to participate in the annual Cleveland air races. He met her when she arrived in New York on a German liner, the *Bremen*. Many of her friends and relations had told her that she would hate America: it was considered a vast soulless and mindless mecca of the machine age where life was business, business was money, and culture was non-existent. Udet, on the other hand, had assured her that she would love it. He was right: Hanna loved America, and America loved her—as he had also known it would.

She was thrilled by New York's 'stupendous vistas of naked steel and concrete' and by the beauty of the city at night. American spontaneity and friendliness, and the American sense of humour, appealed to her immediately. Humour, she felt, was a quality sadly lacking in many Germans, and she wished that her fellow countrymen did not have 'such a serious temperament'. Her own ability to laugh, which had so annoyed her teachers when she was a schoolgirl, was undiminished.

Soon after her arrival in New York, her companions pushed her forward to answer a welcoming speech. The idea that she should talk in public in English struck her as intensely comic, but she made a brave attempt. Her use of an expression she had just picked up from the confusing babble around her delighted her audience: 'What a hell goes on . . .' After a moment's embarrassed uncertainty, Hanna joined in the general mirth. Her gaffe was reported in the following day's newspapers, and her unselfconscious but sometimes unfortunate attempts to use their language endeared her to her hosts.

The *New York Times* published a breakfast interview with her. 'Tiny, blonde, blue-eyed, and addicted to tea at breakfast', she was said to have gesticulated with a piece of toast as she promised to land a helicopter on a skyscraper: 'I am come over here next year with a machine, and land on a building.'

She praised the easy equality between men and women, the efficiency of public transport, and the lack of prejudice and preconceived ideas. But she also considered that Americans were in danger of 'absorbing uncritically the opinions served up . . . by press and radio, so acquiring a false sense of values and a uniformity of mind amazing to Europeans'. That precisely this criticism could legitimately be made of Nazi Germany did not occur to her.

On reaching Cleveland, she found the practice of using beauty queens in official ceremonies so unlike the German formality to which she was accustomed that it offended her sense of propriety. When the national flags of the countries participating in the air races were hoisted each day by skimpily clad young ladies, she had to make an effort to accept that this was considered an honour rather than an insult.

Her daily soaring displays during the three flying days at the beginning of September were, by her own account, a rapturously received triumph. She insisted on silence before taking off in a Habicht, a Hans Jacobs glider capable of a full range of aerobatics. It was no easy task to arrange for all the many aircraft engines as well as the usual accompanying music to be turned off, but Hanna was insistent: 'After several hours of events in which the effectiveness was held to be in direct proportion to the amount of accompanying noise, no greater contrast could be imagined than the soundless swoop of that slender shimmering bird, which, despite its name—the Hawk—seemed to come like a dove of peace out of the blue sky.' She performed every imaginable aerobatic figure, and finally landed amid applause which seemed to her never-ending.

After the air races were over, she could have spent several months touring America in response to invitations from German-American friendship groups and other organisations in almost every part of the country. Instead, she and the rest of the German team were recalled by telegram: the crisis in Czechoslovakia had, as she put it, created a dangerous political situation. In America she had at last noticed 'the shadows of the world conflict. I saw them for the first time, without realising that they must mean war: for my thoughts belonged to the wind, the clouds, and the stars, where the world's game of political intrigue cannot reach.'

In September the danger of a war seemed to have been averted when Germany, Britain, France, and Italy agreed in Munich that Germany should occupy the Sudetenland, which Germans felt was rightfully theirs. It was hoped that once Hitler's demand that Czechoslovakia should hand over the areas predominantly occupied by Germans had been satisfied, there would be lasting peace. As Hanna said, the Germans did not want war, but justice, by which they meant the incorporation of all Germans into the Reich. Like many other people, including the British Prime Minister, Hanna assumed that Hitler, too, wanted peace.

National Socialism seemed to her by definition to 'represent the most natural way of life'. She still saw it as an admirable combination of two ideals. 'The seed of nationalism is sown in the cradle where you learn to love and respect your own family,' she explained; 'this love and respect then spreads quite naturally to neighbouring families and thence to your own country and to other nations and peoples with whom you come into contact. Through this appreciation of other nations, the love you feel for your own country becomes deeper than ever before.' Her view of socialism was equally straightforward: 'You are taught as a child to share what you have with your brothers and sisters and your small friends. You are taught to think about others before yourself.' This she considered indestructible, 'the greatest strength that can exist'.

As far as Hanna was concerned, the German people were pursuing the idealistic paths of National Socialism as she saw it, following their leader 'blindly and unquestioningly': she assumed that a leader must, as the highest representative of his people, be followed, and would lead honourably. In 1938, Germany under Adolf Hitler was, as she proudly claimed, 'a progressive, dynamic, and prosperous nation. Even the critics of Hitler had reluctantly to admit that he had done a creditable job in building up the nation and re-establishing her on the map of Europe,' she insisted. 'Never before had the welfare of the masses been so effectively catered for, nor the working man made to feel such a vital part of his country.' She was apparently unaware that Jews were specifically excluded from this benevolence, or that the abbreviated term Nazi had sinister connotations.

Her patriotic idealism received a sudden and severe jolt on the DFS annual outing on 10 November: it coincided with the aftermath of what was to become known as Kristallnacht, the Night of Broken Glass. On 9 November, a German diplomat died in Paris: he had been shot two days earlier by a seventeen-year-old Polish Jew. Indiscriminate reprisals against Jews started immediately throughout Germany, Austria, and the newly acquired territory of the Sudetenland during the night of 9 November.

It has never been satisfactorily proved whether this was officially organised or merely condoned; but on the evening of 10 November Goebbels stated with apparent satisfaction that 'The justified and understandable indignation of the German people at the cowardly Jewish assassination has been vented in a wide degree.' Synagogues had been burned, Jewish shops looted, the houses of Jews had been broken into, and Jewish men, women, and children alike had been dragged from their beds. The streets were littered with the broken glass which gave the night its name.

Hanna's later descriptions of what she saw and of her appalled reaction varied in details: that she protested vehemently has however never been denied by any of those present. In her most detailed account, she described how her attention was first attracted by a disturbance on the other side of the street in a normally quiet market town:

I saw two old people being brought out of their house in their nightdresses. They were protesting and struggling and people were jeering at them. This was followed by a number of shop windows being broken. Then I saw some children coming noisily down the street, dragging behind them a Jewish hearse. They took it to the banks of the River Main, chopped it to bits with axes, and then pushed it into the river.

Her immediate reaction was that 'it must be a Bolshevik uprising at least'. She had been brought up to fear and hate

Communism, and could not imagine that anyone other than a Bolshevik could behave in such a brutal fashion. She shouted for somebody to fetch the police: none of her companions moved.

'How can you stand there and allow such things?' Hanna demanded. 'It is a disgrace that German people should act in such a manner! The Führer would weep if he knew such things were being done in his name!'

She expected that everyone around her would be as outraged as she was. Instead, she found herself being bundled unceremoniously out of the way by Hans Jacobs before she could become the victim of a mob which imagined that she was herself a Jew.

When they returned to their coaches, some of Hanna's colleagues told Jacobs: 'The synagogues are burning.' They did not, he told me, seem unduly disturbed: he had the impression that some of them were even excited by and approved of the violence. Of over a hundred DFS employees, only half a dozen showed any distress at what was happening. Hanna was the most outspoken, and refused to be silenced. She had already been taken to task by Georgii in the past for her open support of Jews, and had complained to Otto Fuchs. 'I agree it's disgusting—but what can we do?' Fuchs had said.

Hans Jacobs gave in to Hanna's insistence that some public protest must be made, and summoned everyone on the outing together as soon as they reached Darmstadt. His announcement was brief and to the point: 'I very much regret that we made our outing on this particular day.' Hanna stated that for the first time in her life she felt ashamed to be German.

Although there were others who agreed with her stance, they did not dare say so. Her apparently anti-Nazi attitude was viewed with disfavour by the majority, who willingly knuckled under to popular opinion to guarantee their own positions. Only Hans Jacobs supported her in public. Associating with Jews was considered a criminal offence, and even standing up for them was suspect: both Hanna and Jacobs risked losing their jobs.

The nephew of the local Gauleiter, the head of the Nazi administrative district, was employed at the DFS. Loyalty to his uncle outweighed loyalty to his boss, and the young man denounced Hanna and Jacobs, who were taken before a committee of local party officials. Although both refused to retract their condemnation of the anti-Semitic behaviour they had witnessed, they were released without further procedures being taken against them. A first-class aircraft designer and test pilot were not easy to replace.

Hanna continued to insist that Hitler could not have known what was happening. It was a relief when an uncle, General von Cochenhausen, assured her that the horror of Kristallnacht had been a mistake, that an order from Goebbels that one subversive synagogue should be burnt had been misunderstood, and that Hitler had been angry and upset: as he needed Goebbels, he had nobly shouldered the blame as 'one of the crosses that a leader sometimes has to bear'. The religious analogy was perhaps unfortunate, and the gullibility of people determined to justify the Führer seems with hindsight astonishing.

For a while, Hanna felt 'utterly broken and disillusioned' that there were things going on in her country that she neither understood nor liked. She nevertheless consoled herself with the belief that now that Hitler knew about it, such things could never happen again. Her brand of patriotism did not include reviling members of other races, and she refused to adopt Nazi anti-Semitic attitudes, or to accept that anti-Semitism was central to Hitler's campaign for Germany.

She was nevertheless aware that Jews were professionally discriminated against through her knowledge of Küttner's experiences. In 1937, he had been banned from all gliding activities in Germany because of the Jewish half of his ancestry. Hanna was incensed at such injustice, and it was largely with her help that he was able both to pursue his meteorological studies and to find employment as an instructor abroad.

Hanna's normally optimistic outlook, and her refusal to see anything but the best in people, soon pushed the doubts caused by the events of 9 and 10 November to the back of her mind. In spite of the danger often involved in the work, test pilots led a sheltered existence. The gliding community at Darmstadt had so little contact with political realities that it was optimistically counting on international participation in an expedition at the beginning of 1939. When France and

Italy, the only other nations which had initially agreed to take part, decided to withdraw—ostensibly for financial reasons—the Germans carried on alone.

The Italians nevertheless gave their full non-participatory support. The venue was an Italian colony, Libya: they paid the Germans' shipping costs, arranged visas and passes in both Italian and Arabic, organised and financed accommodation and sightseeing in Tripoli, provided free petrol and use of their North African military airfields as well as Italian Air Force assistance, and were as friendly and hospitable as possible. The cynical suggestion that the expedition might have a military aim was vehemently denied: the sole intention was stated to be the continuation of the peaceful thermal flying studies started in South America.

Even Italian hospitality could not ease the tensions between the two German groups represented in the team, nor between individual members. Georgii was at the head of an uneasy combination of his own DFS pilots and their traditional rivals, the Darmstadt Akaflieger, led by Otto Fuchs. The mixture was a recipe for dissension. The argument between Hanna and Wolfgang Späte over the Reiher was also immediately resurrected when Georgii decreed that they should fly it in turns. On alternate days, they would each have to make do with a Kranich. Both Hanna and Späte preferred the lighter more manœuvrable Reiher: as Späte put it, to change to the Kranich 'was a bit like driving a lorry after a racing car'.

The rivals remained on outwardly civil terms, but Hanna defected in her free time from the DFS to the Akaflieger contingent. Otto Fuchs commiserated with her about the harsh treatment he considered Georgii was giving her, which on several occasions had reduced her to tears. She accompanied Fuchs on painting excursions, to which some of the others felt he devoted too much of his time. They shared a wide range of cultural interests, and together discussed art, music, literature and even, to a limited extent, politics. Both were considered anti-Nazi, Hanna because of her support of the Jews and Fuchs because of the warnings about the imminence of war which he had been expressing openly ever since he returned from the secret Luftwaffe training base in Lipetsk.

In spite of the tensions, there were some lighter moments. There was, for instance, the Libyan tea ceremony, in which a filthy looking brew was carefully prepared over an open fire in the desert: the Germans, following their own ideas of etiquette, passed the first glass of tea to Hanna—only for it to be whisked angrily away by their Arab hosts, who according to their custom refused to allow a woman any refreshment until all the men had quenched their thirst.

From the point of view of furthering the gliding experience gained in South America, the expedition was not a success. Conditions were less favourable than had been expected, and although some adventurous flights were made, little was learnt. Hanna, however, relished her brief insight into the life and customs of yet another country, making friends with shy Arab children and veiled women and even overcoming her instinctive fear of their men, whose strangeness she initially found threatening.

Film taken on the expedition languished in a cellar until the mid-1980s, when it was put together and shown on German television with a studio commentary taken largely from Späte's detailed diaries: nearly fifty years after the Libyan venture, he still insisted that it was entirely peaceful both in intent and in effect. There were, however, a number of critics who, with the benefit of hindsight, argued in letters published in the press that there must have been an ulterior military motive. If there was, Hanna was unaware of it; the expedition was just another opportunity to fly and to experience new surroundings.

It was clear, nevertheless, when it ended earlier than planned, at the end of March 1939, that war was approaching, although Otto Fuchs was still the only one of the group to suggest that the peace might be temporary. Soon after their return, Späte was called up and sent to Poland, where he suddenly realised the seriousness of the situation: 'During my training it was never suggested that there would be war. Then I was told: last year Czechoslovakia, this year Poland—it was like a bolt from the blue, I'd never thought anything like that could happen.'

'Last year Czechoslovakia' was not strictly accurate: it was not until March 1939 that Hitler took more than was justifiably considered German by adding the rest of the country to his Sudetenland acquisitions. He manœuvred the Czech president into a position where it was made to seem, at least in Germany, that the fate of his people had been 'voluntarily and confidently placed . . . in the hands of the Führer'. Once again, Nazi news portrayed an invasion of a neighbouring country as a welcomed rescue operation.

Equally reasonable noises were being made about restoring the German parts of Poland to the Fatherland. In the Free City of Danzig, Germans outnumbered Poles; Prussia was split in two by the Polish Corridor; and the Polish part of Silesia was considered rightfully a part of Greater Germany. In Hanna's home province, the injustice of Polish occupation of territory which all good German Silesians felt should by rights be part of the Reich was increasingly strongly felt, as was the Communist threat from the east.

Britain's intention to intervene on Poland's behalf should Hitler once again decide to rescue German-occupied territory from a neighbour was not taken seriously: surely, the Germans thought, the British would realise that a strong Germany was an essential barrier for the whole of western Europe against the evils of Boshevism. On 1 September Danzig was proclaimed part of Germany. According to all other European countries, Hitler invaded Poland: the German line was that it was another rescue operation, an unavoidable reaction to Polish aggression. Britain and France declared war on 3 September.

The commercial and military uses of gliding were by then under serious investigation in Germany, although elsewhere it was still no more than a sport. The dive brakes developed at Darmstadt had proved that research at the DFS could have implications reaching far beyond mere pleasure, and the division between civilian and military efforts was increasingly blurred. At the Gliding Research Establishment, Hanna was already involved with work on a troop-carrying glider designed by Hans Jacobs. This had started out as a peaceful project to build a flying weather-station. It then turned into a post office exercise for a freight-carrying glider which would release its tow to land at places where the normal mail planes did not call.

Hanna tested the first prototype transport glider, at a stage when it was still thought that its use would be purely an addition to existing forms of postal communication. Towed by a Junkers 52, she satisfied herself first with its unladen performance; then she added sandbags one at a time until the maximum load was reached before finally taking passengers. It took several months of tests, modifications, and further tests before Jacobs and Hanna were satisfied that the freight-carrying glider was a viable proposition.

By then, the leaders of the armed forces had decided that if a glider could carry freight, it could also carry troops. Hans Jacobs was given the task of redesigning the glider so that ten men plus their commander and essential equipment could land safely and silently on rough terrain. The result was the DFS 230, the largest glider yet built, with a wingspan of 72 ft and a possible speed under tow of 130 mph.

When Hanna demonstrated one of three prototypes built at Darmstadt she had an audience of high-ranking officers. Udet, von Greim, Milch, Kesselring and Model watched as she cast off from the Junkers 52 tow-plane at 3000 ft, dived steeply, and landed near some bushes, into which her ten fully armed passengers rapidly disappeared. Udet immediately told her to repeat the performance, this time with himself and the other four generals on board. Hanna was not used to flying generals: she calmed her nerves by pretending that she was carrying sandbags. All again went according to plan.

As the generals walked away, Hans Jacobs prised himself out of the tail of the glider. He explained to Hanna, who had had no idea that he was there, 'When I saw all those high-ups in my glider, my one thought was that if anything terrible happened with them on board, then I might as well be finished too.'

With his usual showmanship, Udet next arranged a competition between ten troop-carrying gliders towed by Junkers 52s and ten Junkers 52s loaded with paratroopers. Hanna was an anxious onlooker as the twenty aircraft approached the airfield at Stendal. Watched by the Army General Staff, the gliders dived, landed in close formation, and disgorged their passengers neatly and efficiently. The paratroopers were dispersed by a stiff breeze, many of them landing some distance from the ammunition and stores which had been dropped on separate parachutes. The point was taken: in the event of war, troop-carrying gliders could certainly play a role.

From the German point of view, Britain, supported by France, quite unjustifiably declared war on Germany, wilfully ignoring all Hitler's overtures of peace. Poland hoped for military support, but by the beginning of October the whole of western and northern Poland, including Danzig and Polish Silesia, had been incorporated into Hitler's Reich. Under a hasty and ideologically surprising agreement between Germany and Russia, the rest of Poland found itself under Russian domination.

Few Germans had any way of knowing how the rest of the world saw the start of the Second World War: they knew what they were allowed to know, and believed what their leaders wanted them to believe. War was forced upon them. It was their duty to safeguard their country's interests and to follow their Führer.

# 6

# Flying for
# the Future

From the moment that war was declared, Hanna was, whether she liked it or not, committed to the wartime cause of the Luftwaffe. There is no indication that she objected, although she would of course have preferred peace on German terms.

A German glider assault unit was formed immediately, with the intention of using it for an invasion of France in November 1939. Glider troops were to drop on to and overcome the row of forts along the Maginot Line. The troop-carrying glider had already been fully tested, and enough were swiftly produced. The officers in charge of the operation, however, had no gliding experience, while the glider pilots who were to fly into France had no military status. Nor did Hanna. The pilots, who were kept in isolation at Hildesheim, received little relevant training either for the complex co-ordination of gliders and towing aircraft on take-off or for the difficulties of landing and attacking on foreign territory at night.

Although she was eager to put her expertise at the disposal of the armed forces, Hanna was frustrated by military bureaucracy. As a woman, she was not allowed to join the combat troops, nor to arrange training, nor even to communicate with the glider pilots. All her appeals to higher authority failed. The invasion of France was postponed to February: it was a particularly cold winter, and the gliders would almost inevitably have to land on ice. Hans Jacobs was told to provide suitable brakes and to do so quickly. Hanna was to test them.

Jacobs's solution was to devise ploughshares to be fitted one on either side of the landing skids and operated by a lever. They were so efficient that on her first trial landing Hanna was winded. After modifications and further tests, the intensity of the ploughing action was overcome. Hanna, to her delight, was sent to demonstrate the brakes to the glider pilots languishing at Hildesheim; at last she would have a chance to talk to them.

As she had anticipated, they outlined their grievances at some length, and none more vociferously than Otto Bräutigam, one of Germany's most experienced and skilled glider pilots. He was, however, only a corporal: he therefore had no power to introduce the training programme which he considered essential if the operation was not to be a waste of time, money, effort, and lives. Between them, Bräutigam and Hanna enlisted the interest and support of General von Greim. A full-scale rehearsal of the planned glider invasion was held. It was so disastrous that at last the need for detailed practice was accepted.

It was not until May 1940 that the glider assault troops were eventually used, and then it was not in France, but in Belgium. They swooped silently at dawn on to the top of the heavily guarded fort of Eben Emael. The element of surprise enabled 78 men with no previous fighting experience to capture and hold a fort defended by 850 trained soldiers until the German land forces arrived the following day.

In spite of the unmitigated success of the first operation using glider assault troops, their only other active service was an attack on Crete, where the losses and general chaos were so great that even the victorious survivors could take little pride in their achievement.

In the meantime, someone at the Air Ministry had decided that the solution to the problem of transporting guns, men, vehicles, and even tanks into Britain for Operation SEALION, the code name for an invasion planned for November 1940, was a repeat performance of Eben Emael, but on a very much larger scale: not surprisingly, no individual has ever wished to claim the credit for the idea. Two firms, Junkers and Messerschmitt, were told to produce a hundred monster gliders within a fortnight so that they could be used for the planned invasion, an impossible task, allowing no time for tests even if there had been workable designs to start from.

Junkers came up with a Mammoth built entirely of wood: it proved totally inadequate for its task and was eventually converted into the most expensive firewood ever; it had cost 45 million marks, and was used to stoke the boilers of German trains.

Messerschmitt's wood and steel Gigant was marginally less of a white elephant, although it too earned its place in a book called *The World's Worst Aircraft*. At least it could take the weight demanded of it, and would fly once it had somehow been hauled off the ground. The troop-carrying DFS glider was dwarfed by the hastily designed monster. The Gigant was ready for tests fourteen weeks after the initial order had been given, a remarkable achievement, although it was already too late for the original Operation SEALION deadline. The invasion of Britain had, however, been put off until February 1941.

The first problem was how to launch the Gigant, which proved too heavy even when unladen to be towed by a single aircraft. With hydrogen rocket boosters on its wings and a system of three towing aircraft known as the Troika-Schlepp, it was still touch and go whether it would reach the height at which it could be flown as a straightforward but unwieldy glider. Once the rockets had been ignited, there was no way of stopping it; if there was an engine failure on one of the towing planes, or if one of the rocket burners failed to ignite, there was no way of getting it off the ground.

Even when everything worked perfectly, all four pilots had to fly with perfect split-second accuracy, an unusually long runway was needed, and the maximum speed of the towing aircraft with the lumbering weight behind them was only just above stalling point. On the first Troika-Schlepp launch, the pilot only just averted an accident when the main tow attachment snapped.

Hanna was not officially part of the original Gigant test team, but she did not like to be left out of any new development. Fortunately, Franke was with her when she first flew one of the monster gliders. It was inordinately heavy: twin pilot seats were later installed so that two men could wrestle simultaneously with the controls, but Hanna had to handle it from the original single flying position. During her take-off, Franke was in the vast empty space in which troops and tanks

*Gigant*

were to be carried: suddenly he heard a shout of 'Help!' She had banked steeply in the down draught from the towing aircraft and did not have the strength to control the aileron forces.

Although Franke was prepared to let Hanna have her way, some of the other Gigant test pilots were not. Otto Fuchs found her on the airfield with Otto Bräutigam and Bernard Flinch when he called to see her during the trials. 'Just wait a moment, Otto, I'm nearly through,' she told him as she ran to join the others, who were already sitting in the cockpit. Fuchs watched as the boarding ladder was pulled up in front of her and they took off, leaving her standing on the ground.

Hanna was still determined to have her flight. It was, she insisted, Udet's order that she should fly everything. When the Gigant landed, she again left Fuchs waiting while she hurried out to join in the next circuit, although by then there was a thunderstorm approaching. She was on the ladder and about to climb into the cockpit when Bräutigam unceremoniously lifted her and dumped her back on the ground, then pulled up the ladder and again took off without her. Hanna was furious and humiliated, and burst into tears.

A few minutes later, the impending thunderstorm broke. She was distraught when an hour later she heard that there had been an accident: both pilots were dead. 'You saved my life,' she kept telling Fuchs, 'you stopped me going with them.' He kept insisting that it was in fact Bräutigam who had saved her by refusing to let her fly; but it took a while for this to sink in.

On Hanna's last flight with a Gigant, one of the dreaded disasters struck: the engine of an outside towing plane failed before take-off, but after the rockets had been ignited. To avoid slewing the monster across the runway, the Me 110 on the other side also had to be detached. Hanna was, as she put it, 'hanging on one bomber which was like a little fly compared with my giant'. As soon as she could, at 150 ft above the ground, she dropped the remaining tow, and managed to land on a downhill slope in a field just big enough to be an impromptu airfield. Although she escaped unscathed, her two companions were less fortunate: one had two broken knees, and the other was treated for severe shock.

In spite of her escape, a combination of skill and luck, Hanna was shocked enough to pull out of the tests. She tried to persuade Udet and Messerschmitt that the Gigant was too unwieldy to be viable. 'It was so primitively built that it was heavy and difficult to fly,' she said. 'What was too difficult for me in a ten-minute flight was too difficult for a man in a flight of an hour.' Messerschmitt refused to listen to the opinion of a slip of a girl who was not, after all, a fighting man. Unfortunately, more notice was taken of the male aircraft designer than of the female test pilot. A few days later, there was a major pile-up in which 129 men were killed on take-off when the towing planes and the Gigant, which was carrying a full load of troops, ploughed together on the ground. The three tow pilots, the six-man crew of the Gigant, and 110 soldiers were killed.

Production of the ill-fated glider nevertheless continued. Eventually the Gigants were modified into six-engined monsters capable of lifting twelve tons. Hanna found the powered version 'very simple to fly—the engines did it all'. But it was so slow, heavy, and vulnerable to attack that it was never much use.

The Gigant was only one of a number of abortive brainwaves which Hanna had to test during the war. Her work had previously been geared to perfecting workable designs or ironing out problems with gliders already in production. But ideas for use in combat flowed with a touch of desperation, often from men with a greater knowledge of fighting than of flying or designing aircraft. Each project had to be tried before it could be rejected: the submarine had, after all, as Hanna pointed out, initially been considered an impossibility. As one hair-brained scheme after another was tried and failed, the test pilot was often in considerable danger.

She was, in spite of her courage, often afraid, and never more so than in the prototype for a pilotless flying petrol tanker, a glider towed behind a parent machine so that the latter could refuel in the air. Although no pilot would have been on board the final version, it was essential to find out how it would behave: Hanna was chosen to undertake the trials because she was the smallest test pilot available. She had to fight against both airsickness and 'the most primitive and hateful fear' as she was buffeted in the slipstream from the mother plane as well as in any general atmospheric turbulence. The idea was dropped.

So was the 'bed of ropes' on which she made three landings in a glider on the deck of a ship. It was thought that ten 100-ft ropes stretched taut 3 ft apart and 20 ft above the deck could enable aircraft to land on and take off from warships. Hanna was deputed to try it out with a glider. Fortunately she took the precaution of wearing a crash helmet: without it she was convinced that she would have been decapitated on her first attempt when the glider was caught by a cross wind as she was landing, and plunged at an angle between the ropes. Athough the next effort was more successful, it was still alarming, and on the third she overshot and finished suspended above the water with the glider's tail caught in the ropes. Another tempting theory was abandoned as unworkable in practice.

For the first two years of the war, it seemed to Hanna and her family as if God must have a special interest in them.

Hanna repeatedly escaped injury and survived danger. Kurt survived the sinking of his ship, the *Erich Köllner*, at Narvik, although nothing was heard of him for two months. He had managed to fit in a hastily arranged wedding in February 1940 three weeks before leaving for Narvik. For once, the whole family was able to be together for the wedding.

Life in Hirschberg continued as normally as was possible. In July 1940, Heidi gave birth to twins, a boy and a girl. Her elder son was by then a healthy three-year-old. Hanna was a devoted aunt, and looked forward to the limited time she could spend with the children. Willy and Emy Reitsch, who were both beginning to look old and frail, clung doggedly to the conviction that the war was in a just cause and would soon be satisfactorily over. Emy prayed constantly that God would protect Germany and those involved in the German cause.

Almost every day, she wrote to Hanna, sometimes in prose and sometimes in verse. She continued to encourage her in her patriotic self-sacrifice, exhorted her to remain humble (although some would have said this exhortation came too late or remained unheeded), and entrusted her to God. Before she went to bed, Hanna read from the growing bundle of letters, until she knew all her mother's private poems off by heart.

Hanna's faith in God, belief in the Fatherland, and trust in its leader were equally unshaken, although neither she nor any other member of her family joined the Nazi party; as a Freemason, Willy Reitsch would not in any case have been admitted. Some, probably a minority, of Hanna's colleagues, were party members: their job was to test aeroplanes, regardless of political persuasions.

Hanna was employed wherever she was most needed, or wherever she saw most need for her services, which was not always quite the same thing. She took no notice when friends tried to restrain her: 'What do the high-ups care about you?' Otto Fuchs asked her. 'They're just using you. You don't need to wear yourself out and put yourself in danger—let someone else take the risks.' She wanted to be used, and liked to be the first, the only, or at least the most important person to fly anything. Although she was genuinely motivated by a desire to save the lives of future German pilots, her personal ambition sometimes appeared to others to take precedence over her more worthy motives.

She was particularly aware that she was working for the protection of men at war during a series of cable-cutting tests at Rechlin. During 1940, a number of fatal accidents were caused by the unseen anchor cables of the barrage balloons with which the British frustrated German bomber pilots. The barrage balloon was a brilliantly simple idea: an equally simple solution was needed to the problems caused by its anchor cables.

Hans Jacobs designed a cutting device to be fitted to the wing tips of bombers, with an arrow-shaped fender which would, it was hoped, deflect the cable to the wing tips and protect the pilot, cockpit, and engines. Hanna tested his device at Rechlin in a Dornier Do 17 bomber which could be flown, although not landed, from a second pilot's seat in the rear gun turret. The tests started with 2.7 mm diameter steel cables, and worked up painstakingly to cables of 8.9 mm diameter, as thick as those it was thought were used by the British.

On her first trial, Hanna climbed above the airfield until she could look down on the balloon, then circled until she could see the cable glinting against the sky. Then she lost sight of it, but flew at the spot where she expected it to be: her memory served her well, but to minimise the danger in subsequent tests strips of bunting were attached a hundred feet apart so that she could aim half-way between two markers. Flying deliberately into a steel cable required both courage and precision, and it was by no means certain that the protective fender would be effective. The result of the impact was recorded on instruments in the aircraft so that improvements could be made before a thicker cable was introduced.

Hanna was so absorbed in the initial experiments that she carried on for several days with a headache and a temperature. Then she became too ill to fly: she had scarlet fever, which was at that time a serious disease. Complications set in which affected her heart, and for three months she was in the isolation wing of a Berlin hospital. While she was ill, lying in a darkened room, the tests were continued by another pilot.

By the time she recovered, the preliminary trials had almost been completed. The fender had been abandoned: although it had proved effective, its extra weight would have endangered the aircraft if one of the engines were put out of action. The final tests were expensive, as a new balloon was needed for each one, and dangerous, as the pilot had to aim deliberately to sever the cable with a steel strip without the protection of the fender. The problem of removing the free-floating balloons after tests was never satisfactorily solved either by shooting them down or by closing the pressure release valve in advance so that they would eventually burst when they had floated high enough: their trailing cables caused havoc with power cables and added to the expense of the operation.

Although Ritter von Greim had been in command of the later tests, his friend and senior colleague Ernst Udet had never seen one, and did not know that Hanna had been involved. He arrived at the airfield on his way to a conference with Hitler just as she was about to attack the cable of a genuine British balloon, acquired after it had come adrift from its moorings. Unfortunately, although the cable was only 5.6 mm in diameter, not as thick as some which had been successfully cut, it was made up of fewer but thicker strands than any which had so far been safely severed.

If Udet had not been watching, the test would almost certainly have been cancelled because of a strong wind in which the balloon was blown at such an angle that its cable, shorter than usual, seemed likely to give way under the strain. This meant flying alarmingly low into the steeply slanting cable. Hanna was, however, cleared to start. As she flew the twin-engined Dornier into the cable, the strands parted, shaving off the lower edge of two propeller blades. It was, as she put it, 'a race against death', although none of the pieces which landed in the cockpit hit her, as she attempted to feather the propellers to prevent further damage. The onlookers later claimed that the damaged engine tore loose and fell away, although if it did so Hanna omitted to mention it in her own account.

As the Dornier disappeared over the trees, everyone on the ground waited for a mushroom of smoke to tell them that it had crashed. Udet rushed to his Fieseler Storch to follow Hanna: to his relief, she had managed to land the crippled and badly unbalanced aircraft safely. He was, she later said, as white and shaken as she felt: quite apart from his natural concern, he was no doubt wondering how he was going to explain the death of Germany's flying heroine.

At his conference with Hitler, he gave a vivid account of Hanna's miraculously lucky and skilful escape. The Führer was in turn so impressed that he made Hanna the first woman pilot to be awarded an Iron Cross, Second Class, for her courageous survival, as well as a military gold medal in recognition of her general services to wartime aviation. The distinctions did not endear her to her male colleagues, many of whom considered it wrong to award them to a civilian.

On consecutive days in March 1941, Goering presented Hanna with the medal and Hitler conferred on her the Iron Cross, Second Class. Goering, with whom Hanna had had no previous personal contact, offended her with a derogatory reference to her diminutive size. She replied spontaneously, describing his bulk with a sweeping gesture: 'Do you have to look like that to fly?' Fortunately the head of the Luftwaffe was less sensitive about his girth than was the Flugkapitän about her height.

She had met Hitler briefly when she was made a Flugkapitän. Her reaction had been dismayed disappointment. 'I saw Hitler, but I was sad when I saw what sort of a man he was,' she had said to Gisela Holzrichter, adding that she had been so depressed to discover that the Führer, the hero and leader of her country, was ill-mannered and uncouth that she had shut herself in her room for three days to recover. She liked men to look smart—Hitler looked crumpled; to speak well—he had sounded uncultured; and to have fastidious manners—he had picked his nose.

It was a pity that she kept these feelings to herself among her colleagues, who were antagonised by her apparently un-stinting admiration of the Führer. But she considered it a matter of honour and of loyalty not to admit in public that she found her country's leader to be less than heroic and noble. Her instinct was to admire her superiors, and she was flat-tered at being summoned to Hitler's presence:

With a feeling of great excitement, I climbed the steps to the Chancellery at the appointed time. Adjutants led me through the long corridor to a room in which Hitler, Goering, and several other men were waiting . . .

Hitler greeted me warmly and kindly, while beside him Goering stood beaming like a father who has been given permission to introduce his well-mannered child. I sat between them at a round table, on which I remember vividly there stood a vase of sweet peas. Hitler then drew me into a lengthy conversation about my test flights.

The Führer, she claimed, showed a remarkable interest in and knowledge of aviation, although she admitted that it was impossible at such a formal reception to obtain any deeper insight into his personality. Not long afterwards, she bumped into Otto Fuchs: 'Guess where I've been! Hitler invited me!' she told him excitedly. 'Come with me and I'll tell you all about it.' She confided that she found Hitler 'ein widerlicher Kerl'—'a dreadful fellow'.

Only two women had ever been awarded an Iron Cross, a decoration first given early in the nineteenth century: one of them had been killed in battle soon afterwards, in 1813, disguised as a man; the other was a First World War nursing sister. Hanna, as the first woman to be so honoured in the current conflict, received considerable publicity which, to the disgust of some of her fellow test pilots, she clearly enjoyed. She was sent so many letters of congratulation that she needed secretarial assistance to deal with them: Margarethe Böss, a girl employed in Berlin by the Reichsfrauenführerin—the leading lady of the Reich and the coordinator of Nazi women's organisations—was seconded to her for a few hours a day. Gretl, as she was always called, had been an ardent member of the Bund Deutscher Mädel, the girls' version of the Hitler Youth. She was as small as Hanna, whom she admired unstintingly.

Among the fan letters was an invitation to Hirschberg early in April. At every village Hanna passed through in Silesia, the houses were decked with flags, children lined the streets, and the people waved and threw flowers. In Hirschberg, the pupils of the Grunau Gliding School and a Luftwaffe detachment formed a reception committee. Hanna's parents posed with her proudly on the steps of the town hall. She was made an honorary citizen of Hirschberg, a distinction held until then only by the poet and playwright Gerhart Hauptmann, and was presented with a Grunau Baby glider: She christened it the 'Otto Bräutigam', after the colleague who had, as she put it, 'been killed in action', and whose fate in the Gigant she had so nearly shared.

At her old school, she was presented with an unusual memento: a bound volume containing all the less that favourable remarks in class reports about her inability to stop talking and her irritating habit of laughing unnecessarily. She was amused to find that she had been held up for years as a model pupil. It was a strange and moving experience to be treated as a heroine by people among whom she felt so much at home.

Hanna was herself an instinctive hero worshipper, and always needed someone she could look up to and on whose support she could count. A husband or lover might have satisfied her need for a hero, had she been prepared to sacrifice her independence to the former or her puritanism to the latter. When she started flying, she idolised Wolf Hirth, her 'flying father'. Udet then became her flying hero, although she admired him less as a man than as a pilot and as a symbolic superior: he drank and smoked heavily, and had a reputation as a womaniser. Through him, she had been given opportunities to further her own career; she did not mind that he had used her public reputation and effervescent personality for German and Luftwaffe propaganda ever since her helicopter flight in the Deutschlandhalle.

On 17 November 1941, it was announced that Colonel-General Udet had tragically met his death while testing a new weapon in the fulfilment of his duty. Even his colleagues at first believed the statement: it was thought that the weapon must be Germany's secret rocket plane. That he had, in fact, shot himself was hushed up—it would undoubtedly have upset morale both within the Luftwaffe and in the country as a whole—and he was given a hero's funeral.

Hanna, among others, blamed Goering for Udet's death, with some justification. Udet was a first-rate pilot, a man whom nobody could dislike, and an excellent figurehead; he was, however, quite unfitted for the job he had been given in charge of Luftwaffe production. The Luftwaffe was underfunded, undermanned, and unready for the major confrontations imposed upon it. After the crippling losses of aircraft in the Battle of Britain, and the inability of the air force to cope with the demands of the Eastern front, he was Goering's scapegoat. Without him, Hanna was professionally vulnerable: she could no longer call on his support, or use his name to open doors which might otherwise have remained closed. Milch, who replaced him, considered a woman test pilot an embarrassment, and was not inclined to give her preferential treatment.

Her new hero was another general, Ritter von Greim, a quiet and reserved man who had been one of Udet's closest friends since they had been colleagues in the First World War, during which he had been knighted. Increasingly, she turned to him for advice and support. They shared deeply held convictions about patriotism, honour, and loyalty. Hanna's family liked and admired von Greim, as did everyone who served under him.

The war which had begun so well for Hanna was gradually taking its toll, and it was inevitable that eventually tragedy would hit her family. A month after Udet's suicide, Hanna's brother-in-law Gustav-Adolf Macholz was killed, leaving Heidi heavily pregnant with her fourth child. A fortnight later, Kurt was sunk for the second time, 200 miles off the North Cape with heavy losses on his destroyer. Heidi's baby was from the start sickly, and survived only eight months.

In 1943, the thirteen-year-old cousin of Kurt's wife Helma lost her mother—her father had died before the war—and went to live with Helma's parents. She was one of 600 refugee children from Berlin who went to school in Hirschberg, where they were taught in the afternoons and the local children in the mornings. The Reitsch family home became a refuge for Carola, who was hoping to study music. Their musical evenings were 'like a gift from heaven', and Emy Reitsch always had time to spare for the motherless child. 'I shall never forget the warmth and kindness of Mother Reitsch, who was the soul of the house,' Carola later recalled.

Hirschberg was still home for Hanna; nothing would ever

change that, although she was rarely there. As she was often in Berlin (many of her test flights were at Rechlin), she had a permanent small, self-contained apartment at the Haus der Flieger, the former House of Lords under the Kaiser and conveniently near the Air Ministry building. Colleagues who also stayed there from time to time, but who had to take whatever room happened to be available, resented this as yet another sign of preferential treatment; they were nevertheless willing and welcome visitors.

It was there that Peter Riedel brought his American wife Helen to meet Hanna in 1942: it was partly through her influence that he had obtained permission to marry a foreigner during wartime. Helen Riedel spoke very little German; she found Hanna, who was the first of Peter's friends she met in Germany and who spoke English with her, 'just delightful'.

Hanna was always ready to use her influence to help her friends, and at the DFS often helped to circumvent frustrations by going to the top. This was not always appreciated. Even before the start of the war, Hanna and Heini Dittmar had for instance been at odds over her close association with their superiors: Heini had complained to Späte that Hanna paid more attention to 'prettying up new gliders with parsley to impress the generals' than to pioneering test-flying. It was an unfair accusation: although she certainly impressed the generals, it was never at the expense of her fanatical devotion to her duties as a test pilot.

# 7

## High and Low

The peak of Hanna's career as a test pilot was her involvement with the Me 163 rocket plane, one of the most exciting developments in German wartime aviation.

The rocket plane had started as a glider and gained official backing after fifteen years of experiment on the Wasserkuppe. In 1941, Heini Dittmar flew it at 400 mph, then at 571 mph, and then, after a tow to 13,000 ft, at 623 mph. The previous

*Me 163*

world speed record was just under 470 mph. Udet saw Dittmar's 400 mph unpowered flight, and at first could not believe that he had no engine. He was so impressed by its potential military use that he ordered it to be given priority treatment, with an engine. After his death, the Me 163 had to compete for funds with other prestige developments, such as tanks and submarines, as well as the V1 'flying bomb' and the A4 rocket, better known as the V2: work on both unmanned weapons was being carried out simultaneously at Peenemünde, an isolated base off the Baltic coast. The competition between projects for money set production of the V1, the V2, and the Me 163 back by several years. All three were treated as top secret and their individual supporters were convinced that each could win the war.

Heini Dittmar, joined later by Rudi Opitz, continued as test pilot on a military version of the Komet, the Me 163B, which was to be used as an interceptor to split up enemy bomber formations and then attack the bombers individually. It was a strange-looking creation, short, stubby, with a wing span of no more than 30 ft and a tendency to roll over on to its back. The design was based on Alexander Lippisch's long-standing obsession with the idea of a triangular tailless aircraft, which he called a delta. On preliminary tests, it had to be towed into the air. Under power, a revolutionary liquid-fuelled rocket drove it from behind, but once its rocket engine had used the limited fuel supply it became a high-speed glider.

During Hanna's balloon-cutting tests, she and Heini had met and had agreed to forget their old differences: in war, personal rivalries should, they felt, be set aside, an agreement which she had also reached with Wolfgang Späte. In 1942, Späte was recalled from active combat service with the Luftwaffe to take charge of a new series of tests with the military Komet.

Lippisch also wanted to enlist Hanna's services, but was told that Heini Dittmar would refuse to work with her. Dittmar was quoted by Späte as saying that 'There are women who cannot bear it if a man comes into town whom they haven't already been to bed with. For Hanna, aeroplanes are like men for other women. As soon as a new plane appears anywhere, her sole aim is to fly it.' Hanna would have found the comparison offensive, but was determined not to be left out of the project.

When she first flew the Me 163A, in May 1942, it was a one-off flight for which Lippisch had given her permission. When she left the airfield at Augsburg, Späte and Dittmar breathed a sigh of relief. One of their team then suggested that she might after all be an asset in Augsburg: regardless of her ability as a test pilot, her influence would perhaps persuade higher authority to give greater priority to the project. After Heini Dittmar stalled the Me 163A and injured his spine, Hanna became an official member of the Me 163 team.

There could be no more prestigious appointment in German wartime aviation. The Komet was considered a prestige project, a revolutionary design for the future and for success. Hanna did not realise that originally she had not been wanted, nor that it was as a go-between in dealings with the Air Ministry as much as for her ability as a test pilot that she was summoned to work on tests at the Messerschmitt factory in Neuburg in October 1942.

Rumours about the rocket plane, as well as occasional information about Hanna's activities, filtered through to Eric Brown, who was chief test pilot at Farnborough, the British equivalent of Rechlin. Brown considered Hanna's role in German military aviation 'very peculiar'. As she seemed to participate briefly in any prestige project, but rarely to carry the routine testing work through, he decided that she must be 'a freelance test pilot for Nazi propaganda', of which she appeared to him to be a willing tool.

There were a number of fatal accidents with the Komet which, as one of the surviving test pilots put it, 'exploded when it felt like it'. Its engine was fuelled by a highly explosive mixture of hydrogen peroxide (T-Stoff) and methyl alcohol, hydrazine hydrate, and water (C-Stoff). Even ummixed, C-Stoff and T-Stoff were dangerous; together, any quantity, however small, resulted in a massive explosion: it was the careful control of the explosion which provided the rocket compulsion.

Späte was not an easy man to work for—his arrogant manner had earned him the title of 'Count Späte' long before the war—and was determined that Hanna should not fly the fully powered version of the Me 163B. She made several successful unpowered flights. It was essential that the under-carriage, a wheeled dolly, should be jettisoned at precisely the right height, 30 ft above the ground. The Komet could then reach 500 mph in a few seconds and could climb at an angle of sixty to seventy degrees to 30,000 ft in one and a half minutes. In the air, it was considered a joy to fly. Hanna described it as 'fascinating, like thundering through the skies sitting on a cannonball'. The high-speed landing as a glider was, however, even more difficult than the take-off, with no chance of overshooting and having a second attempt. As Hanna was well aware, any error in judgement, however small, or any lapse in concentration, however brief, could mean both her own death and the loss of the aircraft.

On 30 October 1942, she was towed off the airfield at Regensburg in an unpowered Me 163B. It was her fifth flight in the Komet that month. Seconds after take-off, she pulled the lever which should have released the launching trolley: the aircraft started to vibrate. As she continued to climb under tow, Very lights were sent up from the retreating airfield. The tow pilot raised and lowered his undercarriage several times while his companion signalled to her frantically with a white cloth.

To her dismay, Hanna realised that the lever had not released the undercarriage. The fault which had affected the release mechanism had also put the landing skid out of ac-tion. To make matters worse, she could communicate neither with the ground nor with the tow-plane because her radio was not working. The tow-plane was circling over the airfield, but she stayed attached to it, hoping that its pilot would realise what she wanted—to reach a safe height before casting off and seeing if her aircraft would respond to the controls.

The instruction given to all Me 163 pilots was clear: if in doubt, bale out. Hanna knew this, but her instinct as a pilot was to attempt to land: 'No pilot entrusted with the testing of a valuable aircraft would ever bale out and abandon it so long as there was the smallest chance of bringing it to earth safely,' she explained afterwards.

To give herself a little more time to attempt to free the jammed mechanism before making her landing approach, she continued on tow to 10,500 ft. The dolly remained firmly attached beneath the aircraft, which continued to vibrate alarmingly. Below her, Hanna could see ambulances and fire-engines rushing across the airfield. The men watching on the ground were preparing for the worst. So, without panicking or relaxing her concentration, was Hanna.

She had no time to think of her mother, her country, or God as she hunched herself tightly together ready for the inevitable crash. The weight of the undercarriage made her approach even faster than usual, and the extra drag affected the airflow. On her final turn, she lost control.

The Me 163B hit a ploughed field just short of the runway at 150 mph, bounced violently twice, lost a wheel, and came to a standstill after a 180 degree turn. Hanna's first thought was that as she was not hanging in her straps she was at least the right way up, although she was convinced that the aircraft had somersaulted, and that she was alive. Luckily there was none of the lethal rocket mixture on board: had there been, she would have been killed instantly.

She automatically opened the cockpit roof and undid her shoulder straps. Cautiously, she ran her hand over her body to check for injuries: there were none. Then she noticed a trickle of blood from her head. she traced its source to her nose, or rather, as she later put it, a cleft where her nose had been.

'Must I spend the rest of my life without a nose?' she wondered, surprised that she could feel no pain. When she turned her head, everything went dark, so she kept as still as possible. Carefully, without moving her head, she fished her pencil and notebook from her pocket and tried to describe what had happened. Then she tied her handkerchief round her face to spare the rescue party the shock of seeing how badly injured she was, and also perhaps as a brave gesture of vanity. Only then did she allow herself to pass out. 'What a woman!' Späte later commented.

When she came to, the men who had been in the tow-plane were a blur in front of her. Summoning her remaining strength and self-control, Hanna insisted on walking with them to a car, refused to travel in an ambulance, and sat in the front seat on the way to the hospital. She knew that her appearance would cause a sensation at the front entrance, and so asked to go to a secluded back door. There she somehow managed to walk up three flights of stairs before surrendering to the doctors and nurses.

At the Hospital of the Sisters of Mercy in Regensburg, she was X-rayed and then operated on. Her skull had been fractured in six places, her upper jawbone had been displaced, her nose completely smashed, several vertebrae broken, and her brain severely bruised. Her mother and a widowed adoptive aunt, Käthe von Cochenhausen, were at first her only visitors. As soon as Hanna realised that her mother was with her, she felt safe. But she wanted to know her chances of survival, and felt that her friend Edelgard von Berg would be more honest with her than the doctors at the hospital dared to be. Edelgard, whom she had met while she was a medical student in Kiel, was herself a surgeon.

On her way to Regensburg, Edelgard's car skidded on wet leaves and crashed: she was killed. Hanna grew more and more agitated as she waited for her to arrive. Although the doctor advised Frau Reitsch not to tell her about her friend's death as the shock might kill her, Emy took it upon herself to break the news: she felt that Hanna would be able to cope better with the truth than with the feeling that she had been let down. God's will, however cruel it might seem, was more acceptable than a broken promise.

Wolfgang Späte was told by telephone about Hanna's accident. With the rest of his team, he went over every detail to see if anything could have been done to prevent it, and felt it necessary to blame someone or something. He was, however, unwilling to take any personal responsibility: 'How could anyone suggest such a thing!' he protested: 'At the time of the ill-fated forced landing I was after all 800 km away in Peenemünde.' There were, he decided, a number of contributory factors which individually were insignificant. The jammed release mechanism was only one of these. Hanna should, he felt, still have been able to land safely.

Before he returned to Regensburg, Späte wrote a brief report in which he stated: 'Through the impact of the landing Flugkapt. Hanna Reitsch hit her head on the visor. This was made possible because she used a thick cushion behind her back and therefore sat forward and had probably not strapped herself in very firmly.' Sympathy was tempered with criticism: it was implied that Hanna's judgement had been at fault. No one had criticised Heini Dittmar when he had injured his spine so badly on landing that he was in hospital for a year.

Hanna was in no state to feel aggrieved during her fight for survival. It seemed at first unlikely that she would live, let alone fly again. When Goering and Milch heard that she had been seriously injured during the course of duty, they decided that some public gesture must be made on behalf of the German establishment: the problem was to decide exactly what. Her old commandant from Stettin, Georg Pasewaldt, who had taken over some of Udet's duties, was with the two Luftwaffe leaders when they agreed to give her the Iron Cross, First Class. Pasewaldt told me that he opposed the award: it was a military honour, which should be given only to those who had earned it in combat, and would not do Hanna any good.

Emy Reitsch shared Pasewaldt's reservations. Over the telephone, she told Walter Stender, who had known and flown with Hanna since 1934: 'Something even worse has happened now—they've given Hanna another Iron Cross.' It was one thing for her daughter to dedicate herself to flying for the Fatherland, but quite another for her to be made into quite such a public figure. Her mother was perhaps the only person who was convinced that Hanna would live to receive, and to regret, her second Iron Cross, and to realise the danger of being elevated to the status of a Nazi heroine.

Letters, cards, flowers and gifts poured into the hospital for the famous invalid: it seemed almost as if the whole of Germany was willing her to recover. Among the most thoughtful offerings were a bar of chocolate and a bottle of fruit juice, accompanied by a brief but friendly letter: Hanna and Emy were, however, not sure how to react, as the sender was Heinrich Himmler. Himmler, who controlled the Gestapo and the SS, was greatly feared even inside Germany. Emy Reitsch saw him as an adversary of Christianity. When he continued to send letters and unostentatious gifts to the hospital, Hanna and Emy decided they must have misjudged him: no one who behaved so thoughtfully and generously could be evil.

It was the end of March before Hanna was able to leave the hospital. She was determined to fly again, but realised that she was still far from ready to resume her strenuous duties as a test pilot, although she told no one how ill she still felt. Any movement made her feel sick and giddy, and her head ached incessantly. Although she could have gone to any sanitorium she chose, she insisted on staying alone half-way up a mountain in the Riesengebirge in the isolated summer house of some friends.

There she regained her sense of balance by climbing a flight of narrow steps leading from the ground to a protruding chimney stack. At first, it required a major effort of will to reach the top, where she clung weakly to the chimney with her eyes closed; then she forced herself to ignore her vertigo as she focused on each row of tiles separately. Gradually the daily task became easier until, after a month, she was able to let go of the chimney and ease herself along the length of the roof ridge. Sometimes she varied the routine by climbing a pine tree. It was discouraging to find how soon her strength was exhausted: 'Sometimes in my weakness I almost surrendered to despair,' she admitted.

Her mother brought her food every day. Gretl Böss made several visits to the mountain hideout so that Hanna could dictate to her to reassure herself that she could still think clearly and follow her thoughts through logically. At last, Hanna felt able to put herself to the test in the air. With the unofficial help of the commander of the Breslau-Schöngarten military flying school, she flew first a glider, then a powered aircraft. For a few weeks, she practised every possible flying manœuvre.

Doctor Bodewig, the surgeon at Regensburg, had operated on her so skilfully that no one who had not known her before would have been aware that she had a new nose. In August 1943, ten months after her accident, he gave her a full medical check: he could, he informed Milch, see no reason why Flugkapitän Reitsch should not resume her full flying and testing activities. Hanna had willed herself to recover, spurred on as she put it by the burning wish to continue as a test pilot.

The attempt to push further and further into Russia had by then faltered and failed. Although the public was told about imaginary successes, almost the only people still convinced of Germany's superiority in the air were Hitler and Goering. Following the defeat at Stalingrad in February 1943, Hanna felt that 'the German people as a whole realised that it was involved in a life-and-death struggle'. 'After Stalingrad, the shadows which were descending over Germany were visible to everyone,' she wrote in her autobiography. 'We saw them deepen and darken, and in spite of the propaganda, which was still geared for victory, the feeling of inevitable disaster deepened month by month.'

She was more aware of the military position and of the inevitability of defeat by this stage in the war than some of her friends and colleagues gave her credit for: a number of them have told me that they and Hanna fell out, or at best drifted apart, largely because she never admitted that defeat was possible. To admit it in public would, however, have seemed to her as unpatriotic as disowning Hitler.

As soon as she had declared herself fit to resume her service to her country, Hanna became involved with two friends, Heinrich Lange, a Luftwaffe first lieutenant, and Dr Theo Benzinger, the head of the Institute for Medical Aeronautics in Berlin, in a scheme to rescue Germany: before anyone in Germany had heard of the Japanese kamikaze suicide attacks on the American fleet, they were planning a one-way human flying bomb. It was to be a wonder-weapon which would enable Germany to insist on favourable peace terms by attacking enemy shipping and military installations.

The details were at first vague but idealistic, and the scheme was kept secret. Hanna, however, could not resist spreading the word that she was working on a top-secret, highly important, and eminently honourable project. As she put it, the 'immediate circle' of those who knew about it 'continually widened as more and more of our associates were initiated into our plans'. It was to be several months before the suicide mission became more than an idea. In the meantime, Hanna was expecting to be re-employed on the Komet.

When she reported to Goering that she was ready to resume her duties, she was, to her surprise, invited to his luxurious private residence for lunch. They talked, inevitably, about her crash and about the Me 163, which Goering believed to be already in mass production. When she pointed out that there were no 163s except for those currently being tested, Goering refused to listen. 'It became only too clear that Goering did not wish his comforting illusions to be disturbed,' Hanna wrote later. The head of Germany's air force stormed out of the room to play with his small daughter in the garden. His wife explained apologetically to Hanna: 'It's always the same when anyone tries to tell him the truth.'

If Goering believed that the Me 163 was in production, Hanna assumed that he had also given Hitler this impression. She found it almost impossible to believe the worst of anyone she knew personally, except perhaps Goering: but even he was partially exonerated by her conviction that he must either have been deliberately misled or had lost touch with reality. Yet the realisation that her leaders were so ill informed was deeply upsetting, and she told her cousin Helmut Heuberger that Goering had run the Luftwaffe down to such an extent that it would not be able to withstand future attacks.

For the first time, Helmut questioned his own beliefs. He had joined up voluntarily, had fought with the conviction of an enthusiastic ex-member of the Hitler Youth, had been wounded seriously enough just before Stalingrad to be invalided out of the army, and held the Iron Cross, Second Class. Hanna's revelations led him to the painful conclusion that he must consider his oath of loyalty to have been made not to Hitler, but to Germany: the only way he could help the country was to oppose the leader.

A chance encounter with a distant relative, Fritz Molden, who had founded a small Austrian resistance movement, crystallised his doubts. Helmut became one of the leaders of the resistance in Austria, which was equally supported by the rest of his family. For Hanna, who was unaware of her relatives' political activities, Hitler and Germany were still indivisible; her sense of honour would not have allowed her to support one and reject the other.

She still had some nagging doubts about Himmler, but was relieved to discover when she met him that she could after all respect and even like him. He invited her to dinner and impressed her with his willingness to consider her point of view and his knowledge of religion, history, and art. They sat alone together after the meal in comfortable armchairs in his study, which she found tastefully simple: she told him what her family had always thought of him and he explained that he had been misrepresented. It was 'most important that these tendentious rumours should not get about', he informed her. Hanna left feeling that she could indeed, as Himmler had invited her to do, bring any criticisms or objections to his attention at any time, and that he had been seriously misjudged.

In Hanna's company even the most uncouth of the Nazi leaders always behaved like gentlemen: her willingness to like them apparently brought out the best in them, and it has even been suggested that men with uneasy consciences felt ashamed in her presence and adopted virtuous attitudes to please her. Her inability to be cynical made her unaware of the cynicism with which her goodwill was often exploited.

Her colleagues were not impressed by her support of and continuing association with Himmler: 'You've no idea what a cultured man he is,' she told them. 'Hanna, do you or do you not hear what is going on?' Otto Fuchs asked her. 'Keep away from him.' However much he and others tried to warn her she took no notice. He felt that she was in many ways like a child, and too easily impressed. 'She was too good for what they made of her,' he recalled sadly over forty years later.

Before resuming her duties as a test pilot, Hanna addressed an audience of 2000 leaders of the Hitler Youth and the League of German Girls. The roles assigned to the sexes in Nazi Germany were summed up in the mottoes of the male and female party youth groups: the boys were to 'Live Faithfully, Fight Bravely, and Die Laughing!' while the girls had to 'Be Faithful, Be Pure, Be German!' The youths were being prepared to fight, the girls to breed more Germans who would in turn, according to their sex, fight or breed. Hanna, who had made herself an exception among German women, spoke enthusiastically about her flying experiences, encouraging others to take to the air, but did not mention her growing conviction that only a miracle could prevent defeat.

When she returned to the Me 163 project, which had been moved to Bad Zwischenahn, she and Späte were again at loggerheads. He was adamant that she should not at first fly the fully powered version of the Komet. When he heard that she had been talking about how much she was looking forward to flying two new aircraft which had just been delivered, he told her firmly that it was out of the question. Hanna did her best to persuade him to change his mind, even to the extent of name-dropping: 'The Führer has given me permission to fly any plane I like,' she claimed.

Späte was immovable. He telephoned the offices of Milch and Goering to make sure that no order had been given without his knowledge: his superiors knew nothing about the matter. Hanna's open permission to fly whenever, wherever, and whatever she chose had, it seemed, lapsed.

She was furious, and threw herself on her bed howling like a child and pummelling the pillows with her fists. Mano Ziegler, one of the pilots who had joined the Me 163 team while she was in hospital, found her there, still sobbing: 'It's so mean,' she told him. 'It's not fair!' He tried to explain Späte's point of view: because of her enforced absence from the project for nearly a year, Hanna had had less experience than the other test pilots, and the aircraft were to be tested for use in combat, of which she had no experience. Hanna was not prepared to listen. She was not used to not having her own way, and did not like it; but Udet was no longer alive to support her, and von Greim was on the Russian front.

Her friendship with Ritter von Greim had strengthened. As a mark of respect, she never mentioned him without the title which he had won in the First World War; he almost always called her Flugkapitän. She withdrew honourably from the Me 163 project when he asked her to boost the morale of his troops on the Russian front. In the winter of 1943, anyone defending the retreating eastern boundary of the vast area of Russia and Poland taken by the Germans was in constant danger. The only German woman to have been awarded the

Iron Cross, First Class, would, Greim felt, do a better job of cheering up his men on the front than any general.

Hanna had become a heroine, a symbol of courage, Germany, womanhood, and freedom; her picture and stories of her flying achievements were pinned up as inspiration in barracks or carried with photographs of mothers, wives, sisters, and girlfriends in the rucksacks and wallets of soldiers. The members of an SS Panzer corps wrote her an admiring letter which she treasured:

> We are rough soldiers . . .Carefully camouflaged, we rise from the earth only when the order is given to attack. But sometimes we see above us buzzards and hawks—your birds. We hear and see the great eagles of the air force, your comrades and ours. This lifts our thoughts above the earth into your world. Whenever you feel danger surrounding you, remember that we are thinking of you, wishing you strength, a clear eye, and a calm hand.

She reached von Greim's headquarters in a wood near Orscha in November 1943. Until then, she had never been anywhere near active combat. Test-flying an aircraft with its possible military use in mind was very different from being constantly aware of fighting, with the sound of guns sometimes rumbling like thunder in the distance and sometimes all too near. The insulated life on an airfield was no preparation for the winter cold and damp of the trenches, nor the luxury diet of a test pilot for the basic and meagre fare of soldiers on the Russian front.

On her first night on the front, she cowered in a trench during an aerial attack by the Russians: 'I felt so profoundly terror-stricken that I longed to be able to creep right into myself. Nowhere was safe, nobody could offer protection,' she wrote afterwards. 'This, I thought, is front-line war. This is what our soldiers experience, day after day, night after night. For me it represented the ultimate depth of fear and I sincerely believed that never again could I be truly frightened.' Even worse than the whistling and crashing of shells, and the whine of bombs, was the screaming of the wounded. Afterwards she helped to tend the men who had been injured.

The letter that she wrote to her parents and Heidi that evening gave a more enthusiastic account: 'What I am allowed to experience here is almost beyond my ability to describe . . . I cannot convey to you the pleasure of all the soldiers when the General appeared. They love and honour him greatly—and no wonder!—and their astonishment and delight that I had come right up to the front line was overwhelming . . . I should like to stay out here, and be allowed to fight. But don't worry: in a few days I must alas return to my test-flying.'

The few days became three weeks, during which Hanna accompanied von Greim as he toured desolate front-line positions. He protested that she should keep out of danger: but she had not, she said, come so far just to opt out of her duty on behalf of the women who could not give their menfolk their personal encouragement and support. In spite of the limited facilities available to the commanding officers at their God-forsaken posts they treated her as an honoured guest. She learnt to identify the sounds of enemy and German shells: knowing which were which was comforting.

Her greatest problem was finding a balance between boosting morale and raising false hopes: she was haunted by the knowledge that her leaders, and in particular Goering, refused to acknowledge that the Luftwaffe was hopelessly inadequate and that at best the men were only postponing the day of final defeat.

At Bialystok, in Poland behind the front line, she was helped on with her fur coat by Hans Schütz, a Czech Sudetenland German who had been in Grunau when she did her first gliding course. 'Don't we know each other?' she asked him. It was, as he said, a happy encounter at a sad time and in even sadder surroundings. That evening, after a supper of tinned sardines (one tin was shared between several people), Hanna joined Schütz and the other lower-ranking officers. She had, he was surprised to notice, a small handbag fastened with a safety chain to a bracelet.

'She actually glowed with optimism and encouragement to hold out,' Schütz wrote to me, 'and told us, of course "in the strictest confidence', about secret wonder-weapons, the V1 and the Me 163; actually she only whispered—as if the "high-ups" sitting further away were not to hear, only we few "selected" younger officers!' Neither Hanna nor Schütz were aware that thousands of Poles from Bialystok had been transported to the concentration camp at Treblinka.

Soon after her morale-boosting tour, Hanna visited the Heubergers in Austria. As always when they were together, they sang Austrian folk-songs. Suddenly Hanna broke off: 'We must sing this to Ritter von Greim,' she exclaimed. She managed, by insisting that she should be given a priority rating, to put through a telephone call, and then held the receiver so that the general on the front could hear as they continued to sing in Innsbruck. After a few minutes, the operator interrupted: 'Is this call strictly in the line of duty?' 'Of course it is,' von Greim replied firmly, 'it's most important for the morale of the troops.'

Hanna went down with hepatitis after her return from the front. Her own morale was lowered by her illness and by the depressing insight into the life of the fighting forces: 'The uncertainty, the doglike faith, the agony, the danger, and the cold endured by our men on the Eastern front: all this will never fade from my mind,' she wrote afterwards. Her own loyalty never wavered: 'All I was certain of was that I believed wholeheartedly in Germany, my beloved country. Nothing—nobody—would persuade me to desert her. If she had to fall, then I, too, must fall, for the great things I believed she stood for were those same things that I, and every German patriot, stood for.'

# 8

# Desperate Measures

By the time she returned from the Russian front, Hanna was more convinced than ever that the piloted flying bomb was essential to safeguard German interests. She called it Operation Self-Sacrifice, although it was more often referred to as the Suicide Mission: but this implied desperation and cowardice, whereas she insisted that to sacrifice oneself for one's country was infinitely honourable.

The idea met with general disapproval from the start, both from those who considered it unworkable and from those who found it ideologically and morally unacceptable. 'That we were often not understood is only natural,' she realised, 'for here there was no appeal to the ambitious or those seeking fame, and equally no prospect of a successful outcome for any who felt like dicing with death. Here the complete conquest of self was required.'

While Lange and Benzinger worked on details, it was Hanna's task to approach higher authority. She went first to Milch, who rejected the idea out of hand. It was in his opinion contrary to the German mentality to undertake a task in which the chances of personal survival were nil; and in any case, he did not think it would work. Georg Pasewaldt was another, one of many, who did not believe that a suicide mission was a correct way to wage war. 'Self-sacrifice could bring nothing decisive,' he told me. 'In military circles, this form of heroic, but non-decisive, warfare was totally rejected.' In practical terms, it was seen as a waste of good pilots.

Goering was not approached: Hanna and her colleagues

had no respect for his opinion or leadership, and were determined that he should not have control over their project. In November 1943, at the Aeronautical Research Institute in Berlin, they explained their idea to specialists from various branches of Germany's war industry: Georgii had made the venue available. The meeting was held so secretly that officially it never happened and no list was made of those present, who nevertheless gave the scheme their approval.

There was still no official permission to proceed. Hanna seized her opportunity to put the proposition to Hitler when he presented her with a certificate to mark her second Iron Cross. Over tea in a large reception room at his mountain residence at Berchtesgaden near Salzburg, both Hitler and Hanna attempted to monopolise the conversation. The only other person present was the Führer's adjutant, von Below, who merely listened, but later recorded the confrontation in his diary.

Hitler was not in the habit of allowing other people to talk at any length, and delivered a series of monologues, with

*Me 262*

copious historical references. Hanna eventually interrupted: 'The situation in which Germany now finds herself is without historical precedent and can only be remedied by new and extraordinary methods,' she told the Führer.

After a surprised pause, Hitler embarked on a eulogy about a new jet fighter, the Me 262. Hanna interrupted him again: he had clearly been misinformed. Although the Me 262 had been developed as a wonder-weapon to save Germany, it was still in the development stage and far from ready for use in combat. 'Hitler was living in some remote and nebulous world of his own,' she decided, 'and the appalling implications of this discovery suddenly burst upon me.' She blamed his advisers for not putting him more clearly in the picture: von Below was delighted that she had attempted to do so.

Hitler refused to admit that the situation was serious enough to warrant a scheme such as Hanna suggested, but left a loophole by adding that he, and he alone, would decide when the time was right for desperate measures. Hanna seized on this to extract permission for experimental work to be started immediately, so that as soon as he gave the word the mission could be put into effect: Hitler agreed reluctantly, provided he was not bothered with the details. There were few people who had dared to out-talk the Führer.

The original plan to convert an unmanned V1 was dropped in favour of a low-wing monoplane fighter already in production, the Me 328. The pilot would steer it into the water at an angle guaranteed to ensure that the bomb exploded directly under the keel of the selected target ship. The aircraft was expected to shatter immediately it hit the water, simultaneously killing the pilot and releasing its pretimed 1000-lb torpedo.

There were, Hanna claimed, 'hundreds' of volunteers, although only seventy signed the suicide pledge: 'I hereby volunteer as a pilot for the manned glider bomb. I fully understand that this action will end with my death.' Most were idealistic young glider pilots with little or no experience of flying powered aircraft: throughout the war, members of the male Nazi youth organisations had been able to avail themselves of sponsored glider training, in preparation for entry into the Luftwaffe.

There were personal and ideological clashes from the start. Hanna considered that the colonel who was put in charge of the operation misused the idealism of the volunteers to gain greater glory for himself. He did not offer to sacrifice his own life. Heinz Kensche, the Luftwaffe staff engineer directing technical operations and an outstanding glider pilot, was committed enough to sign on as a suicide volunteer. Hanna insisted that she would gladly have been the first to go, but decided that her influence with Hitler and Himmler could be of more use if she remained an outsider.

Hanna and Kensche tested the suitability of the Me 328, first under its own power and then as a glider to be launched, piggy-back style, from a Dornier 217. In mid-April a factory in Thuringia was given an order for its mass-production; the specifications were then destroyed when the factory was bombed.

The idea of using the V1 was resurrected by Otto Skorzeny, who had become a national hero and a favourite with the Führer after leading the dramatic snatch from a mountaintop hotel of Hitler's ally Mussolini. Skorzeny swept aside objections and refused to accept procrastination. Within a fortnight four manned variations of the V1 bad been produced in an underground workshop near Ainring: single- and double-seater training gliders, a single-seater with landing gear, and a solo one-way-only version for the final flight. The operation was given the code name REICHENBERG from the site of the rapid conversion.

Hanna's services as a test pilot were initially rejected: testing the manned V1 was 'a man's job', she was told. When the first two men to fly it were seriously injured, she was allowed to share the remaining tests with Kensche. In her words, her first flight 'passed without incident': 'the next eight or ten flights were also successful, but not without incident'. Alone in the air on each occasion, Hanna reacted with the calm courage and self-control she always showed when she was flying, although she was often far from calm and self-controlled on the ground.

In one 'incident', the pilot of the towing He 111 had just released Hanna from beneath its wing when there was what she described as 'a loud rending noise': the bomber had grazed the tail of the V1. She managed to keep control and land: the tail had been crumpled and twisted almost thirty degrees to the right.

During another test flight at up to 530 mph a sack of sand which Hanna had asked to have wedged in the front seat for extra weight shifted position. It was only when she tried to flatten out at speed that she discovered that it was blocking the controls. She was too low to bale out but, by pushing the nose down and then up at the last moment as far as she could, managed to land uninjured: the force of the landing splintered the skids and cracked the fuselage.

The landing skids were not strong enough to survive a fully loaded landing. Tests had however to be made simulating flying with the full weight which would be carried during the planned one-way trip. For these a water-tank was built into the fuselage with a plug operated by a lever so that the water could be jettisoned. While Hanna was flying with no engine at 18,000 ft the plug-hole froze. At 4500 ft she attempted to drain the tanks, but the plug was still frozen into its hole as she glided fast towards the ground. It was not until she was only a few hundred feet from the ground that her desperate efforts to move the lever succeeded, just in time for the water to leave the tank before she landed. She was, as she commented, lucky: she would not have survived a high-speed landing had the aircraft still been laden with the water.

Like the Me 163, the V1 was easy enough to fly once it was airborne, but landing it was always both difficult and dangerous: Hanna claimed that it 'glided like a piano'. She tested it in dives of over 500 mph, more than fast enough to ensure the instant death of the pilot and disintegration of the aircraft on impact with the sea. As operational pilots would not be required to land, there was little point in wasting time and risking lives before they were due to be sacrificed: only test pilots and instructors in the two-seater version were therefore expected to cope with the landing.

When the first manned V1s had been tested, Hanna continued as an instructor of the potential suicide pilots in what was called the Leonidas Squadron. Of seven V1 instructors, two were killed and four injured: Hanna was the only one to escape unscathed. No more than thirty pilots were trained to

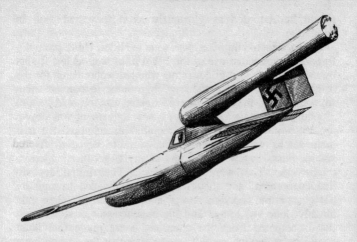

*Piloted V1*

fly the V1, and much of their time was, according to Hanna, wasted in unnecessary physical exercises and pistol practice on the ground. Time after time, again according to her account, she attempted to use her influence to ensure adequate flying experience and relevant target practice.

She was increasingly aware that Germany's time was running out, and was convinced that but for bureaucratic procrastination the operation could have been put into effect before D-Day: by the time the British and Americans had landed in France early in June 1944, she knew but would not yet admit that all her efforts had been in vain.

A few days after D-Day, the pilots who had been training for suicide with the V1 were recalled: Goering, who had previously taken no interest in the scheme, had decided that they were instead to sacrifice themselves with Focke-Wulf FW 190s fitted with 4000-lb bombs. As they were all glider pilots, and few had had any experience with powered aircraft, Hanna was furious. It was little consolation that their deaths, should they not survive their first test flights, would be recorded as gloriously as if they had died in combat.

Hanna went to Himmler, who went to Hitler: Hitler promptly forbade the intended use of the FW 190 as well as test flights by the inexperienced glider pilots who had volunteered for the original project, and a training programme to convert them from gliders to the high-powered fighter was initiated.

Without Hanna's knowledge, a new agreement was drawn up: the volunteers were still required to acknowledge that their deaths were inevitable, but were to agree to fly as suicide pilots in any aircraft and at any target their superiors might select. They were unenthusiastic. Their initial idealism had evaporated, and they were only persuaded to sign by being split into separate groups and told that the others had already done so. Lange and his closest associates, who refused, resigned from the team and were given individual postings far enough away to make sure that they could have no influence on the others.

On 13 June 1944, the original pilotless version of the V1 was at last used in bombing raids on London. The effect was, however, as much psychological as physical: although considerable damage was inflicted to both people and property, and the noise of the approaching missile was terrifying, it proved disappointingly inaccurate. The tests conducted with the manned version were able to detect the cause of the directional deviation, but after the years that had gone into its production the 'buzz bomb' did not after all prove to be the miracle weapon that had been so eagerly anticipated.

At the end of July, Berlin radio reported that Hanna Reitsch, 'a biological phenomenon', had ridden in a robot bomb to discover why these had a tendency to lose their wings after short flights: the explosives were supposed to have been removed so that Hanna could crawl in and lie flat on her stomach to observe the wings during flight through a periscope. She had, it was claimed, been chosen for the task because she was 'insensible to pressure'. Although according to the report the trouble had been found and cured within four days, the pilot had been seriously injured and had been awarded the Iron Cross, First Class, for her efforts.

The American forces newspaper *Stars and Stripes* duly

recorded the report under the headline ' "Freakish" Frau Took Ride in Robot Bomb, Nazis Say'. The story also found its way into the British press, where she was once again called Anna Reitsch. It was an extraordinary mixture of fact and fiction, no doubt intended to scotch rumours about the top-secret Me 163 and manned V1: as the unmanned V1 had by then been used against London, it was no longer secret.

Although the dream of 'rescuing' Germany with the suicide V1 was gradually fading, Hanna's enthusiasm for the scheme remained undiminished. When the initial zeal of some of the volunteers seemed to be fading, she was hurt and surprised, and complained to Otto Fuchs: 'Can you imagine, they don't want to carry on with it?' It was, she told him, difficult to keep her idealists motivated, and she had had to give them a pep talk about honour and patriotism. Fuchs was more sympathetic towards their reluctance than towards Hanna's fanaticism. 'If the best pilots die,' he asked her, 'what do we have left?'

In spite of her claim that there was no shortage of volunteers, she failed to inspire many with the wish to die deliberately for their country; even her most ardent admirers, like a young Luftwaffe mechanic called Irwin Glasenapp, were repelled by the idea. Glasenapp told me that although he had been 'a burning patriot who loved his Fatherland' he would never voluntarily have joined the German kamikazes. That participation should be entirely voluntary was, however, important, and Hanna did not attempt to persuade him.

Glasenapp's ambition was to fly as a pilot rather than as a mechanic or an observer, but in spite of several requests he had failed to achieve a transfer. Hanna offered to put in a good word for him. When he was subsequently summoned by his commanding officer, he expected to be told that she had been successful. Instead, he was severely reprimanded, and told that he should have gone through the proper channels.

In her wish to help those she considered her friends, Hanna had in the past often managed to circumvent regulations. Her intervention in a matter which was not officially her concern was, however, seen as interference: her wishes were no longer respected by her superiors in the way to which she had been accustomed.

She nevertheless managed to enlist the services of von Greim in having the commanding officer of the suicide operation replaced by a popular and successful combat leader, Colonel Baumbach; his only achievement, however, was to have the idea of a 4000-lb bomb abandoned. In a post-war assessment of the Luftwaffe, published as *Broken Swastika,* Baumbach described how he was responsible for dispersing the suicide volunteers to prevent the scheme from being put into operation.

Hanna was convinced that the suicide mission foundered because of the refusal of her superiors to take it seriously. Himmler fell from her favour by suggesting that its pilots should be recruited from 'among the incurably diseased, the neurotics, and the criminals, so that by a voluntary death they might redeem their "honour" ', a proposal which she refused to consider, although it showed an unusual concern on the part of Himmler for the spiritual well-being of his inferiors. Goebbels in her opinion sought to 'exploit the group for propaganda purposes by summoning its members to his ministry and reciting to them a premature panegyric on the theme of heroism'.

It is difficult for anyone looking back on the strangely distorted and fanatical idealism with which Hanna approached the idea of self-sacrifice to see quite how her approach differed from that of Goebbels. On more than one occasion, she had recited a similar panegyric to friends and fellow pilots, most of whom nevertheless refused to entertain the idea of sacrificing themselves; they agreed with Milch that the idea was un-German, that the compulsion to stay alive was insuperable, and that it was moreover impractical to waste good pilots on one mission when they could usefully fulfil many more. Even those who had volunteered and would doubtless have carried through their sacrifice had needed encouragement from time to time to prevent them from withdrawing.

Hanna had pursued the idea with even more than her usual single-mindedness. With retrospective optimism and unquenched enthusiasm, she remained convinced that it could have succeeded, had it not been for 'the total failure on the part of higher authority to appreciate that the self-sacrifice group was no stunt, but a collection of brave, clear-headed, and intelligent people who seriously believed, after careful thought and consideration, that by sacrificing their own lives they might save many times that number of their own countrymen and ensure some kind of future for their children'.

Although Himmler's attitude to the suicide mission offended her, Hanna still showed a touching faith in his integrity. While she was ready to criticise her superiors for their inefficiency and lack of understanding, she was not prepared to believe that they could be actively involved in any deliberate evil. Fighting, even when desperation had begun to set in, was neither cruel nor wicked: it was an unfortunate necessity. Somehow Hanna remained oblivious of the Holocaust.

It has been commonly assumed, since the end of the Second World War, that the majority of Germans knew about the concentration camps, or that they at least realised that something was going on, but did not want or did not dare to think about it. Outside Germany, many people still refuse to believe that it was possible that secrecy about the mass gassing of Jews could have been maintained, and consider that those who claim ignorance are merely feigning clear consciences but did in fact tacitly condone the attempt to exterminate the Jewish race.

Nevertheless, Hanna was only one of many who did not know what was happening. Joachim Küttner has assured me that even he, a part-Jew and a critic of the Nazi regime, knew nothing about atrocities and concentration camps until after the war, and that Hanna was equally oblivious. The propaganda machine was so thorough that the extermination was a well-kept secret known only, or almost only, to those involved with it.

It was easier to probe for the truth outside rather than inside Germany, where fear was a strong deterrent to curiosity. Peter Riedel, who was at the German Embassy in Stockholm, knew a little of what the Jews were suffering. It was however, not until he was sent photographic evidence of atrocities committed at the Majdenek concentration camp in Russia, as well as a full-page facsimile of orders given and signed by Himmler, that he realised that Jews were being systematically tortured and gassed.

Riedel felt that Hanna, who appeared to be on friendly

terms with Himmler, should be equally enlightened. So, while he was in Berlin on leave in October 1944, Riedel visited her, and threw the leaflet down on the table in her flat. 'There's your friend Himmler for you!' he told her.

Hanna picked it up, turned the pages, then screamed at him: 'Do you seriously believe this? In the First World War, enemy propaganda smeared the German soldier with every imaginable barbarity; now it has come to gas chambers! My dear Peter, don't fall for enemy propaganda!'

'Just show it to your friend Himmler,' Peter retorted, 'and if he says he doesn't believe it, I'll try not to believe it too.'

That, said Hanna, was exactly what she would do. Riedel was alarmed: he had travelled on a diplomatic passport, and had smuggled the pamphlet into Germany. If Hanna told Himmler her source, he could be in serious trouble: he asked her to say that she had obtained copies of reports from Swedish newspapers, although when he checked later he found that no articles about gas chambers had at the time appeared in the Stockholm press.

Hanna telephoned Himmler, who granted her permission to visit him immediately. 'What do you say to this?' she demanded. He showed no emotion as he asked her quietly if she believed it.

'Of course not,' she replied indignantly, 'but you must do something to counter it. You can't let our enemies saddle Germany with this.'

Himmler calmly agreed with her. She took his agreement as the denial she had hoped for: she found it impossible to believe that Germans could be responsible for such horrors, and that Himmler, the man of culture and compassion she thought she knew, could have had any part in anything so evil.

When she later described the encounter in her autobiography, she added a sentence explaining that it was not until after the war that she knew the truth about concentration camps. Unfortunately, this rider was omitted from all except the first edition, an omission which was to have serious repercussions for her later. It may seem astonishing that anyone as close to Nazi leaders as Hanna remained ignorant of what was happening throughout the war; but her sense of outrage and her conviction that Germany's enemies were conducting the most appalling smear campaign were genuine.

Soon after Riedel returned to Stockholm, he received a telegram summoning him back to Germany: he decided the time had come for his defection, which he had been considering for some time, and asked for political asylum in neutral Sweden. His request was granted. He told me that he was convinced that had he returned to Germany, he would have been put to death. He did not want to be associated with the losers in a war in which he was unable to support the leaders attitudes and policies.

Although Hanna knew that the war could not be won, she still considered it her duty to stand by her country, whatever the consequences. Not long after Riedel's visit, she was injured on her way to an air-raid shelter in Berlin. In the hospital to which she was taken with concussion and an injured elbow, she met Colonel Rudel, a Stuka pilot who had just had a leg amputated. After an undistinguished start to his wartime flying career, Hans-Ulrich Rudel had more than redeemed himself by destroying 3 Soviet ships, 70 landing-craft, and 519 tanks: he had flown over 2500 missions, an international record, and was revered as the Eagle of the Eastern Front.

Hanna discussed with Rudel a problem which might all too soon arise: the evacuation of the wounded from Berlin once it became impossible to land an aircraft in the smoking ruins. Little was left of the city's former glory, and it seemed unlikely that the Germans would be able to keep control of any of the area for very much longer. The bomb-shattered view from the air haunted her, as did the 'ever more certain foreboding that the city's ordeal was not yet over and that worse was to come.'

She and Rudel agreed that it might be feasible to conduct a rescue operation with a helicopter, which could land on any small flat space such as the top of an air-raid shelter. There was one of these bunkers in the grounds of the zoo, and during the next few weeks Hanna conducted a systematic aerial survey using this as her focal point. In a Bücker 181, she flew low and in all weathers, approaching her bunker every time from a different landmark on the outskirts of the city, and memorising the compass bearing from each, until she felt certain that whatever the conditions she would be able to find it and land on it with a helicopter. She knew that even her self-sacrifice scheme could not alter the outcome of the war, and that it was only a matter of time before Hitler had to admit defeat.

At Christmas that year, there was little to celebrate and considerable need for prayer. The fear inspired by the Russians as they advanced inexorably across Poland was fed by stories of rape and plunder. In Hirschberg, the spectre of Communism seemed closer every day. By January, Hanna knew that the war was entering its final stages. For months, the German armies had, as she put it, struggled vainly to stem the all-engulfing avalanche. In both western and eastern Germany, Allied troops were fighting on German soil, or on soil which Hitler had, only a few years earlier, incorporated into Germany. She telephoned Otto Fuchs, who was still in Berlin, and urged him and his wife to leave while there was time. Although he did not feel able to abandon his position, and his wife had decided to stay with him, Fuchs was touched by her concern, especially as they had all but lost touch because of the divergence of their views.

Twice during the first two months of the year Hanna flew into Silesia, carrying urgent dispatches in and out of Breslau: she had exchanged work as a test pilot for the more urgent role of special flying messenger. The city was already under siege with only one airfield still open to the Germans by the time she arrived there with State Secretary Naumann, Goebbels's assistant in the Ministry of Propaganda. It was beyond the powers of any propaganda to raise the spirits of the inhabitants, who seemed to her already defeated, starving victims of war in whom hope and patriotism had already been killed. It was, in Hanna's words, a city of old men and women with 'pale, fear-ridden faces . . . in whom speech had withered before the terrible fate that they knew awaited them'.

In the middle of February, Hanna's parents and Kurt's parents-in-law left Silesia. Willy and Emy Reitsch abandoned their home reluctantly and only at the insistent request of their friend Blasius, the mayor of Hirschberg. Blasius saw it as his duty to ensure that as many people as possible were evacuated before it was too late; he told Dr Reitsch that he was hindering his efforts because others felt that 'So long as the Reitschs stay here, it's all right for us to stay too'. Willy, Emy, Heidi and her three children, and their maid Anni took what few personal possessions they could carry with them and travelled by train to Salzburg two days after the devastating Allied bomb attack on Dresden and four days after Helma's parents had left Warmbrunn. The Reitsch family were luckier than many of the refugees streaming from the east: they were given accommodation in the attic of Schloss Leopoldskron, an elegant mansion on the outskirts of Salzburg.

Doctor Reitsch was haunted by the memory of the suffering he had seen in Silesian villages to the east of Hirschberg which had already been reached by the Russians. Although he was an eye specialist, he had often been called to give general medical care during the Russian advance. He told his family of women who had been raped and of children ravaged under the hopeless eyes of their parents. As far as he was concerned, the war had been fought to ward off the evil of Bolshevism, which included spiritual and intellectual as well as physical violence: life under Russian rule would, he was convinced, be a fate far worse than death. Even in Salzburg, he could not entirely throw off the depression which threatened to engulf him, but which he kept hidden from his family and friends.

Emy and Heidi were happier and found it easier to form new friendships. They visited and were visited by Hanna's friends Landa Klaus and Elisabeth Scheel. Elisabeth's three children were the same age as Heidi's, and while they played together their mothers talked. Heidi was looking forward to remarrying, and Elisabeth to the birth of her fourth child. She had lost her parents in the raid on Dresden and was convinced that she would soon lose her husband. In Emy Reitsch she found almost a replica of her own mother, and relied on her for comfort and cheerful advice. Emy had, Elisabeth told me, a remarkable ability to live for the day, to put the past and the future into the background, and to remain cheerful and uncomplaining in spite of her own problems. As Easter approached, she wrote a little play in verse for the children and made them all costumes.

Hanna visited Silesia for the last time in April and was able to spend a few days in her home town. There were few civilians left in Hirschberg, where the streets seemed strangely empty: those who had stayed were waiting for the inevitable arrival of the Russians. Blasius had stayed on, in spite of his advice to others. As Hanna said goodbye to him she knew that she would never see him or her home again.

She had been summoned to Munich to reconnoitre emergency landing-grounds for hospital planes near Kitzbühel, just over the Austrian border and not far from Salzburg. Although there was no news of Kurt, the one day that she managed to spend with the rest of her family was happy, in spite of the knowledge that the end of the war was near and the fear of what might follow: 'My parents, my sister Heidi with her three children, and Anni, our faithful servant, were overjoyed at this unexpected reunion. Though we could not fail to be affected by the ominous gathering clouds of national tragedy, the happiness we felt at being together again was all the more perfect and precious because of its rarity and the uncertainty of the days ahead.'

# 9

# Descent into Hell

On 25 April 1945, General von Greim asked Hanna to fly him into Berlin, although the city was surrounded and partially occupied by Russian troops. He had been ordered to report to Hitler, who was still vainly planning for victory in a vast underground hide-out under the Chancellery, a fool's paradise in the middle of a besieged and ruined city. No one knew what Hitler wanted of von Greim, whose sense of honour would not allow him to refuse even such an apparently suicidal duty. As he realised that it was likely to be a one-way trip, he asked Hanna's parents for permission before inviting her to accompany him.

It has been suggested that Hanna insisted on going with von Greim against his wishes, or even that the fact that the two set out on their mission to Berlin together proved that they were lovers. That there was a deep love between them was undeniable; but few who knew either of them well and saw them together believed that it found any physical expression. Both had too high a moral code to indulge lightly in an affair. Von Greim's concept of duty was as clearly defined in private as in professional matters: the sense of honour which bound him and Hanna spiritually also kept them apart physically.

There was an eminently practical reason for Hanna to go to Berlin. Von Greim intended to enter the city by helicopter: as Hanna could fly a helicopter, and had recently made a detailed aerial survey of the area, the general considered that she stood a better chance than anyone else of delivering him safely to the Führer.

There was no time to be lost, but first Hanna had to say goodbye to her family. She arrived at midnight at Schloss Leopoldskron. Her parents were waiting at the door. Heidi's children were asleep in the air-raid shelter in the castle cellar. Hanna hugged each sleeping child in turn, then her sister, and finally her parents. Then she climbed into her car and drove away: Willy and Emy Reitsch stood together watching, two small proud figures. She knew that they were praying silently for her safety, as she was for theirs, and that they did not expect to see her again, although they had not sought to deflect her from her duty.

At 2.30 a.m., Hanna and von Greim left the airfield of Neu-Bieberg near Munich in a Ju 188. They gazed into a still starlit night which was for once undisturbed by enemy aircraft, wondering what, if anything, the future held for them. At 4 a.m., they landed at Rechlin, where the news was bad. For two days, no aircraft had succeeded in flying into Berlin. The only airfield near the city still under German control was Gatow, which was surrounded and under constant artillery

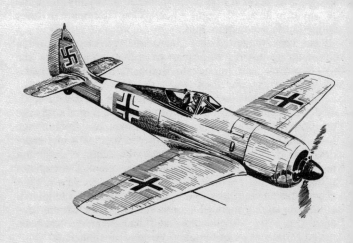

*Fw-190*

attack: it was not known if the runway was still usable. Worst of all, the helicopter they had intended to use had been destroyed in an air attack on Rechlin the previous night.

It seems astonishing that at this point von Greim and Hanna did not abandon the venture. Instead, von Greim decided to continue in a Focke-Wulf FW 190. This was normally a single-seater fighter, but there was one available at Rechlin which had had a second seat fitted in the luggage space. Two days earlier, Speer had been flown in and out of Berlin in it. The air force sergeant who had piloted him was to fly von Greim as far as Gatow, but was then to return to base immediately as the airfield was likely to be captured by the Russians at any moment.

Gatow was some distance from the centre of Berlin. Hanna felt that it was her duty to accompany her general so that he would have someone to fall back on should he need help. As there was no room for her in the cockpit, she wriggled and squeezed feet first into the small empty space in the rear section of the fuselage: she was so tightly wedged against the sharp metal framework that she had to fight to control a wave of claustrophobia. The sight and sound of thirty or forty fighter aircraft noisily preparing to escort the FW 190 was a comfort: as Germany was so short of airpower it seems in retrospect excessive. Hanna could not remember when she had last seen so large a concentration of German planes together.

She was aware that if the half-hour flight did not go well, and there seemed little reason to suppose that it would, she was already incarcerated in her own coffin. She counted the minutes on the luminous dial of her watch, wincing every time the motion caused her position to shift slightly but unable to alter it enough to prevent the pain. The minutes ticked by until she estimated that they must be nearly at their destination. Then the aircraft suddenly pitched and dived. Hanna assumed it must have been hit and waited for the final crash, but the pilot soon resumed level flight: he had been forced to dive to evade attack from Russian fighters.

By the time they landed at Gatow, most of the escort aircraft had been shot down. The FW 190 took off again immediately, leaving its passengers to run for safety. While

Hanna stretched her aching joints, von Greim attempted to telephone the Reich Chancellery. He was eventually able to speak to von Below, who told him that Hitler still insisted on seeing him, but that no one knew why; all roads into the city were in Russian hands, as was most of the city itself.

Although it seemed virtually impossible to reach the Chancellery, von Greim still considered it his duty to obey orders. Hanna felt equally bound to accompany him. There were still two serviceable Fieseler Storch aircraft at Gatow: the one which the couple planned to use was destroyed by artillery fire before they could take off. It was not until 6 p.m. that they were at last able to leave in the other. As they had spent the previous night in the air they were both already exhausted.

Von Greim took the pilot's seat, as he had had experience of flying under fire. Hanna stood behind him, but took the precaution of checking that she could reach the stick and throttle over his left shoulder. She later described the flight into the heart of what was left of Berlin in vivid detail:

> The plane rose smoothly from the ground and von Greim kept her as low as he possibly could. I remember noticing with a sudden longing how remote and peaceful the waters of the Wannsee looked, gleaming silver in the failing light. But the scene only flickered across my consciousness, as my whole being was riveted with animal concentration on the dangers surrounding us on all sides.
>
> We reached the Grunewald without interference, almost brushing the tree-tops to avoid detection by the enemy fighters that were now appearing above us. Then suddenly, from the bowels of the earth, from the lurking shadows, from the very tree-tops themselves, leapt the full fury and force of hell's fire, concentrated from every quarter, it seemed, on us alone. Below us, Russian tanks and soldiers were swarming among the trees. I could see the men's faces clearly as they aimed rifles, tommy guns and anti-tank weapons in our direction. In the sky immediately around us there were hundreds of deadly little explosive puffs.
>
> Then, suddenly, there was a rending crash. I saw a yellow and white flame streak up beside the engine and, at

the same time, von Greim shouted that he had been hit. An armour-piercing bullet had smashed through his right foot. Mechanically, I stretched over his shoulder, seized the throttle and stick, and struggled for all I was worth to keep the machine twisting and turning to avoid the fire. Von Greim lay crumpled in his seat, unconscious. The air around us was so explosive that even the noise of our own engine was drowned.

I gasped with horror as I caught sight of petrol running from both wing tanks. An explosion seemed imminent, I thought; in fact I was amazed there hadn't been one already. Yet the plane still answered to the controls and I was still untouched, although a number of shells hit the plane. My chief concern was for von Greim. Several times he started up, his hand grasping with convulsive energy for the stick and then dropping as he again lost consciousness.

We were approaching the radio tower. The evil-smelling sulphurous air whirled thicker and thicker with smoke, dust, and fumes. Visibility was almost nil. The ground fire was slackening and the area seemed, at any rate, to be still in German hands. It was here that my training flights over Berlin proved their use. To have flown around searching for landmarks would have been asking for trouble, but fortunately this was unnecessary as I could remember the compass bearing for the Ack-Ack tower, which lay directly on our route.

She identified the broad highway which ran across Berlin and at the eastern end of which the Brandenburg Gate still stood. The Storch's low speed, and the short runway it needed, enabled her to land near the gate in spite of the rubble and potholes in the once-elegant street.

Von Greim had by then regained consciousness. Hanna helped him from the aircraft, which they had no choice but to leave in the road. She hoped that someone would come to their assistance before it was seen and both they and it became the targets of another attack from the air. At last, after what seemed an endless wait, a solitary German military lorry appeared. The general was lifted into it, again almost unconscious, and he and Hanna were driven through the

Brandenburg Gate, along Unter den Linden and Wilhelmstrasse, and into Voss-strasse, all little more than rubble under a pall of smoke.

At the air-raid bunker into which Hitler and his court had retreated, von Greim was carried by half a dozen SS guards to an underground operating theatre. Hitler's latest private doctor, an orthopaedic surgeon called Stumpfegger, dressed his wound. Then the general, on a stretcher, and Hanna were led two floors further down under the earth to discover from the Führer the reason for their visit.

On the way down the stairs they met Frau Goebbels, who had been living voluntarily in the bunker with her husband and their six children for a few days, but for whom any visitor from the world outside was clearly a relief. She and Hanna had never met, but recognised each other from photographs: Magda Goebbels allowed her surprise and emotion to overcome the normal formality of a first meeting, and embraced Hanna tearfully. Before the two women had had time to talk, Hitler appeared.

Hanna was shocked to see that he looked both physically and mentally ill: his head drooped, his arms twitched, his eyes were glassy, and his voice was expressionless. When von Greim, still lying on his stretcher, had given a report of the journey, Hitler turned to Hanna and, according to her own emotional account, exclaimed:

'Brave woman! There is still some loyalty and courage in the world!'

He then told them that Goering had sent him a telegram suggesting that he, as Hitler's right-hand man, should assume leadership of the remnants of Germany. 'Goering has betrayed and forsaken me,' he ranted, his voice strengthened by rage. 'I have had him put under arrest and have stripped him of all his offices.'

Von Greim was told that he was to succeed the traitor as commander-in-chief of the air force, and was promoted to field marshal. The announcement was greeted with exhausted silence. The telephone call which had summoned von Greim to Berlin could equally well have imparted the news of his unexpected and unwanted promotion, and he and Hanna could have been spared an unnecessary and hazardous journey.

There were only two possible reasons why Hitler had insisted on promoting von Greim in person: either he was so unaware of the situation that he did not realise the danger and difficulty to which he had subjected one of his most loyal servants (it was after all not at his suggestion that Hanna too had risked her life); or he could not bear to be robbed of a new audience.

Hanna realised that von Greim's 'entirely immutable and selfless' sense of honour would compel him to stay in the bunker with Hitler to the end. There was, after all, virtually no air force left for him to command. She felt that her own loyalty, whether to von Greim, Hitler, or Germany, but principally to von Greim, gave her no choice: she too would stay. There could be no psychological escape from the unreal and desperate atmosphere of the bunker, and there seemed equally little chance of escaping from it physically.

The people living in Hitler's underground retreat were a microcosm of all the characteristics of the Nazi regime: loyalty and sycophancy, idealism and fanaticism, patriotism and racialism, love and cynicism were all represented. Once in the bunker, normality was left behind, although the presence of six boisterous children was a bizarre reminder of a previous life of fresh air and clear minds: they were the sons and daughters of Goebbels and his wife, both willing underground companions of their lord and master. The names of all six began with H, apparently in bizarre homage to Hitler: they were all angelically blonde-haired and blue-eyed—ideal Aryans. Their mother was the perfect example of Aryan womanhood, blonde and statuesque, although no one could have claimed any form of physical perfection for their father.

By the time Hanna joined the subterranean madhouse to which Magda Goebbels had, of her own free will, brought her children, their fate had already been sealed. Hitler had informed the inmates of their bunker that he would never leave, and that if—or rather when—the end seemed inevitable he would take his own life. To those he thought might wish to die with him, he had distributed phials of poison. Joseph Goebbels had protested that of course victory was still just round the corner, but that should Hitler nevertheless see fit to 'seek eternal rest from the burdens of an ungrateful people' he too would naturally take his own life.

Magda Goebbels was equally determined to follow, and to ensure that their children were not left alive: without the Führer, she insisted, life would have nothing to offer them. Hitler was so overwhelmed by her promise of ultimate loyalty that he promptly undid the golden party badge which had adorned his breast for fifteen years and pinned it instead on hers.

When the newcomers to the bunker were allowed to withdraw from Hitler's presence, Hanna gratefully accepted Magda Goebbels's invitation to have a much-needed wash in her private quarters. The six children were in bed but awake, and gazed at her with unconcealed curiosity from their bunks, bombarding her with questions. Throughout her stay in the bunker, Hanna spent as much of her time as possible with them, telling them stories about flying and foreign countries, teaching them how to yodel, and singing her favourite folksongs with them.

During the day, the children competed to see who could guess correctly how many direct hits would be scored on the bunker; when the younger ones occasionally forgot that it was a game and cried in fear, they were told that 'Uncle Führer' was busy conquering his enemies so that they could soon go home and play in their garden.

Although Hanna longed to be able to fly the children to safety, this was clearly impracticable, and she felt that it would in any case have been wrong to separate such a closely knit family: 'One could only pray that the magic and fantasy that enriched their little lives and provided an escape from the grimness of the bunker would remain with them to the end, whatever that had to be.' Because of the children, there was something approaching friendship, a friendship of mutual support in adversity, between Hanna and Magda Goebbels, who told her proudly how Hitler had given her a ring and his prized party badge.

Hanna had previously not known any of the inmates of the bunker well and few personally, apart from von Below and Naumann, possibly General Krebs and General Burgdorf, and probably Hitler's pilots, Hans Baur and Betz. She met a dozen others, including Martin Bormann and his secretary, Eva Braun's brother-in-law Hermann Fegelein, Hitler's two secretaries, and of course Eva Braun, to whom she took an instant dislike. She saw more of Dr Stumpfegger than any of the others, but only because she spent most of her time looking after the injured von Greim.

In spite of her exhaustion, neither Hanna nor anyone else slept much during her first night in the bunker. The artillery fire above them was almost unceasing, and so accurate that even fifty feet below ground plaster fell from the walls and ceilings. During the next two days, there was no improvement, although Hitler and his associates continued to talk as if there was help at hand and hopes were raised by snippets of almost favourable news. To Hanna and von Greim, who felt that they were the only sane and realistic people in the insanity that surrounded them, it seemed scarcely credible that Hitler could still talk optimistically about relief from the army of General Wenck, who was supposed to be gathering his forces and coming to the rescue: Wenck had as they knew no forces to gather, and had already abandoned the attempt.

It was rumoured that Fegelein had been accused of attempted desertion and shot: Hanna felt, as she later put it, as if the very ground beneath her feet was beginning to give way. Even in the extremity of their position, in the knowledge that defeat and probably death were inevitable, and that Hitler and his immediate circle 'were living in a world of their own, far removed from the reality outside', neither she nor von Greim considered deserting their country's leader.

Twice, von Greim refused to leave: once when a Ju 52 was sent specifically to fetch him and Hanna, and again when an Arado 96 managed to reach the centre of Berlin. Hanna greeted the arrival of the Ju 52 as a miracle, and would gladly have taken the opportunity of escaping with von Greim and even with Hitler, had either been willing to leave.

They were not entirely cut off from the outside world: there was still one telephone line between Berlin and the rest of Germany. Von Greim used this to tell Colonel Rudel and General Koller that he had no intention of abandoning the Führer in his hour of ultimate need. Hanna also talked to Koller, who recorded in his diary that to free the line for more important calls he hung up on her hysterical and long-winded account of her trials and tribulations. He felt that both Hanna and von Greim were as out of touch with reality as everyone else in the bunker.

On 27 April, when Hanna had been in the bunker for twenty-four hours, Hitler sent for her: he gave her two phials of poison, one for herself and one for Field Marshal von Greim, so that they would have the 'freedom of choice'. If Wenck's army did not materialise, he told her, he and Eva Braun had already decided to end their lives. Hanna did not believe that, even if Wenck arrived, Hitler could live much longer in his obviously feeble state of health: his vital energies were, as she expressed it, too depleted to sustain him alive. He had in any case made it clear that he did not wish to escape.

Another long day passed. During the next night Hanna felt that 'the entire force of hell had been unleashed' as the Chancellery was directly bombarded. She spent that night, as she had done the previous two nights, in von Greim's sickroom so that she could tend to his every need. Shortly after midnight, Hitler appeared in the doorway, his face ashen, a telegram and a map clutched in his hand: he looked, Hanna said, 'like a dead man'. Himmler, he told them, had betrayed him—the telegram was proof of his betrayal—and a Russian attack was expected on the Chancellery the following day. Hanna and von Greim were ordered to fly out in the Arado. They protested, but Hanna did not, as she is commonly assumed to have done, weep and cling to the Führer's feet: this was a figment of the dramatic imagination of film-makers. Their protests were overruled.

Von Greim was given his first unrealistic task as commander-in-chief of the Luftwaffe: he was to organise an air attack on the enemy in the streets leading to the Chancellery. Hitler was clearly 'living in a world of illusion', Hanna realised. She thought of the scenes she had witnessed throughout Germany in the previous few weeks: 'the roads blocked and overflowing with fleeing civilians, the troops flooding back from the front, the nights spent amid the moan and crash of bombs, the bombardment under which the Reich Chancellery had lain for days'. Hitler had not ventured above ground to see the real Germany of April 1945, a country of fear and despair.

Bormann and Hevel gave von Greim letters for the Reich offices in Berchtesgaden and Salzburg. Hanna was entrusted with Magda Goebbels's ring, a present from Hitler, as well as letters from Eva Braun for her sister and from both the Goebbels for Magda's son by her first marriage, Harald Quandt.

Goebbels wrote that 'alive or dead, we will not leave the shelter unless we leave it with honour and glory'. He was still, as he approached his chosen death, a master of propaganda, attempting to safeguard his own reputation in the glorious reassessment of Nazi Germany which he confidently predicted: 'Germany will outlive this terrible war, but only if it has examples upon which to guide its reconstruction. Such an example we want to give here! . . . The lies will one day break under their own weight and the truth will again triumph. The hour will come when we will stand pure and undefiled as our beliefs and aims have always been.'

Magda Goebbels's expressions of Nazi loyalty were as strong, although interspersed with a greater show of parental affection. 'We are here to give our National Socialist way of life its only possible and honourable ending,' she told her son. 'Life will not be worth living in the world that will come after Hitler and National Socialism.' This, she explained, was why she had felt compelled to take the children of her second marriage with her, first into the bunker and then into death: 'They are too precious for the life that will come after us; a merciful God will understand me when I help them to a merciful deliverance.' She and her husband, who had rarely been noticeably close in life, were of one mind—'to be true unto death to the Führer'.

It seems hardly in keeping with Hanna and von Greim's joint sense of honour that they read the letters entrusted to them. That they did so is clear, for Hanna later admitted to destroying Eva Braun's letter undelivered: she and von Greim considered it childish, but were afraid that it might glorify her as a Nazi martyr. She reconstructed it from memory under interrogation: Eva Braun was sorry for those left 'in the chaos that will follow', 'glad to die at the side of the Führer' and 'glad that the horror now to come is spared me'. 'What could life now give me?' she asked. 'It has already been perfect. It has already given me its best and its fullest. With the Führer, I have had everything. To die now, beside him, completes my happiness.'

It was night when Hanna and von Greim left. The Goebbels children were asleep, but Magda Goebbels said an emotional farewell. Von Below accompanied them to the exit of the bunker, where instead of fresh air they met sulphurous fumes, smoke, and flames, and the whining and crashing of shells. They made their way in an armoured car to the zoo, where the Arado was waiting under cover near the Victory Column. It had been flown in by the pilot who had taken von Greim and Hanna as far as Gatow only days before. To have landed in Berlin, under continual fire, was as Hanna said an amazing feat.

Although enemy searchlights swung endlessly across the east-west axis, the pilot managed to take off on a 400-yard strip of road which was free of craters. He headed towards the Brandenburg Gate, a solitary symbol of former glory amid the rubble. As they flew across the province of Brandenburg, lakes gleamed silver below them in the moonlight and burning villages made dots of colour against the dark countryside. At Rechlin, they were welcomed in despairing silence by the remnants of the operational staff. Hanna was cold, tired, and depressed. Even in the fresh cold night air, she could not rid herself of the smell of 'fire, doom and death'.

While they were in the air, a bizarre and macabre marriage ceremony was being conducted fifty feet underground in the bunker: Eva Braun, who had been able so recently to conceive of no greater happiness than dying with the Führer, was granted her dearest wish—to be able to die as Frau Hitler. Suicide rather than marital bliss was the main topic of conversation at the nuptial breakfast.

The bridegroom then spent the rest of his wedding night dictating public and private last wills and testaments. Self-justification and denunciation were the themes of Hitler's last political testament, according to which neither he nor anyone else had wanted the war: he blamed it entirely on 'those international politicians who came either of Jewish stock, or worked for Jewish interests'. That the war had been lost was, he claimed, the fault of all those who had betrayed him, and in particular of Goering and Himmler.

While the Führer was dictating, Hanna was trying vainly to get warm; the new field marshal, still hobbling painfully on crutches, was issuing his first empty orders as commander-in-chief of the air force which had once been Germany's glory. There were no aircraft to be mustered, but the instruction had nevertheless to be given.

From Rechlin, Hanna flew him on to Plön to talk to Admiral Dönitz: the head of the air force wanted to discuss the future with the head of the navy. The next stop, in a two-seater Bücker, a small slow aircraft in which Hanna could fly low enough to avoid detection, was to Dobbin to see another field marshal, Keitel.

At midnight on 29 April, von Below was sent, by land and river, out of Berlin. Later that day, news of Mussolini's death reached the bunker. In the afternoon, Hitler had his Alsatian Blondi poisoned and two other dogs shot. In the early hours

*Bücker two-seater*

of the morning, he conducted a silent farewell ceremony of handshaking. As soon as he left, the mood changed to one of relief: Hitler was about to die, and all those who had protested their undying loyalty were delighted. The atmosphere which Hanna had experienced in the bunker, an atmosphere of the grave, became almost festive.

When Hitler and his bride had carried out their suicide pact, Joseph and Magda Goebbels kept their word: they killed first their children and then themselves. Hanna and von Greim had in the meantime proceeded to Lübeck, where the field marshal was anxious for a situation report from his generals in the area. It was there that late in the evening of 1 May they heard the announcement of Hitler's death.

The following day, Dönitz, whose appointment as the Führer's successor had taken everyone by surprise, made a statement: the Führer had died 'a hero's death', and the German people must bow in deepest grief and respect for the leader who had 'early recognised the frightful danger of Bolshevism' and had 'dedicated his being to the struggle against this evil'. 'His mission in the battle against the Bolshevist storm-flood is valid for Europe and the entire civilised world,' Dönitz finished, tactfully making no mention of the parallel struggle against the Jews. To protect civilian refugees and retreating troops, the fight against the evil of Bolshevism must, Dönitz told the nation, be continued.

The future looked bleak as Hanna and von Greim continued to scurry from place to place, and the sense of living in a nightmare became even more overwhelming. When Dönitz summoned his new government to Plön they made their way back there. Hanna confronted Himmler for the last time in Plön: she accused him of betraying his Führer and his people 'in the very darkest hour'. 'History will weigh it differently,' Himmler replied. 'Hitler wanted to continue the fight. He was mad with his pride and his "honour". He wanted to shed more German blood when there was none left to flow. Hitler was insane. He should have been stopped long ago.'

Even at this stage, Hanna was not prepared to allow anyone to accuse Hitler of insanity: she told Himmler that far from being insane, Hitler, whom she had left less than thirty-six hours before, had died for the cause he believed in, bravely and honourably. Himmler would have done better to think of saving German blood before he became identified with 'the useless shedding of so much of it,' she suggested, according to her later interrogation report.

Hanna and von Greim flew on after the conference at Plön to Königratz, headquarters of Field Marshal Schöner, the commander of the German troops still in Czechoslovakia and Silesia. Von Greim wanted to order Schöner to hold on as long as possible. It was an unnecessary journey; the order had been given before they arrived. By then von Greim was so ill that for four days further travel was impossible. Hanna nursed him until he was able to continue. They then left in a Dornier 217 to see Kesselring in Graz, another wasted and alarming flight: they were shot at by their own side as they came in to land, and Kesselring had left for Zell am See.

Undeterred, although exhausted and depressed, they switched to a Fieseler Storch in pursuit of the elusive Kesselring. At Zell am See, they found instead General Koller. As far as Koller was concerned, von Greim had simply vanished for a week, then had telephoned him in the morning before appearing in person, still accompanied by his faithful pilot-cum-nurse. He was shocked at von Greim's appearance, on crutches, clearly in pain, his face sunken and with an unhealthy yellow tinge, and told him he should be in hospital: this temerity did not come easily to one accustomed to respect rank, nor did talking in front of Hanna. Von Greim, however, insisted that she should stay.

Koller recorded his amazement that the two enthused about Hitler, regretting that they had not been allowed to die with him in the bunker, and that Hanna even said: 'We must kneel before the altar of the Fatherland and pray.' To Koller's suggestion that Hitler had betrayed the country and the people, and that his suicide was the most cowardly betrayal of all, von Greim replied with an attack on the man he considered the true traitor, Goering. Hanna, according to Koller's account, wept as she entreated him not to protect Goering, while von Greim said that he would like to shoot him himself— harsh words from a man who was normally so mild mannered and gentle. 'The situation is not lacking in drama, and I feel very sorry for myself,' Koller wrote in his diary: there seemed to be no sensible person to whom he could turn.

Koller's account of the next stage of their journey, by car, varies considerably from that given by Hanna. Hanna's von Greim was noble, loyal, the most honourable man that had ever lived, struggling bravely in spite of injury, illness, and mental anguish to fulfil his duty. Koller's von Greim caused the young officer assigned to him considerable problems; he was desperate to escape, unbearably stubborn, and either afraid to take what was coming or delirious. 'He got out [of the car] in the country, wanted to put on civilian clothes and escape to the mountains,' Koller reported.

That a man who had been badly injured, had barely had time for medical attention, and who was running a high temperature should have reached a stage of psychological and physical collapse was hardly surprising. For a fortnight, both he and Hanna had been under the greatest strain, with very little sleep, and both had reached the point where they were incapable of rational thought. Von Greim was obsessed with the need to muster opposition to the Russians, and Hanna with the task of looking after him. Her only comfort was the thought that her family was safe in Salzburg.

At Zell am See, they learnt that the capitulation was to be on 8 May, a day earlier than they had thought. They had failed to find Kesselring, and in the few hours that were left before Germany's final surrender they set off for Kitzbühel, where a doctor whom Hanna knew and respected had recently opened a hospital. It seemed, she admitted at last, as if any further efforts on their part would be useless, although von Greim still wanted to encourage resistance against the Russians.

At last, on the morning of 9 May, Hanna delivered her patient to the hospital at Kitzbühel. She, too, was in need of medical attention, for exhaustion and delayed shock. In the afternoon, Captain Eric Brown tracked her down there through a chance remark overheard in a bar. He had been given a list of Germans whom he was to find for the British: it included Wernher von Braun, Dr Ernst Heinkel, and Professor Willi Messerschmitt, Messerschmitt's chief test pilot Gerd Lindner, Focke-Wulf's designer and test pilot Kurt Tank, and Hanna Reitsch. He was tempted to kidnap her, but decided reluctantly that he must 'play the game': instead he reported her whereabouts to the Americans, in return for a promise that he would later be allowed to interview her.

Koller visited von Greim the next day, and afterwards made an entry in his diary: 'He was always a most honourable and worthy man, exemplary in his behaviour and a gentleman from head to toe. A supporter of the Nazis, he was suffering because what had in his estimation been a good idea had been shamefully corrupted.'

Von Greim was indeed, as Koller suspected, tortured by agonies of conscience, which he discussed day after day with Hanna. He knew that he would sooner or later be brought to trial, and that if he were to be honest he must then denounce Goering; but this offended his sense of loyalty to a fellow German and an officer. He still had his poison capsule, as did Hanna, and they talked about suicide. They were both aware that if they were to die together, it would give rise to gossip and speculation about their relationship.

Nothing, Hanna determined, should be allowed to besmirch her hero's honour: she decided that if he felt compelled to take his own life, she would follow, but only after an interval of a week so that their names would not be dishonourably linked. Whether or not they reached a formal agreement to this effect, Hanna considered it a binding pact.

# 10

# The Prisoner

It was rumoured before the capitulation that all Germans would be returned by the Allied victors to their place of origin. For the Reitsch family, this would have meant living under the Russians. Landa Klaus, who knew how greatly Dr Reitsch feared being sent back to Silesia, found them rooms on a farm in a valley where she hoped they would be able to live secretly. She even organised a horse and cart to move their belongings. But Dr Reitsch refused to move: if Hanna was still alive, she would expect to find her family at Schloss Leopoldskron.

Although General Koller claimed in his diary that he had telephoned both Hanna's and von Greim's families immediately he knew they were safely out of Berlin, he cannot have done so: four days later, Willy and Emy Reitsch were still waiting for news. Doctor Reitsch had given up hope of ever seeing either Hanna or Kurt again, and was more deeply depressed than even his wife realised. He was convinced that he would be separated from the women and children who depended on him, and that without his protection they would be brutally treated by the Russians.

On 4 May Landa called at Schloss Leopoldskron. She was met at the door by the caretaker. All the Reitsch family were ill, he told her: they had upset stomachs after drinking some fruit juice that was off, but would probably be better by the next day. The following day, she called again, expecting to find that they had recovered.

There was a horse-drawn cart in front of the house. On the cart were six bodies, all covered—the corpses of Dr and Frau

Reitsch, Heidi and her three children, and their maid Anni. Willy Reitsch had shot first the others, and then, after the police had been called, himself. The stomach complaint of the previous day had been caused by an abortive poison attempt with cyanide. As far as he was concerned, he had done his ultimate duty.

He left a letter for Hanna. If by some miracle she had survived, he wrote, he knew that she would be reassured by, and even happy in, the knowledge that her loved ones were safely with God and that no torture or unknown death could befall them.

It was only the certainty that she would soon see her family that had kept Hanna going since she left Berlin. On 10 May, she sent a letter to Salzburg with a doctor who was going there, and waited confidently for an answer from her mother. She was asleep when the doctor returned: he told von Greim what had happened. Von Greim broke the news to her as gently as he could in the morning. She appeared to take it calmly, too numb with shock to show any apparent emotion.

Only von Greim was aware of the depth of her wretchedness. 'At least, thank God for him, for one person who knew them,' Hanna thought. She told herself that her father had seen no alternative but to take upon himself 'the heaviest responsibility of all'. But how, she asked herself, could she continue to live without her mother, and what cruel fate had determined that she should survive so many close brushes with death, only to be robbed of everything that really mattered to her? More than ever she needed someone to rely on, and that person was, of course, von Greim: but she knew that he too might soon choose to die.

A few days later, Koller visited von Greim again. The curtains in his room were drawn. Photographs of Hanna's dead relatives were displayed on a small table, surrounded by flowers; a candle was burning on the shrine. Koller thought Hanna and von Greim were both distant, unnaturally closed in on themselves, and felt deeply sorry for them. He asked that von Greim should not be moved, fearing that he would not survive any further upheaval in his present condition.

On 22 May, Field Marshal von Greim was officially arrested. He was to be taken to England as a prisoner of war and then to stand trial at Nuremberg. On 24 May he took what he saw as the only honourable way out: at the hospital in Salzburg, he used the cyanide capsule that Hitler had given him on his promotion to commander-in-chief of the Luftwaffe less than a month earlier.

After von Greim's suicide, Hanna felt more alone than she had ever imagined possible. She had to survive for a week before she too could use her poison capsule. Her only regret was that she was not allowed to cross the border between zones in Austria to visit her family's grave first.

Half-way through the week, she was visited by three American officers, who stood beside her bed while they issued a pressing and flattering invitation to go to America. She would, they promised, become even more famous, not to mention rich, and would be able to fly to her heart's content. If she refused, they would, however, be powerless to protect her from imprisonment by the CIC, the American Counter Intelligence Corps. Although she was equally unimpressed by the bribe or the threat, she was given three days to think the matter over.

She had not changed her mind by the time her visitors returned: it was, she told them, better to die or live without flying but with honour in her own country than to live and fly without honour in another. She nevertheless accepted their offer to escort her to Salzburg: she had not questioned the decision to keep her word to von Greim, and intended to kill herself as soon as she was brought back to Kitzbühel.

The Americans who escorted her had just returned from Dachau concentration camp, and confronted her with photographs of the atrocities they had seen there. Hanna was reminded of 'that fearful pamphlet' which Peter Riedel had thrust under her nose and with which she had confronted Himmler. 'I was speechless with horror,' she later wrote, 'but didn't believe a word of it.'

'Such things could *never* have happened in Germany,' she tried to tell herself. If it was true that her own countrymen could be capable of such horrific deeds, then there was nothing worth saving: this was not the Germany to which she had devoted her life. Her patriotism soon regained control, and she decided that she must fight for the good name of

Germany, and defend her countrymen 'against this most vile and devilish defamation': 'The name of my country must be cleared and the people must know what atrocities have been committed behind their backs and in their name,' she resolved. It was a half-acceptance of a possibility with which, like many other Germans, she found herself incapable of coming to terms.

The journey continued in silence. Hanna struggled with her conflicting loyalties until they reached the vast park-like cemetery where von Greim's grave, marked by a simple soldier's cross in a long line of similar crosses, lay only a few steps away from that shared by her parents. Her companions stood at a respectful distance as she wordlessly begged von Greim, the man she had loved and respected more than any other, to understand that she would have to break her word. The decision to stay alive, to fight for the honour of Germany, now seemed as inevitable as her earlier resolve to die.

Hanna returned to Kitzbühel, fired with new missionary zeal, and perhaps secretly relieved that she did not after all have to use her poison. Her Mission made it even more impossible for her to contemplate a new life in a new country, although several further approaches were made to her by the Americans. 'I am the German test pilot Hanna Reitsch,' she insisted proudly. 'I will always remain a German, and especially in this time of her misery.'

If anything, Germany's downfall had hardened Hanna's attitude and strengthened her patriotism: 'As a German and one who was happy to live under Hitler's rule when our country had never had it so good before, how could I suddenly point a jeering finger against it at this time when fortune was against it, with my eye on a fat American carrot?' she asked, adding: 'I may appear in some eyes to be a hopeless idealist. But dishonest and a hypocrite—never!' Perhaps this is as good a summary of her character and attitudes as any.

With the division of Germany's territories between the Allies, the French were to take over the area of Austria around Kitzbühel. It was rumoured that they would be tougher than the Americans: America had, after all, not been occupied, and the French were in a mood to extract retribution.

With the connivance of the Americans, the hospital in Kitzbühel was evacuated to their zone of control before the French took over.

Hanna travelled with the hospital contingent on a Red Cross train as far as Innsbruck, where she stayed for a few days with the Heubergers. For the first time she learnt that her relatives had rejected Hitler, and had been active in the Austrian resistance. They avoided political discussions or recriminations: it was more important that they had all acted in the way that each thought honourable, had survived, and were together.

The Heubergers were, as far as she knew, her nearest surviving relatives—there was no news of Kurt—and they did all they could to make her feel that she belonged with them. As she had left Kitzbühel with no time to pack her belongings, Helmut went by motor bike to sort them out for her. The French had not yet taken over the hospital, where it took him all night to collect together her innumerable dresses, coats, blouses, underwear, towels, creams, soaps, perfumes, and piles of papers—she had tipped everything out of drawers and cupboards in her room before her hasty departure. Helmut hid her cases and a crate of hospital instruments from the French in a hayloft.

Obsessed with the idea that she must be near the family she had lost, Hanna decided after a few days to leave Innsbruck. As she was about to board a train to Salzburg, she was accosted by a man in an American officer's uniform: he told her, civilly and in fluent German, that she was to go with him to Zell am See. There she was taken into custody by the chief of the Air Force Intelligence Unit in the American zone, Captain Robert Work.

The aircraft in which Hanna had landed at Zell am See with von Greim was still there when the Americans occupied the area. Intelligence units had been instructed to find where she was and to establish the identity of the male passenger she had taken out of Berlin: as no one knew for certain what had happened to Hitler, it was thought that she might have flown him to safety. Even if she had not, as one of the last people to see him she was wanted for questioning about his last days in the bunker. Work, who already knew of Hanna's flying activities, immediately dispatched some of his best agents, Austrians who had co-operated with the Allies during the war, to look for her.

'I knew that she was a figure of some import in Luftwaffe research and aircraft testing, which alone made her a prime target for air force interrogation,' he told me, 'but here was the possibility that she was the key to the fate or perhaps even the whereabouts of Hitler. I would say that at that moment she was probably one of the most fruitful sources that any interrogator could hope to have before him. The magnitude of my possibly being the person who would be instrumental in finding Hitler was overwhelming.'

Work kept Hanna in Zell am See for a few days, to give her time to recover from the wild sequence of events of the previous month. She was not, he told her, under arrest, but in his custody as the guest of the American government, a distinction which Hanna defined as being 'free, but not free'.

Although she was aware that each of the Allies was anxious to interrogate her, she assumed that their interest was in her work with the V1: she was afraid that this might classify her as a 'war criminal'. Work did not enlighten her about the true reason for the interest of Allied intelligence. He gave her the impression that he wanted to protect her from the Counter Intelligence Corps and other Allied organisations who were looking for her, including the Russians.

He was determined to gain her trust so that she would talk to him openly and honestly, and so that he could play a significant part in establishing what had happened to Hitler. She seemed, he thought, a little frightened: 'She was not exactly timid, but she spoke softly and with care. There was something believable and sincere about her right from the beginning.' Hanna accepted his friendship at face value. She was too emotionally exhausted, and to instinctively trusting, to suspect his motives and to wonder why one American should be so anxious to shield her from other Americans.

At first, Work allowed Hanna to stay at Schloss Leopoldskron, which had been occupied by the American Property Control Commission, represented by a Captain Bird. She was given the flat in which her family had lived during the last few months of their lives, and which she called her 'only home'.

Either Bird or Work visited her every day and brought her food. Not surprisingly, she was still clearly deeply upset by the deaths of members of her family and by her experiences at the end of the war, and often spoke of suicide and of joining von Greim.

Although Hanna was on her honour not to make any attempt to leave, she was allowed to go by bicycle to visit her parents' grave every morning. Landa Klaus was the only person apart from Work and Bird whom she saw regularly. Together they sorted out the possessions left by Hanna's parents. Hanna was all for throwing almost everything away except her mother's verses, family photographs and letters, and the phial of poison given to her by Hitler: she might one day want to use it, and it was her last link with von Greim.

Landa was more practical and parsimonious, and often retrieved something which Hanna had discarded. While Landa was going through the mounting piles of rubbish, she came across a box in which she found Eva Braun's visiting card, with her family address on it: Hanna did not want anything which would remind her of Eva Braun, and so Landa kept it.

Hanna was equally impractical when it came to normal domestic matters, in spite of her training at the Koloniale Frauenschule: when Landa left her one day to cook some noodles, she admitted that she had no idea how to set about the task. In spite of their macabre situation, they laughed together over this as over many other things: nothing could quench Hanna's ability to laugh for long.

Whenever she had been in Austria during the war, Hanna had sung with Landa and a girls' choir: when her fellow singers discovered where she was, they serenaded her from a distance. The strains of yodelling and Austrian folk-songs carried clearly across the lake behind the castle.

With Captain Bird's connivance she was able to make several trips to visit friends at Ainring: although she considered this a kindness, the excursions were reported to Work. When she heard a rumour that her old boss, Professor Georgii, was in prison at Reichenhall, she made a genuinely illicit trip across the border of which her custodians remained unaware. She claimed later that she then went on a five-day hunger strike which forced Work to obtain Georgii's transfer. Work told me that he knew nothing about this, but that as soon as Hanna told him where Georgii was he made a telephone call and had him handed over: he was delighted to have found Georgii, who was high on his list for interrogation.

It is not surprising that the traumas of the end of the war had strengthened, rather than weakened, the feelings of loyalty between friends and colleagues, as well as between relatives. Tightly knit groups had been scattered and did not at first know what had happened to each other. Finding out was difficult, and rumours often replaced facts. Gretl Böss, Hanna's occasional wartime secretary, was convinced that she must still be alive and travelled anxiously from place to place trying to find her.

At last, she heard in Ainring that Hanna had recently been seen there with an American officer, presumably Captain Bird, that she was apparently a prisoner of the American air force, and that she was expected to visit Ainring again soon. A few days later Gretl did indeed see her there, with the same American officer, who gave permission for them to meet at Schloss Leopoldskron.

After a few weeks, Work decided that if he was to gain all the information he wanted from Hanna she would have to be moved: 'So many topics of importance in addition to the "last days" information began to surface that I recognised as vital information on the inner workings of Luftwaffe research.' It would be easier to interrogate her about the suicide squadron and the V weapons, about which little was known, at Villa Glanzenbichl in Traunkirchen bei Gmunden, where the Americans were already interrogating some of Germany's leading military and civilian scientists. He also hoped that her appraisal of top Nazi leaders, particularly Himmler and Goering, would help to explain how the German high command had worked and how it fell apart.

When Hanna was told that she was to be moved, she interpreted it as a triumph of her will over Work's that Georgii was to join her at Traunkirchen, and felt that leaving Salzburg was a fair exchange.

On the day that she was to leave Salzburg, Hanna was visited by her sister-in-law. Helma was a Marinehelferin, the equivalent of a Wren, and in co-operation with the Allies after the end of the war she was escort to the last Wrens returning to their homes in Salzburg. She had been trying anxiously to find out what had happened to her parents-in-law, as well as to Hanna. The two women were allowed to spend ten minutes together: Helma was able to reassure Hanna that Kurt was alive and in Kiel.

Later in the day, Gretl Böss was, as she had been promised, escorted to Schloss Leopoldskron to visit Hanna, with whom she spent half an hour alone. They swopped watches—Hanna's watch had been given to her by Udet—and Hanna gave Gretl her poison capsule for safe-keeping. Work had suggested this: although he would dearly have loved to have it himself, he knew Hanna would not willingly have handed it over to him.

At Traunkirchen, she and Georgii were under relatively luxurious house arrest. Although they were not free, they suffered few restrictions, and were able to walk and talk unsupervised in the spacious grounds and even to swim in a lake within the boundaries of the estate. The Americans appeared to be treating them as friends; they took their meals together, talked over their past experiences, and discussed the future.

Work's German was good—he had lived in Germany until he was nine—and Hanna almost forgot that their countries had so recently been enemies. 'We discussed every subject under the sun, but inevitably flying, being our *métier*, was our favourite topic,' she wrote later. 'Just as in a family, we discussed freely the planes we had tested and our experiences in doing so, and readily answered the enthusiastic questions fired at us by the Americans. They were, of course, particularly interested to hear my account of my flight into Berlin and my meeting with Hitler in the bunker.'

On several occasions, Work suggested that Hanna should write about the last days in the bunker. She was not yet ready to do so, she told him. He did not press the point, but was at pains to ensure that his own report reflected her opinions accurately so that her eventual account would not contradict his. She did, however, write several other reports for him, including one on the Suicide Mission and a condemnation of Goering.

The villa was, as Work put it, 'abuzz with people writing reports'—the German 'guests' as well as their interrogators: 'As long as they were busy writing they were enjoying my hospitality and participating in the most fascinating meal-time discussions I have ever participated in—and all the while the table we sat around was well supplied with items most of the guests had not seen for years.'

Work often asked Hanna to remain at the table after the others had withdrawn, and to correct him as he recited what she had already told him. She always complied: the war was over, and it was time for the truth. 'Sometimes when I had exhausted my powers of retention I would plead an upset stomach and retire to the wash room,' Work told me. 'There, sitting on the pot, I would review what I had, make notes on what I had just heard, pull the flush cord, and return to the dining-room.' His 'tender stomach' became a standing joke. Hanna was also interrogated by an officer from USAF Technical Intelligence, who talked to her several times in a rowing boat on the Traunsee and with whom she was on as friendly terms as with Work.

She was not aware that the stories she had told with her usual expressive enthusiasm were to play a significant role in proving whether or not Hitler was dead. Work, whose name appears on several interrogation summaries based on his conversations with Hanna and on her own written reports, told me in 1987, some years after he had retired from the United States Air Force with the rank of colonel: 'I still view my interrogation of her as a memorable event of the early postwar time—particularly as it was largely her testimony through which we were able to furnish data to the Nuremberg trials which was pivotal in helping that body firm its conviction that Hitler was indeed dead.'

Gradually, as he built up a relationship of trust with Hanna, Work began to think that there could be 'a role for this remarkable and competent woman in post-war Germany'. The fact that she had not been a Nazi party member would make it easier for her to take 'an early role in the rebuilding of Germany'. He was determined to use every opportunity to establish her as a reliable witness, including her co-operation in American plans for the future of Germany.

When he was told that his time with her was to be curtailed, and that she was to be handed over to a higher authority, the dreaded CIC, he protested, but was overruled. Hanna was taken back to Schloss Leopoldskron, where she was fetched by a CIC contingent which included the colonel in charge. As she knew that Work had attempted to thwart the Counter Intelligence Corps on her behalf, she was worried that he might get into trouble, and wrote to his superior explaining how well he had treated her.

She was taken first to the Salzburg prison, where she was locked in a tiny bare cell and subjected to the same harsh treatment as the other inmates. Her feelings during her first night ranged from gratitude that her parents had been spared knowledge of the indignity to which she was being subjected, to overwhelming despair. In the next few weeks, she spent many of the long, empty hours scratching verse after verse written by her mother on the cell wall with her nails.

From snippets of conversation she overheard, she gathered that she was being held because it was suspected that she had helped Hitler to escape from Berlin. She claimed that she was never told this officially, and was never interrogated: she still did not regard the friendly conversations in Traunkirchen as interrogation.

The Americans kept their promise to allow Eric Brown access to her in July. His brief was for a technical interrogation on the Me 163. 'She was an emotional wreck when I was allowed access to her,' Brown told me, 'and poured out more than she intended.' Although they met occasionally afterwards, he was convinced that Hanna always tried to avoid him because he could have been 'a grave embarrassment' by revealing their conversation, which in his opinion confirmed that she was a 'fanatical Nazi'. His report, which I have been unable to trace, even classified her as such. Work, who came to know her far better, reached the opposite conclusion.

In September the British intelligence authorities in Germany gave a young man called Hugh Trevor-Roper the task of collecting all available evidence to ascertain once and for all whether Hitler was dead or alive. Trevor-Roper interviewed a number of the survivors from the bunker personally; others were interrogated on his behalf at various camps.

Although Trevor-Roper made one attempt to see Hanna, the Americans were either unable or unwilling at the time to arrange a meeting. Instead he was given a copy of a confidential interrogation summary, 'The Last Days in Hitler's Air Raid Shelter', signed by Work (see Appendix 2). Trevor-Roper relied heavily on Work's report in the initial report which he had to submit by the beginning of November.

Yet another attempt was made to persuade Hanna to go to America when she was taken from the prison for a reunion with Wernher von Braun, General Dornberger, and a number of other men who had worked on the V2 and who had all been recruited by the Americans. The suspicion that she was expected to be weak enough after the rigours of her confinement to welcome the chance of a new life strengthened her resolve: she would stay in Germany, whatever the consequences. She was moved yet again, first to a cell in Freising and then, at the beginning of November, to another prison cell in Oberursel.

There she was, she claimed, treated as a top Nazi criminal. Nothing had prepared her for the misery, discomfort, and hatred she encountered. She was indignant: she felt that she had merely done her duty as a German, and was unable to understand the intensely bitter feelings of her captors. Her only comfort was that she knew that her brother was alive, although they were unable to contact each other.

Work submitted two more interrogation summaries while she was in the Oberursel prison. Both were based on her own written reports as his 'guest'. One was a detailed and bitter criticism of Goering, whom she held responsible for the disintegration of the Luftwaffe and for the deaths of Udet and von Greim. The other described the V1 Suicide Mission, about which there had previously been only vague rumours.

After a few weeks in the Oberursel prison, Hanna was suddenly removed from her cell. She was convinced that she was about to die. Instead, she was taken to a house not far from the prison which had been a home for retired teachers and which the Americans had taken over as a detention centre for some of their more elevated prisoners. Camp King, as the Americans called it, was a considerable improvement on the prison, although to the German inmates it was known as Haus Alaska.

Hanna was the only woman among a constantly changing group of fifty or so political and military leaders awaiting interrogation and trial and, in some cases, execution. She resented what she considered the unnecessarily antagonistic attitude of some of their guards: as a number of her fellow prisoners had held high Nazi office, anyone more politically aware might have found this less surprising. That she was with other Germans, and in many cases men whom she had admired from afar, Hanna considered a privilege: 'Binding us together was the fact that we were all Germans who had gone through the same process of torment and degradation, who understood one another and belonged together. Each one's suffering was the suffering of everyone. But suffering was the one thing we never discussed.'

During the day, the prisoners were allowed to mix freely, although at night they were confined to their rooms: Hanna enjoyed the luxury of a private and comfortably furnished and heated bedroom. They formed the habit of giving and attending morale-boosting lectures, reading plays together, and sharing domestic duties on a rota. Their only grievance about their physical treatment was the quality and quantity of the food served in a communal dining-room.

Hanna and Schwerin von Krosigk, Hitler's former finance minister, formed a mutually supportive friendship. They went for leisurely walks in the grounds and discussed the past and the future: the present was a matter of psychological survival. Among their topics of conversation, and later of correspondence, was Hitler's health. Hanna was relieved to discover that he had suffered a personality change as a result of treatment by the less reputable of his doctors: she felt that this explained and therefore partially excused his loss of touch with reality.

On 4 December, a press release was circulated by the public relations office of the American forces in Germany, announcing that Hanna Reitsch would be available for interview the following day at the Oberursel Interrogation Center. The press release included a one-page biography of Hanna which she had, it was claimed, dictated, and which stated that although she was 'not an ardent Nazi, not even a party member, the final days of the war in Germany were yet to her a tragedy'. Her personal description finished with the comment: 'She is 33 years old, she says, adding that she is not considered beautiful.'

A fifteen-page interrogator's account of her story was attached, with an embargo until after the press conference: although it did not carry Robert Work's name, there is no doubt that he had prepared it. In a lively, largely conversational, style, it described the experiences of Hanna and von Greim in the bunker and her observations on the other occupants, including the Goebbels family, Bormann, Eva Braun, and Hitler himself. Translations were included of the letters Hanna had carried out of Berlin from Goebbels and his wife to his stepson Harald Quandt, as well as a reconstruction of the letter from Eva Braun to her sister which Hanna and von Greim had destroyed.

'Her story does not pretend to add any sensational details to what is already known,' the report stated. 'If it is kept in mind that this material is a statement of her own opinions and observations, the information may be considered as completely reliable.'

Hanna's attitude to Hitler was reported in what were claimed to be her own words: 'Hitler ended his life as a criminal against the world, but he did not begin it that way. At first his thoughts were only of how to make Germany healthy again, how to give his people a life free from economic insufficiencies and social maladjustments. To do this he gambled much, with a stake that no man has the right to jeopardize—the lives of his people.'

Hitler the idealist had, in Hanna's opinion, died, the report continued, and his country with him, because of the incompetence of Hitler the soldier and Hitler the statesman: 'She frequently remarks that never again must such a person be allowed to gain control of Germany or of any country, but strangely enough she does not appear to hold him personally responsible for many of the wrongs and evils that she recognises completely and is quick to point out. She says rather, "A great part of the fault lies with those who led him, lured him, criminally misdirected him, and informed him falsely.

But that he himself selected the men who led him can never be forgiven.' '' Goering was the arch-villain.

The question to which everyone was still seeking a positive answer was whether Hitler might have escaped: 'The possibility that Hitler might have gotten out of the bunker alive, Reitsch dismisses as completely absurd. The Hitler she left behind in the shelter was physically unable to have gotten away.'

The press conference at which Hanna was expected to repeat at least some of her criticisms was, by her own account, a farce. A Captain Cohn had briefed her in advance, and had given her a choice: to denounce Hitler and his regime, and be rich and famous; or to stand up for him out of some misplaced and pointless sense of loyalty, and regret her folly and her obstinacy for the rest of her life. Hanna resented being bullied and bribed: she threw back the questions about Hitler defiantly, claiming that she had supported him willingly, would do so again, and denying that he was in any sense a criminal.

After a few questions, she was removed by Cohn, who she claimed was furious and told her she would be sorry for her stupidity. She was convinced that the Americans were deliberately choosing Jewish staff to make life more difficult for the Germans in their custody. Cohn in turn no doubt thought that she was making his life, and indeed her own, unnecessarily difficult through her stubborn and incomprehensible attitude. As the reporters who had been assembled to question her already had the interrogation summary, her gesture of defiance was a wasted effort. It was, however, an inevitable and logical reaction to the way she had been treated.

It was not long before newspaper articles based on Work's interrogation report started to appear. Work's original classification of his report had been 'confidential'. It was, he told me, declassified without his knowledge and to his intense annoyance at the request of a senior intelligence officer in Washington whose brother-in-law edited the *Princeton University Quarterly Review*. He was sent eleven copies of the issue in which the report was published. That, Work told me, was the only material gain he ever received from his association with Hanna Reitsch.

In Britain, a series of three articles at the end of December in the *News Chronicle* claimed to give Hanna Reitsch's 'eye-witness account' of the last days in the bunker. By then, the American forces paper *Stars and Stripes* had already carried a similar article on 6 December, and a copy of this eventually turned up in Haus Alaska.

Hanna was incensed. It was not that she minded talking about her experiences. But, she complained, much of what it was claimed she had said was pure invention. She had, for instance, never said that Eva Braun had spent most of the time polishing her nails, nor that Bormann was writing a diary; nor had she described Hitler as raving like a maniac, supervising suicide rehearsals, and 'running almost blindly from wall to wall'. She objected vehemently that the article was so cleverly written that anyone who read it must be angry with me, both those who were for, and those who were against Hitler'.

This was perhaps what really upset her: she felt that Hitler's critics would consider her more of a devotee than she was, and that his supporters would feel that she had been disloyal. Either way, her personal honour was threatened. Initially, she blamed Captain Cohn. Later, when she was told that Captain Work had been present at the press conference, she blamed him: he was, however, not there and knew nothing about it, although the articles were based almost entirely on his reports.

There seems no reason why Work would have put words into Hanna's mouth: her story was quite sensational enough without additions. It is possible that misunderstandings had crept in during his translation. He was convinced that he had given an accurate account of what she had said to him, and made it clear in his reports that he believed that she was making an attempt to be honest, and that honour was all important to her, although he did not think she always knew exactly what she meant by it: 'The use of the word amounts practically to a fetish complex . . . and is almost an incongruous embodiment of her entire philosophy. Her constant repetition of the word is in no manner as obvious to her as to the interrogator, nor is the meaning the same, nor does she recognise the incongruous use she makes of the word.'

It seems likely that with hindsight she remembered the events in the bunker or her conversation with Work differently, or wished she had said less and eventually persuaded herself that that had been the case: it all came down, as usual, to a question of 'honour'; and if in cold print what she had said did not seem honourable, she decided, quite unconsciously, that she had not said it, or had been misunderstood or misinterpreted.

She even persuaded herself that she had been neither interrogated nor told that anything she said was being taken down: she had, she protested, never seen or signed any interrogation report. Normal peace-time conventions, however, were not adopted by the Allies when in the years immediately after the war they questioned members of the nation they had defeated. Hanna had assumed that she would see and sign any report based on what she had said: it was a trusting and naïve assumption, as a result of which she felt betrayed when her conversations with Work were repeated and embellished without her permission.

When I told Robert Work about her reaction to the accounts based on his reports, he said that he could understand the change in her attitude: 'When we encountered each other I was probably, almost certainly, the first ray of hope that she had found in that bleak German desolation of the immediate after war. So she spoke freely and openly because she did so want a role in the rebuilding—and saw me as a bridge toward that end just as I had planned.' He was not surprised when he heard that she had been unco-operative towards her later captors and interrogators: the trust that he had been at such pains to build up had been wasted. At Oberursel, she was caught between two opposites: the antagonistic captors, who in her view attempted to destroy her self-respect, and the self-justifying captives, who reacted by glorifying the past in their efforts to come to terms with their country's downfall.

Hanna spent Christmas and New Year at Haus Alaska. At Christmas, a small tree was decorated with condoms, which had been blown up and rolled in flour and sugar. It was left to an embarrassed general to answer Hanna's question when she saw the tree and exclaimed in delight: 'How lovely! Where did you manage to get balloons?' It was, however, a cheerless festival; Hanna spent the evening alone in her room, overwhelmed by homesickness, sorrow over the lost war, the ravaged country, and the millions who, like her, were refugees from their homes in the east, and of course grief for her dead relatives. After her release it became her custom to spend Christmas alone, or rather, as she preferred to put it, with her loved ones in spirit. The New Year was celebrated a little more cheerfully, with poetry recitals and music: Hanna's contribution was to sing.

Six months later, Hanna was still smarting over the public slur to her honour. In her determination to put the record straight, during June 1946 she spent many hours composing a letter to her brother, giving him her own detailed account of the bunker episode: if her story was going to become part of history, she wanted it told her way.

Although the inmates of Haus Alaska were cut off from the outside world, Hanna, who was suffering from swollen legs and feet, possible symptoms of heart trouble, was occasionally allowed out, under escort, for medical treatment at a nearby sanitorium. It was there that Gretl Böss again tracked her down. It was only in the treatment room that Hanna was not under military guard, and on several occasions Gretl crawled in through the coal-hole so that she could talk to her there. In spite of her proud boast that nothing could touch her soul, and that she never allowed herself to become depressed, Hanna was according to Gretl Böss 'very up and down': 'During this time, Hanna often wondered why she was still alive—but she was filled with a sense of mission.'

# 11

# Suspicion and
# Persecution

Hanna was released, as the Americans put it, 'in her own custody' at the end of July 1946. She was offered accommodation in a luxurious guest-house for high-ranking American officers, but refused: it would have put her in an invidious position by making it seem as if she had sold herself to her country's enemies.

In theory, Hanna was 'free to dwell and travel as she pleased'. She was, however, in no fit state to do so: she was suffering from shock as the result of her long confinement; her legs and feet were badly swollen; and her lips had a bluish tinge suggesting heart trouble. An American colonel, William R. Philp, arranged for her to spend her first few weeks of freedom in hospital in Bad Nauheim, 'until such time as it may be convenient for her to reside elsewhere': friends who visited her there were shocked at her appearance.

For the next nine months, one American organisation, USFET (United States Forces, European Theater), was contemplating employing Hanna, while another, CIC, was convinced that she was involved in a Nazi plot. Philp at USFET believed that she had been badly treated: 'She had been arrested by CIC for some obscure reason, or for no reason at all, as she was not a member of the German Armed Forces, nor of the Nazi Party, nor a security threat, nor in an automatic arrest category.' He considered her 'a personality to be reckoned with in Germany, with the power to influence thousands', who would therefore be much better as a friend of America than as an enemy.

CIC, on the other hand, immediately put her under surveil-

lance. Less than a week after her release, a letter was inter-
cepted from an ex-Luftwaffe pilot, Rudi Storck, in which he
reported that he had just had a pleasant surprise: Hanna
Reitsch had turned up for treatment in his home town of Bad
Nauheim, and they had met. 'She has not changed, is filled
with idealism, and has the indomitable heart of a flyer!' he
wrote. Storck and Hanna had already arranged a meeting with
old flying comrades.

Hanna was not losing any time in picking up the threads of
her old life, and in the months which followed was soon
actively involved in further reunions with wartime colleagues.
CIC suspected her of being one of the chief organisers of a
Nazi plot to reform the Luftwaffe and kept a careful watch on
her activities in an operation they codenamed SKYLARK: Gretl
Böss, because of her connection with Hanna, was thought to
be a courier.

At the same time, Colonel Philp was, unknown to CIC,
encouraging Hanna to attend meetings of former Luftwaffe
pilots and other Germans. It was his contention that 'as she
knew a great many individuals high in Nazi circles, and was
known throughout Germany, especially by influential persons
. . . she would be able to spread democracy to the people that
counted and were in a position to help the Americans in their
occupation'. His approach was in fact similar to that adopted
by Robert Work, with whom he had a long discussion about
Hanna. Work told me that their conversation convinced him
that Philp would be able to inspire her renewed co-operation
and help her to play a role in the new Germany.

When she left the hospital, Hanna was unaware that she
was either suspected of being a subversive agent or was being
used by the one American whom she trusted as a friend. For a
few weeks, she lived in Kronberg/Taunus with two women,
whose husbands were prisoners, and their children. They
shared the work in the house and garden. With Marianne
Berg, who had no idea that her house was being watched,
Hanna had long earnest conversations about their religious
beliefs, about the world, and about life and death. Hanna was
much in demand by the children as a story-teller, sang to
them, and prayed with them for their fathers' safe return.

It was there that she was at last reunited with her brother

Kurt. It was an emotional occasion, on which both cried and laughed in equal measure. Kurt was in Lübeck, where he was employed in the minesweeping operation on which the British and German navies co-operated: at nine o'clock every morning, he had to report to a series of British intelligence officers. With one, called Arthur Pavey, he shared his Christmas cake, and later visited him in England.

From CIC reports on Operation SKYLARK it is clear that almost anyone Hanna contacted was suspected automatically of subversive activities. Any ex-pilots were added to the investigation list. CIC was, however, finding it difficult to plant an informant among Hanna's 'inner circle' because the 'personalities contacting [the] subject are highly nationalistic and idealistic', certainly a fitting description of Hanna herself.

There was a less flattering reference to her in an Intelligence Division Summary: 'Reitsch, Hanna, who flew von Greim out of the Berlin bunker in a Storch, has recently been turned loose by the Americans and is earning a number of free dinners and parties, if [the] report speaks true, on her story of "the last hours of the Third Reich". She is undoubtedly a very potent propaganda factor if nothing else, and is almost openly queuing up for der tag.'

When Colonel Philp decided that the time had come when it would be convenient for Hanna to reside elsewhere, he found her accommodation in Oberursel, conveniently near the headquarters of USFET. He was anticipating that sooner or later she would be engaged in some project for the Americans. Hanna moved in November 1946 into two rented ground-floor rooms. Gretl Böss, who went with her as her secretary, had a small attic room. One of Gretl's many duties was to push-start Hanna's car, a small Fiat provided by Philp; he also arranged a regular supply of fuel for a stove which was their only heating.

For a nominal salary of ten marks a month, Gretl Böss did the shopping, cooking, cleaning, washing, and ironing, as well as typing letters from dictation—Hanna was a copious letter-writer, but even her closest friends found her large dramatic scrawl almost impossible to decipher. She also listened whenever a sympathetic ear was needed: 'Thank God you're here and someone understands!' Hanna would say when she was, as often happened, tired, depressed, or frustrated. Although she knew that she could rely on Gretl to be discreet, she rarely told her the names of her many visitors, who would arrive at almost any time of day or night.

Philp was a frequent guest. Once Hanna had recovered her health, he decided both to boost her morale and test her reliability by arranging for her to go to Salzburg. She was anxious to collect her few remaining personal possessions from Schloss Leopoldskron, and to revisit the graves of her family and von Greim; he wanted to 'give her a chance to meet and mingle with all classes of Germans to learn what they thought and how they were reacting to the American occupation'. Hanna agreed to submit her contemplated itinerary with a complete list of the people she intended to visit: most were relatives or old friends like her music teacher Otto Johl, Landa Klaus, and the Heubergers, but it was always possible that she might provide a useful lead or contact.

Philp provided her with a letter stating that she was on an important United States government mission. When Hanna's car broke down, she used her official letter to obtain a replacement from CIC in Regensburg, where a German undercover man was assigned to accompany her as her driver. This was, however, so clumsily done that she was immediately aware of his role. This, as far as Philp was concerned, meant that the entire operation was wasted.

CIC thought differently. Their agent, Franz Bredl, provided a day-by-day account of the people Hanna visited, and of the conversations at which he was present. He was told by Kurt Schnitke, a former Luftwaffe pilot who Bredl claimed was 'definitely up to no good', that Hanna was trying to get in touch with German scientists and technicians working for other powers, so that when Germany was again able to build aircraft they would be able to keep up with technical developments elsewhere.

Further CIC suspicion was aroused when a former Luftwaffe officer employed by CIC and code-named 'Saturn' discovered that Hanna, Elly Beinhorn, and Rudel had visited Wolf Hirth: 'All three [Hanna, Elly and Rudel] were fanatical Nazis,' Saturn stated, 'or were regarded as such by other less indoctrinated Luftwaffe personnel.' He reported that, according to

Hirth, Hanna 'was of the opinion that something had to be done about German aviation and that she did not concur with many other former Luftwaffe personnel who had written off Germany completely and wanted to leave Germany for good'; she maintained 'that all prominent persons in German aviation were honour-bound to assist her in creating a secret organisation which for the time being would have to be completely undercover'.

The CIC conclusion was that Hanna was involved in what they called the Oberst Rudel Movement, thought to be a group of former German air force officers who were maintaining their own intelligence unit, although it was not considered to have any subversive intention: indeed, it was not even definitely known to exist at all.

There was some acrimonious correspondence between CIC officers in charge of Operation SKYLARK and Philp. The CIC men were annoyed that Philp had 'aided and abetted a German national, believed to be a fanatical Nazi', and claimed that Hanna had misrepresented herself by claiming to be on a confidential mission. It was suggested that Hanna had infiltrated Philp's organisation and was 'using personalities and facilities of that organisation to her own advantage'.

Philp retorted that Hanna's involvement with any undercover organisation was connected with her efforts towards better understanding between America and Germany, and that any such organisation had to remain undercover as otherwise its members 'would lose a great deal of their effectiveness with other Germans who would need to be converted from an anti-American position'. She had only infiltrated his outfit to the same extent as she had CIC, Philp insisted, 'just enough to permit this organisation to control her movements somewhat, learn of her activities, and obtain as much information of an intelligence nature as possible through her connections'.

It was impossible to reconcile the CIC conviction that Hanna was a dangerous and notorious Nazi with Philp's belief that she was not and could be useful to the Americans. In March 1947, it was agreed that both CIC and USFET would cancel their conflicting interests in her. It was officially recorded that she was 'found to have been unsuitable and relieved of any further responsibility'. Philp appears to have been reprimanded for his association with her. In one of two sets of surveillance reports I received from different American sources, every reference to him had been censored, as well as any mention of Fritz Bredl and 'Saturn'.

Hanna had made as much use of Philp as he of her: he had enabled her to travel round as she pleased, in a car provided by the Americans, and to meet old flying friends more openly than would otherwise have been possible. She was certainly thinking of the future, and preparing for the day when Germans would be allowed to fly again; like Philp and Work, she believed that co-operation between Americans and Germans was essential. It was hardly surprising that she saw the American occupation as a protection against the Soviet Union, given the attitude of her own family and many other Germans towards Communism.

In April 1947, Hanna applied for a permit to cross the Austrian border so that she could visit her family's grave on the anniversary of their death. She had not been informed that her mutually agreeable association with Philp had been terminated, but it became apparent that she was no longer under American protection when her request was refused. The refusal struck her as callous and unnecessary, and she crossed the border with a false passport. She was promptly arrested. When her identity was revealed, she was after all allowed to visit the graves, but her arrest for crossing the border illegally was reported in the press. This gave rise to renewed suspicions that she must be involved in some undercover operation.

The CIC order that all interest in Hanna should be dropped was reversed, but it was only occasionally, during surveillance on other people, that her name appeared subsequently in intelligence reports. In 1948, she was suspected of involvement with an organisation furnishing false discharge papers and assisting people to escape from Germany. A young man chosen because he was cool-headed, intelligent, trustworthy, and 'a large and Nordic type' was sent to test her.

Hanna was immediately suspicious of the false Mr Winter, supposedly an SS officer who had just escaped from an internment camp at Moosburg. Although her sympathy was aroused by his story, she noticed that his hands were surprisingly well-manicured, and wondered how he came to have an expensive fountain pen. 'Winter' believed that Hanna was sincere when she told him that she would have helped him if she could, but that she had no way of doing so.

Hanna saw the episode as part of a deliberate campaign against her, which she blamed chiefly on Hugh Trevor-Roper. His book *The Last Days of Hitler* had been published in Britain in March 1947, and was immediately accepted as the authoritative account of the circumstances surrounding Hitler's death. Once again, Hanna found that her so-called eye-witness account had been quoted without her knowledge.

She wrote to Trevor-Roper, offering to tell him her own story. He declined to meet her, although he contacted the Americans from whom he had received Work's interrogation summary. As Hanna Reitsch was denying the report, he explained, he was in a quandary, and wanted to know whether it could be considered reliable. The reply was in the affirmative, with the proviso that 'Hanna Reitsch could have lied to the interrogators'.

As far as Trevor-Roper was concerned, this should have been the end of the affair. But Hanna refused to let it drop. A lengthy and acrimonious correspondence followed, during which Hanna threatened legal action and a number of her friends wrote to Trevor-Roper on her behalf. There were 104 points in his book to which she objected: to anyone who examines her version alongside Trevor-Roper's text, it is often difficult to understand why. Nevertheless, Trevor-Roper made a few minor alterations in the second edition, which was published in 1950: Hanna became, for instance, 'tenacious and tearful', rather than 'weeping and posturing', 'terrible' was changed to 'dramatic', and Hitler no longer 'stormed with indignation'—he was 'white with indignation'. Hanna was not mollified.

Trevor-Roper's version of Hanna's story was subsequently regurgitated in newspaper articles, books, and even films. Only one writer, an American called Michael Angelo Musmanno who published his own book about Hitler's last days, *Ten Days to Die*, bothered to interview Hanna rather than relying on Trevor-Roper's book. It is not an exaggeration to say that, however trivial the affair may have seemed to Trevor-Roper, Hanna felt that he, along with Cohn, had ruined her reputation, and all but ruined her life.

Her name was continually linked with that of Hitler. The fact that she had never joined the Nazi party, and that no reason was found to prosecute her (she received her de-Nazification certificate in December 1947) was of less general interest than that she had spent part of the last week of Hitler's life in the bunker in Berlin.

The feeling that she had been unfairly branded as a Nazi did not deter her from her mission, which involved her in speaking about flying at camps: she hoped by her example to inspire goodwill and faith in the future of Germany. This she felt was undermined by the unfairness of the Nuremberg trials, particularly that of Field Marshal Kesselring, whom she described as 'well known and loved by the German people for his chivalry, humanitarianism, and fairness'.

To von Krosigk, who was still in prison, she wrote: 'All those who "hope" should not be deceived and disappointed again, by mistaking might for right as was done during Hitler's regime.' It seemed to her unjust that only the leaders of the defeated nation should be called to account, and not those of all nations which waged war. 'As long as different laws exist for the victors and vanquished, a nation cannot be re-educated,' she wrote: her intentions were, she claimed, the same as always—to build up understanding and fight against hatred.

Hanna was increasingly convinced that she was a victim of a deliberate policy to destroy the reputation of all German heroes. 'It was not sufficient for the victors that Germany was conquered,' she wrote thirty years later. 'Her backbone must also be broken. They knew that there were some backs which would refuse to be broken, those that belonged to people who had been idols during the Third Reich and who would be prepared to be cut to pieces rather than to surrender their souls. Such people they could murder, but murder would only make of them martyrs. The remaining course open to them was character assassination. They did everything possible to wipe out their names to besmirch them with such shameful deeds that the people would no longer accept them.'

She was in no doubt that she was one of the idols who were to be besmirched. That she had been elevated during the war to the status of a national heroine had not been through her own choice, although she had accepted it willingly enough at the time. But that she should now be made to suffer because she had done her duty rather more in the public eye than most seemed to her unfair, particularly when she suspected that her own countrymen were being used to assassinate her character. Even one of her V1 suicide volunteers was, she was informed, in the pay of the Americans; another ex-pilot claimed that an article he had worked on had been rewritten to show her in an unfavourable light before being published in France.

There were rumours that she was living a life of luxury, driving a large American car, and earning favours by sleeping with Americans; it was even claimed that she had been the mistress of more than one of the Nazi leaders, including Hitler himself. To anyone who knew her well, such gossip was clearly ridiculous, but it was widely believed by those who did not. The thought that she had broken her word to von Greim by staying alive, only to be constantly slandered, added a burden of guilt to her despair.

She had many acquaintances, but few close friends, and her trust had proved so often ill-founded that she began to wonder if there was anyone who was as open and honest as she considered herself. At night, she lay awake, tormented by self-pity, or cried herself to sleep. During the day she was able to exercise enough self-control to seem as calm as anyone so naturally effusive and emotional could ever be. Her misery affected her health, and for several years she had recurring liver and circulation problems which she attempted to cure through diet: but a well-balanced diet of fresh food was almost impossible in the years of privation which followed the war.

She had retrieved her poison capsule from Gretl Böss and was often tempted to use it. Had it not been for the friendship of a Catholic priest, Father Friedel Volkmar, she was later convinced that she would indeed have committed suicide. Volkmar, an old friend of the Heuberger family, discovered her one day in tears. She poured out a muddled confession of hurt pride, guilt, despair, loneliness, and hopelessness. He encouraged her by pointing out that if she allowed herself to be destroyed by rumours and slurs on her honour, she would merely be playing into the hands of her enemies.

'You must stick it out,' he told her. 'Walk through the streets with your head high, even when other people are pointing their finger at you. With God you are stronger than all of them together!'

His belief in her gave her strength. She had found someone whom she could admire and respect, and with whom she felt able to talk about her deepest feelings. As far as anyone could ever do, Volkmar replaced her mother, her father, and von Greim. At the same time, he reinforced her faith both in herself and in God. He became her closest friend, her confidant and adviser, and her most ardent supporter.

When a notice was pinned up at the Oberursel town hall announcing that the de-Nazification hearing on Hanna Reitsch was to be held in the middle of December 1947, it was Volkmar who contacted her friends and relations and spurred them on to write letters in her favour. One of the first people he contacted was Joachim Küttner: a testimony from someone known to be half-Jewish would be a point in Hanna's favour. Küttner responded with a glowing affidavit.

Volkmar even attempted to defend Hanna in the press. In the spring of 1948, he composed a lengthy appeal on her behalf, which he persuaded seventeen other friends to sign, But although it was sent to numerous newspapers and magazines it was never published. Hanna considered this part of the plot against her. It is, however, equally likely that it was considered too long—indeed one of her supporters had refused to sign it for that reason—or that it was not at the time thought to be of any general interest.

Among those who signed it was Lotte Schiffler, a Catholic who was involved with the rehabilitation of refugees. Volkmar, who had introduced the two women, thought that Lotte would be able to help Hanna, and that Hanna might forget her own problems by helping with Lotte's voluntary work. Lotte, who had been active in the resistance during the war, was dubious: politically they were clearly poles apart. As soon as she saw Hanna, and heard how her parents had died, all her doubts vanished: 'There was a tiny girl, small, dainty, with clear searching eyes,' she told me. 'I felt immediately protective. She had suffered so much. I was determined that nothing more must be allowed to happen to that child!' She felt that

Hanna was destined to suffer, and considered her stoic acceptance of her fate heroic: 'It was her cross that God's hand was on her.'

It was through Lotte that Hanna formed another unlikely but long-lasting friendship, with a French woman called Yvonne Pagniez, who had been awarded the Légion d'honneur for her work in the Résistance and later won several major literary awards in France. They met in Wiesbaden, where Yvonne was giving a talk aimed at establishing cordial Franco-German relations: it was based on her own time as a prisoner-of-war of the Germans and her escape from Ravensbrück concentration camp, about which she was writing a book. Throughout her lecture, she was aware of a young woman leaning against the door at the back of the hall and listening with intense concentration: she was so small that her head scarcely came above the rows of those who were seated. When the room was nearly empty, the unknown woman approached silently and took Yvonne's hands in hers; her eyes were filled with tears. 'Who are you?' Yvonne asked. 'Hanna Reitsch.'

Yvonne had heard that Hanna Reitsch was a 'war heroine' and a woman of 'indomitable courage', but also that she was a 'confirmed Nazi', the 'intimate friend of Hitler'. 'My astonishment was boundless,' she wrote later, 'when I saw before me not the Valkyrie I had imagined, but a tiny person who looked so modest, whose body seemed so frail, and who smiled hesitantly at me as she wiped away her tears.' Their prison experiences, their fervent patriotism, and their conviction that good relationships between nations were essential for the future, formed a bond which was reinforced by Yvonne's resemblance to Hanna's mother: she had the same small, neat figure, the same way of talking and moving, the same expression in her eyes, and was almost the age Emy Reitsch would have been.

Lotte Schiffler and her husband translated Yvonne Pagniez's book about her escape from Ravensbrück into German, and encouraged Hanna to write her own autobiography. Hanna decided that this was indeed the only answer to the lies which she felt were destroying her, and went into retreat to work on her life story. With the help of the abbot of Maria Lach, a Benedictine monastery in the French zone, she spent several weeks in the secluded house of an elderly widow. The monks brought her fresh fruit and vegetables, new-laid eggs, home-cured ham, milk, cheese, and sausage—food such as she had not had for years. She was happier and healthier than she had ever felt in Oberursel. Her pride in the finished manuscript was, however, dashed when she showed it to her old flying friend, the actor Matthias Wiemann: it was, he said, far too personal, and only someone who knew her would find the idealism it expressed convincing. She must rewrite it.

Writing came less easily to Hanna than talking, and her second draft was dictated into a microphone hidden in a vase of flowers. She worked with intense concentration, talking for hours at a time, and gave the tapes to Lotte Schiffler to type. The entire book was completed in a fortnight, and was accepted by a publisher in Stuttgart. There were a few disagreements during the editing: a number of alterations were suggested, each of which Hanna rejected—it was her life.

While she was waiting for her book to be published, Hanna approached a new newspaper, the *Frankfurter Allgemeine Zeitung,* with her usual complaint that she had been misrepresented by Trevor-Roper. The editor sent a reporter called Thilo Bode to investigate. Bode, a wartime submarine commander who had himself been interrogated after the war in Washington, was convinced after several interviews with her that Hanna had indeed been badly treated. He suggested that Robert Work was as much to blame as Trevor-Roper, and Hanna became convinced that the interrogator had made money by writing about her.

Bode sent the first draft of a long article based on her account to a German historian, Professor Rheindorf. Rheindorf, who knew Hanna well, made a number of suggestions and cast doubts on Trevor-Roper's professionalism. The final version was submitted a month after Hanna's initial approach to the newspaper, and was to have been run as a series of five articles. To Hanna's fury, it was not published. Bode was philosophical: 'The political climate then was such that a German newspaper could not start an acrimonious controversy with a man like Trevor-Roper, who made it quite clear in his arguments with Hanna Reitsch that the word of any occupation authority was not to be doubted.'

Hanna's version was more dramatic: according to her, the editor had refused to publish an account which was favourable to her because it would appear to be 'a glorification of the Third Reich', and Bode refused to stay in a country where democracy and freedom of the press were a farce. He did indeed subsequently leave Germany, but two years later and as press attaché to the German Embassy in New Delhi.

Thilo Bode remembered Hanna as 'a very impressive lady, full of energy, full of laughter, single-minded, a daredevil, always slightly in the clouds, always very enthusiastic, brave as many soldiers would have liked to have been, fiercely devoted to everything she did, a "reiner Tor", as they say in German—that is: the kindest form of a fool, never suspecting anything devious. She was a "Schwärmer", easily in raptures: she enthused about nature, about children, flying, mankind . . . but also about Hitler, about [von] Greim . . . Her large blue eyes and her niceness were certainly attractive, but there was also an element of "don't touch me" about her . . . She was very close to her family, I believe that all the love she had in her (and there was a lot of it) went to her family . . . She was very slightly hysterical, one might say. In a not unkindly sense, one could regard her as highly strung; she was deeply religious, easily moved to tears.'

On one of their meetings, Hanna drove him from Frankfurt to Oberursel in an old Volkswagen which had been given to her by the VW firm. The Fiat which Gretl Böss had so often had to push had long since been returned to the Americans, but the Volkswagen was equally temperamental, and the engine caught fire. Hanna braked immediately, and used Thilo Bode's mackintosh to beat out the flames: her reactions to a practical emergency were those of a pilot, rather than of a highly strung or hysterical woman.

Hanna's book, *Fliegen mein Leben* (literally 'Flying My Life'), was published in 1951. With the natural pride of a new author, she was delighted to see it displayed in the window of a bookshop in Frankfurt, and assumed excitedly when the display was no longer there a few days later that it must have sold out. To her dismay, she was told instead that it had been removed in response to an anonymous threatening letter. The same thing had apparently happened in four other bookshops. Hanna blamed Captain Cohn.

In her introduction, she stated that in spite of the so-called eyewitness accounts which had appeared over the years, the truth was that she was herself speaking for the first time in her book. 'Anyone who follows my development from my youth and can read between the lines . . . will understand that there could be no other path for me in the war than the one of which I tell,' she wrote. 'My meetings with leading personalities arose from my professional activities. I report about them as truthfully as about the rest of my life: what I am like, how I came to my profession, and what it has been given me to experience since as a pilot.' Her aim was, she explained, to help 'young people, flyers, those who seek and struggle'.

She hoped that the book would vindicate her and that its honesty would put paid to the belief that she had ever been politically motivated. Instead, it seemed to many to reinforce the view that she had been, and probably still was, a supporter of Hitler: she had refused to take the stand of those who were wise after the event.

Nevertheless, the book sold well enough to bring her a small income, the first money she had been able to earn since the war. Her meagre wartime savings had been decimated by the devaluation of the mark, and she had been living virtually on charity. As she had never been a member of the armed forces, she was not eligible for a military pension, and it took her some years to fight for her right to a small injury pension after her accident with the Me 163.

In spite of her conviction that she was reviled because of the association of her name with that of Hitler, Hanna still commanded considerable favourable attention, even adulation. From time to time, gifts of money were sent through the post or pushed by the donor through her letterbox. From an elderly American of German origin, Edwin Flaig, she received regular parcels of food and clothing for two years, and occasional cheques for some time afterwards.

Gretl Böss and Hanna parted company in November 1951, by mutual agreement. Living with Hanna was a full-time occupation, and Gretl wanted to lead her own life. She worked for a while for a distant relative, and then ran the insurance department of a large food wholesaler: she rarely saw or heard from Hanna.

Fräulein Anna Walter took over Gretl's role with self-effacing adoration and efficiency. She dedicated the rest of her life to Hanna, living entirely for and through her employer. Their relationship was clearly defined, with a strict old-fashioned formality: they never used Christian names or the familiar *du*, and although when no one else was present they ate together, Fräulein Walter never presumed to join Hanna when she had visitors. Their duties too were defined: Hanna left all domestic details to her secretary, who shopped, cooked, cleaned, washed, ironed, and typed. Hanna was fully occupied with the various demands of her mission.

Not long after the publication of her book, Hanna moved to Frankfurt, where she hoped to be able to evade publicity and where she had found a philanthropic outlet for her energy. Through Father Volkmar, she had met another, younger, Catholic priest, Karl Pehl, who had initiated a scheme similar to the later Samaritans. Frankfurt was a depressing place after the war, with a high suicide rate, particularly among the many refugees from the Russian zone.

Hanna, who knew all too well what it meant to be homeless and in despair, worked with Pehl's team of assorted Christians for eighteen months. She felt that by telling people, who felt that life was no longer worth living, her own experiences, she could give them new hope: although she was a good listener, she was an even better talker.

Much of Hanna's free time from the emotionally exhausting demands of voluntary social work was spent with Fathers Volkmar and Pehl. They became a closely knit threesome, spending at least one evening a week together. When the Opel family allowed Hanna to erect a small wooden chalet on land they owned high on a hillside in the Taunus, she and the priests often drove together from Frankfurt to spend some time in the clear country air.

Through her close association with them, Hanna gradually felt herself drawn towards the Catholic faith of her mother. Eventually, in 1954, she was received into the Catholic Church. She could never bring herself to accept that the Pope was infallible, but by joining their church she felt nearer to Volkmar, Pehl, and her mother.

# 12

# At Home
# and Abroad

In August 1949, an American intelligence report noted that 'Reitsch, Hanna, much publicised woman pilot . . . supposedly attended a meeting of gliding enthusiasts held at the Wasserkuppe . . . although a Military Government ban on such meetings, and the formation of para-military sport organisations, specifically forbids glider clubs and glider flying'. The Allies had learnt after the First world War that if German flying enthusiasts could find any loophole in a post-war ban on flying they would: that was after all how gliding had developed. After 1945, even the making of model aircraft was forbidden.

So, in theory, was talking about flying. When Hanna and a number of others were allowed to do so in public early in 1951, it was a sign that the Allies were relaxing restrictions. In February Hanna gave a lecture about gliding at the town hall in Frankfurt. It was her first public appearance since the war, and had been widely advertised. In spite of a number of anti-Nazi posters and slogans outside, the hall was filled; the audience gave her a rapturous reception and the *Frankfurter Allgemeine Zeitung* printed a brief but enthusiastic report.

For Hanna, it was the first of many similarly heartening occasions. When she took her place in front of a hall full of people, she looked small and fragile, until she started to speak. She was an extraordinary public speaker, and no one who heard her once ever forgot the experience. Although some who heard her several times commented unkindly that anyone who had been present at one of her lectures had heard them all, each was carefully and individually prepared.

Every pause, every gesture, every inflection arose naturally from her familiarity with her subject matter as if it had been rehearsed for maximum effect: her spontaneity was always genuine. To say that she lectured is misleading: each speech was a performance, during which her voice sank to a whisper, rose to a crescendo, and died into anticipatory silence without losing the attention of her listeners. Her strong, slim hands were as active as her vocal chords.

In Frankfurt, she talked about her gliding experiences, about gliding's mystical power for good, and about her conviction that it was the best possible spiritual training for the young, in whom it could inspire qualities such as self-discipline and team spirit. She longed for the day when the ban on flying would be lifted, and cherished an idealistic vision of the youth of Germany working towards world peace through the international family of gliding.

A few months after Hanna's lecture in Frankfurt, glider pilots from all over Germany gathered for the annual celebration of Lilienthal's birthday at the Wasserkuppe: Lilienthal was considered the father of gliding. For the first time since the war, their meeting was allowed to take place uninterrupted. They arrived on foot, by bicycle or motor cycle, and by car, with sleeping bags and tents but, of course, no aircraft. Hanna drove to the gathering in her old Volkswagen and shared a caravan with Wolf and Lala Hirth. It was an emotional reunion for many who had not met for years and were relieved to find each other still alive.

The way for a resumption of flying was prepared when the German Aero Club was reinstated. Wolf Hirth was unanimously elected president. Although Wolfgang Späte was convinced that Hanna deliberately ignored him when they passed in a crowd, they spoke later and agreed that nothing should spoil the atmosphere of camaraderie.

By the end of the year, the Germans were at last given permission to start gliding again. Four firms, one Wolf Hirth's, immediately started to fill the demand for training gliders. Within a few months there were, according to an article in *Stars and Stripes,* 750 gliding clubs in West Germany with a total membership of 35,000: gliding had regained its preeminent position as the national sport, with the assurance that never again would it be perverted to military ends. In March, Hanna was towed into the air by a Pan American aircraft in the first post-war Focke-Wulf glider.

A West German team competed against eighteen other countries in an international gliding championship in Spain in July 1952. As the only woman, Hanna was singled out by name in the opening speech. She was gratified to find that thirty-two of the fifty-nine aircraft entered were pre-war German models, and that the war had not destroyed the spirit of international goodwill among gliding enthusiasts. But instead of a favourable mention in the press at home for her bronze medal, Hanna's photo was published: she was shown with Otto Skorzeny, who was living in Madrid, and it was suggested that her object in going to Spain had been to meet a fellow Nazi.

During the next six years, Hanna threw herself wholeheartedly into rebuilding the gliding movement in Germany. Her efforts were rewarded in June 1953 by an official announcement of appreciation from Wolf Hirth on behalf of the Aero Club: 'Frau Reitsch devotes herself to this work with her well-known thoroughness,' Hirth wrote. Her services to gliding included test flights, lectures and visits to clubs and schools, assistance with competitions, and sitting on commissions. They were all undertaken in a voluntary capacity, although she received a small fee as an aviation consultant in Westphalia. At last it seemed as if she could forget her association with Hitler.

Reluctantly, she turned down a request for her services as a helicopter pilot in Pakistan: she had been asked to fly stores for a Baltoro expedition (Karakoram) into the base camp, but considered that the sudden changes in altitude and the rarefied atmosphere were more than any helicopter of the time could cope with. The expedition leader, Dr Karl Herrligkoffer, was looking for a scientist, and she put him in touch with her cousin Helmut Heuberger: in 1954, Helmut went on the best-known Himalayan expedition led by Herbert Tichy, a fellow Austrian.

Hanna was to make her first post-war visit to England that year, as a member of the West German team at the international gliding championship at Camphill. She had already been granted a visa when, on the Saturday before the competition, she was informed that the government in Bonn had instructed the Aero Club to withdraw her. Several British newspapers had linked her name yet again with Hitler, to the alarm of the West German Embassy in London.

Hanna had no choice but to accept her last-minute disappointment. The other members of the team wanted to stand down in support, but were told that it was important for international relations that Germany should be represented, provided it was not by Hanna Reitsch.

An official announcement was made that Hanna had 'suddenly withdrawn from the competition for personal reasons'. She was incensed. 'The Bonn authorities have forced me to stay behind, but they can't force me to keep quiet,' she told a *Daily Mail* Berlin reporter, to whom she complained of 'disgraceful and unjustified attacks' on her in the past: for nine years, she told him, 'certain circles in Germany' had been trying to make her a political figure.

Her outspokenness attracted support from the German press, but was considered by some of the gliding fraternity to be disloyal. Heinz Kensche wrote an open letter accusing her of having put her own interests before those of the rest of the team: 'Could you not for once have put yourself in the background and have kept quiet for the sake of gliding and of your colleagues?' he asked.

The publicity forced the Aero Club to issue a belated statement explaining that it had 'decided upon recommendations of competent German institutions to withdraw the entry of Mrs Hanna Reitsch in order to avoid any personal false statements in the press, which might eventually result in unpleasant political consequences'. Although this made it clear that the Aero Club believed political accusations against her to be unfounded, it seemed that elsewhere in Germany she was still considered guilty although proved innocent.

Hanna was generally felt to have been badly treated, and withdrew to the Taunus. She was upset by the intrusion of politics into a sport which she felt should transcend all differences between nations. At the next international contest, in France in 1956, she competed without political repercussions, although members of the British team felt that she was on the defensive when they met her.

The venue in 1958 was to be Poland, the first time an international gliding contest had been held behind the Iron Curtain. It was the convention that any host country would grant visas to the teams of all competing countries. Although Hanna was selected, she did not intend to compete, but was determined to go to Poland as a supporter: as her homeland of Silesia had become part of Poland at the end of the war, she felt that her visit would be a significant gesture of international friendship.

She had decided to make a grand and generous gesture by relinquishing her place to Dr Ernst Frowein, a pilot who had often just failed to make the team. Before she consulted him, she started a campaign on his behalf which split the Aero Club into pro- and anti-Frowein factions; or rather, one group which wanted to make Hanna's generosity known as an example to German youth of public-spirited unselfishness and another which felt that Frowein's performance was erratic and his personality abrasive.

There was also a technical problem: according to the selection procedure, Hanna could only stand down in favour of the next pilot on the list. This was not Frowein, but a younger and less experienced pilot called Rolf Kuntz. She felt that this would have been taking her unselfishness too far: Kuntz would have his chance sooner or later. The situation was further complicated when Frowein said that he would not in any case accept, although at some point his name had been published as a team member instead of that of Hanna.

After numerous letters, meetings, and telephone calls, and a certain amount of dissension, Hanna was officially reinstated. On the afternoon of Friday, 6 June, two days before the team was to leave for Poland, she was refused a visa, although visas had been granted to the rest of the West German contingent. No reason was given. She attempted unsuccessfully to contact the current president of the Aero Club, Harald Quandt, to ask what she should do.

It was Saturday evening before the West German team was together in Braunschweig and could discuss the problem, still without any guidance from Quandt; their departure was scheduled for early the following morning. At first, two of the other team members were in favour of making a stand; the one who argued that they should go anyway was Haase, who had been one of the team in England and whom Hanna had always considered a friend.

Eventually it was agreed that everyone except Hanna should proceed as planned to Leszno, and that a protest would be made there both to the Polish Aero Club and to the FAI. Hanna did not voice her own opinion, as she was the interested party. But she did not doubt that if her visa was still not granted, the rest of the team would withdraw in support.

She went forlornly back to Berlin. Four days later, she heard that although the Poles were still refusing either to grant her a visa or to state their reasons, they had promised to issue one immediately for a replacement. Quandt announced that the West Germans would compete and that Rolf Kuntz was to take Hanna's place. Hanna felt betrayed. Although Haase became the world champion, she could see no honour in a victory gained at the expense of team spirit.

The Poles never gave any explanation for refusing Hanna a visa. A few people suggested that she should have realised that she would not be welcome in Poland, and should therefore have saved everyone embarrassment by declining her place in the team. This was not a view which Hanna could accept. Nor could she understand Harald Quandt's contention that, as the refusal to grant her a visa was a political matter, he would have been confusing sport and politics if he had withdrawn the West German team, and might have jeopardised East–West relations. She felt rather, that by not withdrawing the German team, he appeared both to be making a political statement about her and to be putting political expedience before team loyalties. A number of Hanna's supporters, including the ever-loyal Volkmar, wrote letters on her behalf.

Hanna was quite prepared to forgive and forget, provided the Aero Club made a public apology. The Aero Club was equally prepared to resume an amicable relationship, provided she dropped her demand for an apology. Both were equally intransigent. The Alte Adler, an association of veteran pilots of which Hanna was an honorary member, entered the fray on her behalf and set up a commission to consider the evidence. It found Hanna innocent and the Aero Club guilty, and demanded a public reinstatement of her reputation. Louis de Lange, a Dutch pilot who was then at the head of the international gliding commission, OSTIV, investigated the affair and also came down on Hanna's side. Matters were not helped by a newspaper article accusing Quandt of gross ingratitude to Hanna, who had brought him his mother's and his stepfather's last letters from the bunker.

Gradually even Hanna's most devoted supporters advised her to let the matter drop: but it had become a question of honour not to give in. She announced that until an apology was forthcoming, she would sever connections with the Aero Club, which meant withdrawing from all flying activities in West Germany. Whereas she had once proudly said to the Americans that she would rather stay on the ground in Germany than fly anywhere else without honour, she now felt that her own country was the only one in which she could not fly with honour.

Hanna's rift with the Aero Club was followed by an unexpected ambassadorial project to India. It was ironic that she should be asked to be a representative of the West German government which, only four years previously, had refused to allow her to represent her country in England, and that she should be a missionary for gliding when she was on neither speaking nor flying terms with her sport's national umbrella organisation.

The Indians had a number of gliding clubs, including one in Delhi. However, a jet fighter had crashed into a hangar at the Delhi club, destroying its gliders. At the suggestion of a West German diplomat in Delhi, Georg Steltzer, the West German government decided in 1958 to create goodwill by presenting a replacement glider to the Delhi gliding club. Hanna had been an excellent aerial ambassadress before the war: her fame as a glider pilot, her effervescent personality, and her ability to charm and instruct simultaneously were undiminished, in spite of her tendency to fall out with anyone who offended her sense of honour. The Indians professed themselves flattered and delighted that such a distinguished pilot should agree to visit their country.

Instead of the two weeks originally envisaged, Hanna stayed

for two months. On her arrival, in April 1959, she was overwhelmed by the heat but enthralled by a kaleidoscope of impressions. During her first week she endured a constant round of receptions and cocktail parties—she had always hated large gatherings. The people she most wanted to meet were Nehru and his daughter Indira Gandhi: the West German Embassy said that this was impossible.

Eight hundred prominent Indians watched the impressive and comprehensive aerobatic display in which she demonstrated the Ka-7 glider's capabilities during the official handing-over ceremony. She was far more nervous about her first public speech the same evening, but proved as energetic a public speaker in English as in German, and was invited to speak to the assembled Indian parliament the next day. Her performances in the air and on the ground were repeated in Bombay, Poona, Bangalore, Madras, Pondicherry, Calcutta, Patna, Benares, and Allahabad, and she spent a week free of duties in Kathmandu. She gave seventeen speeches, all in English, some to experienced pilots, some to total novices, often to several groups in one day, and flew with student pilots and their instructors.

Hanna was fascinated by the serenity of the Indians. She had had no previous contact with Eastern religions, and felt that meditation could answer her own spiritual needs. With an Indian air force captain, Pauli Soni, she made a pilgrimage to an ashram at Pondicherry where an elderly Frenchwoman was revered as 'Mother' by a vast multinational family of religious enthusiasts. They were devout meditators who had abjured all worldly wealth, although the ashram had its own schools, university, and laboratory, as well as a sports field, a swimming-pool, and tennis courts.

The eighty-year-old Mother of Pondicherry granted her an audience. She had seen Hanna's photo and was convinced that they had met in some previous incarnation: 'I recognise you,' she told her. 'You don't only fly aeroplanes, your soul flies higher than any aeroplane. We shall see each other again and shall meet in another world.'

The day after her return to Delhi, Hanna was summoned to meet Nehru: he wanted her to take him gliding. A twenty-four-hour guard was put on the new glider until the appointed time. To prove that it was safe, Hanna first took Georg Steltzer for a flight: the project had after all been his idea. Then it was Nehru's turn: he enjoyed himself so much that he did not want to come down. For two hours they soared above an assembly of ministers and diplomats, who had no choice but to wait beneath them in the broiling midday heat. When they eventually landed, Hanna went up again, this time with one of Nehru's friends, Swami Ranganathananda: it was the first time an Indian yogi had flown in a glider. He later visited her in Frankfurt and taught her yoga. Her final passenger for the day was Air Marshal Mukerjee.

The following day, Hanna was invited to lunch with Nehru and Indira Gandhi. She had considerable difficulty in eating with her fingers, as they did, but none in talking. Nehru had heard the imaginative rumour that Hanna had been Hitler's mistress, and for several hours listened to her account of her dramatic flight into Berlin and her time in the bunker.

One invitation was followed by another: when Hanna returned from a moonlit excursion to the Taj Mahal, she was told that she was to move into the Prime Minister's house for her last few days in India. She was the first German to be his personal guest since the war, and considered it a great honour, especially as the German Embassy had said that she would not even be able to meet him.

Her guides round Delhi were Nehru's grandsons: Rajiv was fifteen and Sanjay thirteen. She took them gliding and admired their model aeroplanes. They and their mother accompanied her to her final public appearance in India, a lecture in Delhi's largest hall which was attended by everyone of any importance in the city, including Nehru. It was another triumph.

Bonn was delighted that Hanna's visit had received wide and favourable publicity. Georg Steltzer considered her mission to India 'most successful', although he found her intensity and idealism exhausting, and her inability to stop talking 'a pain in the neck'. At one official function, he and his wife had watched in fascination as she raised a forkful of noodles to her mouth and then embarked on a lengthy story: the fork and noodles remained poised for twenty minutes.

'We all enjoyed having you at the house, and I think you did a lot of good to Sanjay,' Mrs Gandhi wrote in July 1959.

Hanna sent Rajiv and Sanjay model gliders from Germany and the following year gave Sanjay a movie-camera and Rajiv a stopwatch and penknife: she received handwritten thank-you letters addressed to 'My dear Hanna'. Mrs Gandhi's letters were longer and chattier; for several years she and Hanna corresponded on first-name terms.

Nehru wrote to her more formally and less frequently. Hanna's admiration for him was unbounded, although she found it necessary to point out to him his international duty and lectured him in writing on the plight of the unwilling inhabitants of East Germany. She thought it so important that he should understand the evils of Communism and of the division of Germany that on one occasion she even arranged to fly to London to talk to him for a few minutes between his official engagements.

Hanna assisted the progress of gliding in India by arranging for a team of Indian pilots to visit West Germany in the summer of 1960. Her visit to India had a deep and lasting effect on her own spiritual life: she added the self-discipline of daily yoga and meditation to the physical exercises she had always done early in the morning, long before most people were awake. The enthusiasm with which the Indians had responded to her belief in the moral value of gliding as character training for the young restored her own faith in her mission. She now saw this more in terms of using flying to train a future generation than of vindicating the past.

Her absence in India gave rise to a rumour among flying acquaintances that she was suffering from religious mania and had even had a mental breakdown: when Hanna became aware of this, she saw it as yet another instance of victimisation by the Aero Club.

Until her feud with the West German gliding community, Hanna had had little time to spare for old friends. In 1959, there was for the first time a reunion of schoolfriends, both staff and pupils, from Hirschberg. They were scattered around West Germany and still felt that they were refugees. Hanna was inevitably the centre of attention at the annual reunions which followed: she had the most exciting adventures to relate and told them in the most stimulating way. They sang together as they had done in Otto Johl's choir, and hers was still the most enthusiastic voice.

An old school reunion without Hanna was, the others felt, unthinkable. When one year she said she could not go, one of the others fetched her by car. On the return journey, Hanna suddenly leant forward from the back seat and flung her arms round the startled driver: 'I'm *so* glad you all persuaded me to come,' she said. Her own driving was alarming: she drove fast, talking all the time, and was frequently stopped, although she was usually let off with a caution as soon as her identity became known.

There were Koloschule reunions too. Although Hanna attended these less regularly, She often saw Gisela Holzrichter and her husband Armin: they lived not far from Frankfurt. Gisela sometimes accompanied Hanna to the dressmaker who made most of her clothes to her own design at a reduced charge. She liked good-quality material and had adopted a distinctive semi-military, semi-folk style. Her hairdresser too gave her a special rate; she had given up her earlier tightly permed bangs for a softer, more becoming, look. Although she never used make-up, she always looked both smart and feminine, and wore a heady perfume and small pearl earrings.

Gisela and Armin were among the few of her friends that Hanna introduced to her brother Kurt. It was rare that people from different parts of her life met each other: she was inclined to be possessive, particularly about her brother, and preferred to keep them in separate compartments. Everyone who knew her was aware of her strong feelings for her family: as the years passed, she felt spiritually even closer to them, and still relied on her mother almost as if Emy were still alive.

Her mother's sister, Hanna Heuberger, became almost a substitute. Her cousin Wolfgang's children replaced her own nephews and nieces: one was the Hanna of the next generation. As a small child, the third Hanna adored her aunt, but as she grew older she became more critical of the older Hanna's exaggerated way of speaking and precise enunciation, and by the way in which she had created a cult around herself and her values. Her famous aunt seemed both eccentric and egocentric, was apparently incapable of objectivity, and constantly attracted trouble. After her marriage Hanna Schantl became much more appreciative and more tolerant, although she still felt that Hanna's habit of telling younger people how to think and behave created a generation gap. Hanna was unaware that she appeared dogmatic or patronising: she was just certain that she knew best, and took an ingenuous pride in her own achievements.

In 1960, she went back to Finland: the Finns were delighted to see her again, and she remembered every flattering reference to her pre-war visits. In the quarter of a century since she had helped to pioneer Finnish gliding, they had built on the expertise and enthusiasm she had shared with them. She brought back a three-roomed Finnish sauna: it was put up at her retreat in the Taunus, next to a mountain stream where a natural pool of clear water was almost as cold as a Finnish lake. At weekends, she and her two priestly companions, and other friends whom she occasionally invited to go with her, chopped and stacked wood so that she could benefit from her extravagant souvenir.

Her nostalgic trip to Finland was followed six months later by another return visit, this time to the United States. Wernher von Braun had suggested that 'an old girlfriend, Hanna Reitsch' might 'make a big hit': 'Hanna has an unusually intriguing personality,' he said, adding that she had 'done all kinds of crazy things' as a famous soaring champion and a wartime test pilot. The fact that her English might be 'a bit rusty' would, he felt, make her talks 'even more spicy'. He was right.

She was received at the White House by President Kennedy, with nine other women helicopter pilots. They belonged to an international association called the Whirly Girls founded in 1955 by Jean Ross Howard. Hanna was Whirly Girl No. 1 because she had been the first woman ever to fly a helicopter. Jean was Whirly Girl No. 13. On the day after their reception by the President, the group of women helicopter pilots flew to the Sikorsky factory. Hanna felt that meeting Igor Sikorsky, the elderly pioneer of the American helicopter industry, was almost as great a privilege as being introduced to Kennedy. The sense of privilege was mutual, and after an official luncheon Sikorsky invited Hanna to his home.

*Saturn Rocket*

Hanna's furtherance of international and personal relations included giving a talk about her own test flights at the Edwards Test Center in California to an audience of test pilots, among them the then unknown Neil Armstrong. At Huntsville, Alabama, she stayed with Joachim Küttner, who was working with Wernher von Braun at the space centre where American success relied heavily on expatriate German expertise. There she gave a lecture about her experiences in India: she was apprehensive about her reception as someone had draped a flag with a swastika over the reading desk, but it was a lone gesture.

Earlier in the day, she had stood beside Wernher von Braun during the launch of the second Saturn rocket. She remembered how he had talked to her about his dream of launching a rocket into space when they were both learning to fly more than thirty years earlier, and was delighted that he had achieved his ambition, even if it was not in the country where he had initiated rocket research.

The warmth of her reception in America reinstated Hanna's faith in the country and its people, although she felt that she was a prophet without honour in her own country. In spite of her continuing feud with the West German Aero Club, she was still revered at individual West German gliding clubs. Even those who disapproved of her on political grounds conceded that she was an outstanding pilot.

In the autumn of 1961 she was presented with a tangible expression of appreciation by the club at Velbert: a Zugvogel 111 glider. Until then she had for ten years, ever since the resumption of gliding, had to rely on the generosity of others for her flying. Among the people who had contributed to the cost was her cousin Helmut's father-in-law, Gustav Hardop. 'I can't tell you how happy I am that now I have my own plane,' she wrote to him, 'and don't always have to be tactful about asking other people to lend me one.'

# 13

# Flying for Nkrumah

Whenever Hanna's morale was boosted abroad, it plummeted again at home. Not long after her return from America, she and Peter Riedel met for the first time since the war, at an aviation reception. 'We were both in the dog-house,' Peter Riedel told me, Hanna because of her 'bad press' in West Germany and her feud with the Aero Club, by then well into its fourth year, and Riedel because it was his first time in the country since his defection. When he and Hanna entered the room, the only person who greeted them was Messerschmitt: everyone else ignored them. They made an early departure. As Riedel escorted Hanna to her car, she looked so unhappy that he bent down and kissed her forehead.

Once again, an unexpected invitation was to take her away from her problems in Germany: President Nkrumah of Ghana wanted her advice about setting up a gliding school. She had never, she realised as she pondered the invitation, thought of black-skinned people as equals. About Ghana she knew only that it had formerly been called the Gold Coast, that it had recently gained its independence from the British, and that part of it had once been a Germany colony. Nkrumah was merely a name, although she had read that he was a dictator.

The West German government was eager to avail itself of any opportunity in Ghana, where Western and Eastern powers were competing for influence. After her success in India, Hanna was on excellent terms with Dr Sattler at the West German Foreign Office in Bonn: he gave the Ghanaian venture his blessing as a way of 'reinforcing bridges between countries'. Hanna was cautious: she would go for a week in March, she decided, before committing herself any further.

On the flight to Accra, she prepared herself by reading Nkrumah's autobiography: she formed a favourable impression of 'a son of the bush' who had, in spite of humiliations and sacrifices, studied theology, philosophy, and sociology in the United States, and law in England.

Hanna was naturally inclined to see the best in anyone, and to admire leaders. In Nkrumah she saw nothing but good. He looked good, for a start: ascetic, slim, youthful (he was in his fifties, a year or two older than she was), and simply but elegantly dressed. His dark eyes seemed to her to radiate charm and goodness. In the furnishing of the small book-lined room in which they met she divined taste, culture, and international understanding: above the bookcases was a politically and spiritually eclectic array of photographs of dignitaries. Budgerigars chirped and chattered in an aviary outside the window, and multi-coloured fish swam beside the desk in an illuminated aquarium. It was not the office, surely, of an unscrupulous dictator.

By the time Nkrumah had told her that she had been recommended by Nehru, and she had explained to him that gliding would provide an ideal way of training the character of young Ghanaians, she felt that they understood each other. Nkrumah had, as she put it, 'an ability to concentrate immediately and totally on a person and a problem, as if there was nothing more important in the world for him at that moment': it was a talent which Hanna both shared and appreciated. She responded for forty minues on the temporal and spiritual values of gliding.

There was already a gliding club in Ghana, started in 1957 and patronised by the British and a few other Europeans; it was not deliberately all-white, but the Ghanaians were not interested. The chiefs who owned its site, a few miles east of Accra at Afienya, were paid the ground rent in gin. The villagers' cows shared the unfenced scrubby field peacefully with the twenty or so active flying members, who disturbed them only at weekends. Nkrumah's doctor Albert Hawe, who referred irreverently to his most distinguished patient as 'His Nibs', was a senior member of the Accra Gliding Club, which welcomed the suggestion that their airfield should become the site of a gliding school. Its chairman, Frank Handscomb, was the only white person on a committee set up by Nkrumah to consider Hanna's advice, and looked forward to sharing the improved facilities.

Hanna visited Afienya on her second day in Ghana. She found a makeshift way of going about things: gliders were launched by a tow-line of fencing wire attached to an old and unreliable Chevrolet. With some trepidation, she agreed to go up in the club's Spatz: a 12-volt car battery was fitted behind the pilot's seat to supplement her weight. She was released 750 ft above the ground and was relieved not to land on a cow.

On her third day in Ghana, Hanna presented her proposals to the committee: initial boarding accommodation for twenty pupils, later rising to forty, as well as three instructors and a minimum of four mechanics, an administrative office, a canteen and kitchen, a hangar with carpentry and metalwork facilities, and a classroom for theoretical instruction. At least four gliders would be needed, two double-seaters and two single-seaters, a winch, and a second-hand tow-plane. In addition, she suggested that seven Ghanaians should be sent to West Germany for training: three officers who would then become instructors, and four mechanics who would learn how to build and repair gliders.

It was an ambitious programme. The only building on the airfield was a small wooden hangar belonging to the Accra Gliding Club, which would continue to operate as usual at weekends and during the holidays. However, by the end of Hanna's third day in Ghana, the committee had agreed to her proposals, which had in turn been approved by the President. All Hanna had to do was supervise the team of Ghanaians in West Germany and return to Ghana in January to start up the school with their help. The committee would ensure that all building work was completed and arrange the purchase of gliders.

Hanna, who was staying at a hotel where she had a maid, a cook, a waiter, and a chauffeur with a Chevrolet, spent the rest of the week meeting Ghanaian VIPs and visiting Mr and Mrs Nkrumah. They entertained and enlightened her with a three-hour film showing the 1957 independence ceremonies and the 1961 British royal visit. She was delighted at the insight this gave her into the people of Ghana and their customs. By the time she left Ghana at the end of the week, her doubts had been dispelled: she was looking forward to renewing her friendship with the admirable President and to inspiring a love of flying in his beautiful country among the people she had already taken to her heart.

As soon as she arrived back in West Germany, she reported to Dr Sattler. The Foreign Office issued an official invitation to a team of Ghanaians, whose fares were to be paid by the Ghanaian government and who were to stay for six months. When they arrived in May, Hanna met her first problem. Ghana was short of pilots and mechanics, and had sent a group of young men from the Ghanaian Young Pioneers, 'nice boys, but neither old enough nor sufficiently experienced for their task'. She could not send them back without causing a political incident.

Some were sent to the Schempp-Hirth factory to learn basic maintenance. The prospective pilots went first to Dr Frowein's flying school on the North Sea island of Juist, and then to Freiburg-Breisgau, where she invited a young woman called Waltraud Bals to join their course for a week. Waltraud, who had recently made her first solo flight, was thrilled: she considered Hanna almost a goddess. The Ghanaians looked upon Hanna as, and even called her, 'Mother'.

Hanna fussed over 'her boys' like a mother hen, explaining to them how they should behave. They took her admonitions to heart, and made promises about 'concentrating entirely on learning for my country'. She elected the most promising as team leader, but he too had to be called to order: 'You will find me more behaved and will enjoy me,' he assured her, adding: 'Since your letter I had thought of nothing but death.'

In spite of the difficulties encountered on both sides, by the end of the year three Ghanaians had qualified as gliding instructors, one had achieved a Silver C, and the others had learnt some basic maintenance. Before they left Germany, Hanna escorted them, at West German government expense, on a sightseeing tour: Frankfurt, Berlin, *Don Giovanni* at the Berlin Opera House, the Volkswagen factory at Wolfburg,

Hamburg, Bonn, a steel-works, a chocolate factory, and a dairy.

The operation was voted a success, particularly as a number of Ghanaians had recently acquired anti-Nkrumah attitudes in West Germany. Hanna's boys would hear no criticism of the great man: when an attempt was made on his life, they and she were equally upset and flying was cancelled.

However it was clearly not going to be possible, as Hanna had hoped, for any of them to work without supervision. As a further self-interested gesture of goodwill, the Bonn government agreed to pay the salaries of two German assistants of her choice. Her own salary was to be paid by the Ghanaians, but she envisaged staying in Ghana for only two or three months. In December, she wrote to Nkrumah: 'I hope with all my heart, that through our establishing a gliding school in Ghana the friendship and mutual understanding of our two countries will become still deeper.' A German gift of a high-performance two-seater glider was already on its way to Accra.

She left for Ghana in March, after frequent requests to postpone her arrival. Ignoring a spate of parties and receptions which had been planned for her first two weeks, she set out at 6 a.m. to inspect her school and found, instead of the buildings she had asked for, a half-finished British clubhouse with a bar and showers, and a long hangar with heavy manually operated doors. She went straight to Nkrumah. It was the start of a close friendship with the President and the prelude to a head-on clash with the British.

A new committee was set up, under the chairmanship of the minister of defence, Kofi Baako. At his suggestion an abandoned British camp two and a half miles from Afienya was renovated as temporary accommodation. Frank Handscomb remained on the committee, and on ostensibly good terms with Hanna, for a few months. He had, as he understood had been agreed, ordered two T21 Slingsby training gliders: although Hanna would have preferred German aircraft of metal construction, the Slingsbys had been chosen because, as they were wooden, they would be easier to repair in primitive workshop conditions. Handscomb had decided on the hangar design because it was reasonably cheap, simple, and seemed adequate: it had been assumed that there would be enough manpower at the school to cope with the doors.

At an early meeting of the committee, Hanna outlined her long-term plans for eight regional gliding centres, each with its own full-time instructional and maintenance staff. The more Frank Handscomb thought about the proposals the less he liked them: 'They seemed to envisage that at some time every man, woman, and child in Ghana would be strapped into a glider, at a cost which did not bear thinking about,' he explained to me. He suggested in a letter that Hanna's scheme was 'on a far larger scale than the circumstances warranted' and that the committee 'should be content with something on much more modest lines'.

The cost to the Ghanaian government of the two gliders and the hangar was around £6000, a large sum for a struggling country. Handscomb had been in Ghana since 1949, and felt that he knew the situation there better than Hanna. He had in fact suggested during her absence that the cost of the school buildings she envisaged put them out of the question, and that money should be saved by giving training only at weekends. Hanna felt that he had been deliberately working against her.

She was exhausted and frustrated, and in Handscomb's words unleashed against him a diatribe the like of which he had never heard before and never heard again: 'She stood in front of me, jabbing one of her long, thin fingers at me and constantly saying: "You, you, you." My occasional efforts to say something were simply met with: "Be quiet!" '

To Hanna, it was a simple matter into which cost did not enter. Nkrumah, or Osagyefo (Saviour)—she preferred to use the affectionate title given to him by his people—wanted the gliding school, she wanted it, and that was that. She had her way, but at the cost of a permanent rift with the British flying community. Nkrumah told Dr Hawe, in strictest confidence, that Hanna would have liked to have had Frank Handscomb deported.

Before the school could be opened, there were several months of work which was to be harder than Hanna had ever anticipated. Her German colleagues, Täwe Löhr and Ernst Wieser, arrived in time to share the burden. Hanna wore herself out with official engagements, supervision, and a spate of lectures to instil interest in flying. She was at first living in a controversial mansion, the home of a Ghanaian minister who had been disgraced when his wife ordered a solid gold bed from London. It had since been turned into a guesthouse for official VIPs. She was its first occupant, and slept in a circular bed—not the gold one—surrounded by mirrors.

Although she felt uncomfortable in such grand and notorious surroundings, she appreciated the swimming-pool, which she used at four every morning before her daily meditation and yoga. By six she was making telephone calls and had been joined by her German colleagues for a business breakfast. Although she was constantly rushing from one place to another, she always looked cool, in white trousers and a loose patterned cotton overblouse, and never wore either a hat or sunglasses: the African climate appeared to affect her less than the other Germans. Nkrumah's wife lent her a red Volkswagen, which made the frequent journeys between Accra and Afienya easier.

The school was opened at a grand ceremony presided over by Nkrumah and attended by Ghanaian and foreign dignitaries, the members of the Accra Gliding Club, and Dr Sattler. Hanna gave an aerobatic display which even her most ardent detractors admired, and which caused an African ambassador to murmur audibly that she must have a hidden engine.

She dedicated herself to the International School of Gliding with even more than her usual singlemindedness. She and her German colleagues moved into separate single-storey huts at the renovated camp until purpose-built bungalows were erected for her and Löhr in Accra; Wieser stayed on site. The promised buildings gradually materialised, but teaching young Ghanaians to fly proved a more daunting task than Hanna had anticipated. She, Täwe Löhr, and Ernst Wieser had all their meals together and discussed the problem endlessly.

Reluctantly, they came to the conclusion that the young Ghanaians, lovable and enthusiastic though they found them, were culturally not ready for flight and that too much was being asked of them. Technology was in its infancy in Ghana, and few of the pupils had had more than basic education.

They lacked concentration and co-ordination, and found European attitudes difficult to understand. Hanna had strict ideas about discipline, which included a healthy diet with meals at set times and in the right place: lounging around eating outside, as the boys had always done, was somehow wrong. Eventually she had to give up the attempt to make them sit indoors round a table.

There was considerable resentment that she made them work through the heat of the day, and so little general enthusiasm for flying that grounding was considered a privilege rather than a punishment. When Wieser introduced making and flying model aeroplanes to the curriculum, more progress was shown: at last it seemed that a way had been found to inspire an interest in flight.

Hanna wanted perfection. This included clearing the airfield of all possible obstacles, and fencing it in to keep the cows out. The fencing annoyed the gliding club, and deprived the cows of a large area of grazing; but cutting down a tree had more serious repercussions. No one had told Hanna that it was sacred. After it had been reduced to a stump morale in the school inexplicably declined. Only when a gory ceremony of sacrificial cleansing and apology by the villagers had taken place was morale restored.

It was not so easy to clear the air of international tensions. Hanna was on good terms with her pupils and with the people in the village of Afienya, and on excellent terms with Nkrumah, whom she saw or spoke to on the telephone daily. She felt honoured to be the close friend and even the confidante of such a great man, and ran to him with every problem. This caused ill-will in expatriate and diplomatic circles, where it was considered that Hanna's history was repeating itself: once again, gossip accused her of being associated with a dictator.

There were three German ambassadors while she was in Ghana. The first, Dr Lüders, told Frank Handscomb that he found her a 'serious embarrassment' because 'she represents the Germany we are trying to convince the world no longer exists'. Like his successors, he nevertheless kept on outwardly good terms with her.

The second, Dr Walter Reichhold, was predisposed against her by first-hand reports that because she always considered herself in the right she was unpopular in German flying circles, by what he had read in Trevor-Roper's book, and by his own anti-Nazi activity in Switzerland during the war. The third was Georg Steltzer, who still secretly thought her a pain in the neck.

Reichhold found Hanna's pre-war colonial attitude to black Africa, her hero worship of Nkrumah, and her Nazi reputation equally unhelpful in his attempts to smooth strained relations between Germany and Ghana. Worse still, she attempted to intervene in matters of diplomacy, and upset West German relations with the British, the French, and the Libyans: the Israeli ambassador was amused at the Germans' predicament, and the Indians and Pakistanis thought she was wonderful. The American ambassador, William Mahoney, admired what he called her 'free world' philosophical viewpoint, and was not surprised that as a loyal and traditional German citizen from a part of Germany overrun by them she 'literally detested' the Russians. The Russians found her presence in Ghana and her friendship with Nkrumah useful propaganda against the evils of Western influence in Africa.

Instructions were issued from Bonn that Reichhold must put up with Hanna because the gliding school was Nkrumah's pet project: 'We should make use of the opportunity this presents,' he was told. In one of several communications from Reichhold to Bonn, he said that he did not expect her to stay long: 'I believe that Hanna Reitsch overestimates her own physical endurance and the capabilities of her pupils. We should be prepared for a collapse.'

Hanna was nevertheless still there when he was recalled in July 1964, and welcomed his removal even if she did not actually, as was suspected, procure it. She considered her influence on Nkrumah to be greater than it perhaps was: it seems, for instance, unlikely that his sole reason for not officially recognising East Germany can have been that he did not want to upset her, and he continued to associate politically with the Russians in spite of her feelings.

She met Reichhold's replacement, Georg Steltzer, at the airport. Before leaving Bonn, he had discussed her role in Ghana with Dr Sattler, who was aware that she was creating less goodwill in Ghana than had been the case in India.

Steltzer and Hanna were at first on friendly terms: she gave him occasional useful information and told his wife that she was enjoying her political involvement through Nkrumah. She was, however, as he put it, 'often bitter and cross'. Nkrumah respected Steltzer more than his predecessors, and Steltzer and Hanna fell out when the President rejected her advice in favour of a discussion with the ambassador.

Diplomats were not the only people Hanna upset. She annoyed Nkrumah's fiercely protective secretary, Erica Powell, by assuming that she could see the President whenever she liked, and an RAF flight lieutenant, Clifford Boxsey, had a number of brushes with her. Boxsey, who had been seconded to the Ghana air force to take charge of air safety, was the technical member of the gliding school's management committee. As principal of the school, Hanna attended its meetings, but only in an advisory capacity, a fact of which Boxsey frequently felt compelled to remind her.

When the school's tow-plane, an old Piper Super Cub, had been grounded, Hanna walked into the hangar at Accra and demanded to use it. Boxsey refused, whereupon Hanna threatened to go to the President. According to an amused bystander, 'At that, Boxsey became very stiff, in a way only RAF officers can, and replied: "I am not working for the President of Ghana, but for Her Majesty the Queen!", saluted and left.'

Many of the British and Germans in Accra considered that Hanna's efforts to teach young Ghanaians to fly, and thereby to train their characters, was little more than a neo-Nazi attempt to introduce an African form of the Hitler Youth movement. This view was reinforced both by her frequent condemnation of the lack of discipline and devotion to duty among modern German youth, and by the fact that her first pupils were members of the Young Pioneers. She had not chosen them, and found them able to respond to tuition only when model-making. Her attempts to have this introduced in schools throughout Ghana, as a way of inspiring the technical awareness which she found so lacking, were also seen as somehow sinister.

The pupils on the school's second flying course were more mature and coped better with the demands of flying, although it took them twice as long to qualify as would have been normal for a European. Hanna's critics latched on to a fatal accident which they blamed on her method of teaching, but which she insisted was caused entirely by pilot error. It was not her fault, she protested, if no one had seen fit to tell her that the pilot in question had already been thrown out of air force training because he was not considered suitable pilot material. It was the only accident in the three years that the school operated.

The more she was beset with problems, the greater was Hanna's dedication both to her task and to Nkrumah: 'In pioneering work one must expect opposition and jealousy, and the more enemies arose against us amongst foreigners, i.e. among non-Ghanaians, the clearer it became to us that our path and our work was beginning to bring success and help to Ghana.'

Hanna's brother Kurt and her two priestly friends visited her in Ghana. Like her, they saw a noble leader who was often misled or misrepresented and who needed Hanna's

*Piper Super Cub*

advice and protection against his enemies, in particular against those unscrupulous people who were trying to influence him in favour of Russia.

Her unquestioning and vociferous support of Nkrumah also made her enemies among Ghanaians, especially when she stumbled across a bribery scandal. More than twelve million marks had been paid into special accounts in Germany, London, and Syria. Hanna's suspicions were aroused when a German glider was sent to Nkrumah as a present for the gliding school. Further treachery was revealed by an abortive attempt on Nkrumah's life, in which he overcame his attacker but was bitten on the cheek and scarred for life. Hanna's admiration of his courage was exceeded only by her relief at his survival, and her indignation that he should have been so betrayed.

By the end of 1965, the National Gliding School had, after three years of intensive work, reached a point where Hanna felt that her efforts had not been in vain. Three Ghanaian instructors were working alongside the Germans. Several successful open days and flying displays had been held in Accra and Takoradi as well as in Afienya.

A few African heads of state had visited the school during the first Organisation of African Unity conference, although fewer than had been hoped. None had availed himself of the invitation to fly: the disappointment this caused after weeks of preparation was made up for by a personal visit and individual thank-you gifts from Nkrumah. Model-making was at last being introduced in ten schools, and Hanna had had another idea: she would support the President's national literacy drive by using the school and its literate pupils to teach the villagers of Afienya to read and write.

She had, it was true, had to drop some of her more grandiose plans: financial restrictions made the idea of opening further gliding centres throughout the country unrealistic. Little cost had, however, been spared in realising her dreams at Afienya: the National Gliding School had become a showpiece. It looked what she fully expected it to be, a permanent and flourishing establishment, with a large ancillary local workforce, a police guard round the perimeter fence (this had been introduced after a break-in) and flower-beds which were her particular pride outside all the buildings. Although the two or three months she had anticipated spending in Ghana had stretched to three years, she had no thought of abandoning the project or the country which had come to mean so much to her.

The year 1966 started well. Hanna returned to Ghana on 1 February to resume her duties after her annual Christmas break in Germany. An army sports instructor was to be seconded for one day a week to the gliding school. Voluntary yoga and meditation classes were to be introduced.

On Monday, 21 February, Hanna was with a number of ministers, officers, and other loyal supporters of Nkrumah who waved goodbye to him as he left Ghana on a Vietnamese peace mission. On the evening of 23 February, she met the education minister, Suzanne el Hassan, to discuss the provision of books, paper, and pencils for her literacy scheme.

By the time Hanna awoke the next morning, a military government had been established. At five, she heard machine-gun fire in Accra. For the next half-hour, she telephoned every minister she knew, starting with Kofi Baako, the minister of defence, to find out what was going on. There was no answer either from them or from any other of her Ghanaian acquaintances.

Then the Ghanaian wife of an employee at Flagstaff House phoned her in tears and told her that her husband had been arrested: 'Hanna, it's a revolution!' she sobbed. Hanna instructed the police who stood guard day and night outside her bungalow to shut the big iron gates and not to let anyone in, and telephoned Wieser at Afienya. The revolution had not reached the gliding school, and she advised him to keep the pupils busy and calm.

At six, she listened to the news: Nkrumah had been relieved of his post *in absentia,* his party had been dissolved, his ministers had been arrested, and all key positions had been taken over by a military regime. General Ankrah, who had been dismissed from his position as army chief of staff the previous year, was ruling the country as head of the National Liberation Council, the name adopted by the revolutionaries. Hanna was appalled: she had never imagined that there could be such treachery or such ingratitude.

During the next few days, she began to feel like a boomerang as she was repeatedly stopped by police and soldiers. She was escorted unwillingly backwards and forwards between Accra and Afienya, sometimes contemptuously at gun-point, sometimes courteously, alternately under arrest and free.

The gliding school was soon under siege, surrounded by armed men who were afraid that Nkrumah might try to land there if he decided to return and mount a counter-attack. The majority of her pupils had turned from ardent support of Nkrumah to equally ardent declarations that he was a criminal, and had abandoned all semblance of discipline and respect. The Ghanaian newspapers announced that Hanna Reitsch had turned the gliding school into a systematic experimental concentration camp, and had criminally diverted Ghanaian money for corrupt building purposes.

Steltzer was in Germany during the coup, but flew back immediately. To her horror, he told Hanna that he considered the coup to be in Germany's best interests: furious, she told him that he was a traitor. 'She made herself very unpopular because she didn't believe that the saviour could be put aside, and tried to get this reversed,' he told me. 'She rang everyone she could think of for support.' There was, however, no one who was not already in prison who was prepared to give it.

On 3 March West Germany officially recognised the new regime, the first Western country to do so. Hanna, who felt ashamed and betrayed, was deported that evening. She did not in any case feel that she belonged in the new Ghana, a violent and treacherous country which she no longer felt she knew.

Before she could settle back into life in Germany, Hanna wanted to reassure herself that Nkrumah would not risk his life by trying to return to Ghana. To evade reporters, she travelled to Guinea under an assumed name and in disguise, a journey that was reminiscent of her surreptitious trips across the German/Austrian border after the war.

As soon as she saw Nkrumah, she burst into tears: the deposed and exiled President had to comfort her, rather than she him. His apparently calm and cheerful acceptance of his fate confirmed her view of his greatness: God's will worked in mysterious ways, he told her, and she should stop worrying about him. She poured out everything that she had seen and heard during her last ten days in Ghana and left as secretly as she had arrived, after promising to make sure that Erica Powell, who had been his secretary since long before he became President, was all right.

Erica had, like Nkrumah, been out of the country during the coup. The two women had not been particularly friendly in Ghana, but their shared loyalty to Nkrumah was a strong tie in adversity. Hanna spent a cold fortnight at the Powells' rambling family house in Norfolk. During the next few years, Erica visited Hanna several times in Frankfurt, where they worked together on an English version of Hanna's life story. It was, however, never published.

Hanna was offered another assignment abroad, both by Dr Sattler and by the Indian government; but she still felt so deeply rooted in Ghana that instead she devoted her energies to writing a book about her experiences there. It was published in 1968, under the title *Ich flog für Kwame Nkrumah (I Flew for Kwam Nkrumah)*, as was a new edition of her first autobiographical book. Her vision of Nkrumah as a rejected and misunderstood saviour reinforced the belief that she was, as Frank Handscomb put it, 'a quite unregenerate Nazi', and had again fallen under the spell of a dictator.

It was, however, unfair either to compare Nkrumah with Hitler, or to suggest that Hanna had the same attitude to both. Her admiration for Nkrumah was perhaps as politically naïve as her acceptance of Hitler, but was based on a far closer acquaintance. Unwittingly, and as usual with the most sincere of motives, Hanna had again set herself on a political stage.

The gliding school inevitably fell into the hands of the club, as Hanna had feared it would and as she was sure the British members had plotted, although half-hearted weekend tuition continued for a while. Her only comfort was that seven of the assistant instructors she had taught were admitted in 1967 to the Ghanaian air force as pilot officers, and that a few of her pupils wrote to her from time to time calling her 'My Saviour!' or 'Dear Fly Captain'. 'This is the voice of your son writing,' one informed her, and another promised:

'Never at any time will I turn my back against you, but in case
I do may God curse me!'

Hanna kept in touch with Nkrumah until his death, although they never met again. When he died, she and Erica
Powell exchanged grief-stricken eulogies.

# Success but No Escape

In the years following her return from Ghana, Hanna became a grand old lady of the air, an aviation celebrity and the champion of younger women pilots. She and Elly Beinhorn were founder members of the German Association of Women Pilots and of a German branch of the 99s, an international women pilots' organisation founded in America in 1929. She was recognised immediately at airports and airfields, and treated with deference. When she met friends off commercial flights at Frankfurt, she was ushered respectfully on to the tarmac.

It would never have satisfied her to be purely a VIP, gratifying though it was to be treated as such. Flying was still her life, and from 1969 onwards she found a way of getting round her own self-imposed ban by spending a few weeks each year in Austria, at first with her Zugvogel and then with a new Standard-Cirrus. With the Cirrus, she trained both in Austria and at a privately owned airfield at Varese in Italy for long-distance flying over the Alps. Early in the summer of 1970, she created a women's alpine gliding record. That it was a record was a bonus as she loved nothing more than flying in the Austrian Alps, which was demanding, sometimes alarming, always potentially dangerous, and spiritually releasing.

When she was not flying, she was able to relax in a way which she found impossible in Frankfurt. She sang with friends, including the women who had serenaded her across the lake at Schloss Leopoldskron, went to concerts, and walked in the mountains. In 1974, she took out Austrian citizenship. She felt that in Austria she was accepted and liked for herself, whereas in Germany she was always aware that many people still judged her instead by her past.

Although she had not flown at the Wasserkuppe for many years, Hanna could not miss its golden jubilee in August 1970, especially as she and Joachim Küttner were to accompany the guest of honour, the astronaut Neil Armstrong. As well as being the first man on the moon, Armstrong was a keen amateur glider pilot. He was invited at the suggestion of a young man called Helmut Dette, a Wasserkuppe enthusiast and one of Hanna's most ardent admirers, who had read *Fliegen mein Leben* several times and had appointed himself her unofficial press officer.

There had never been so many people at the Wasserkuppe. As part of the celebrations, a small gliding museum was opened near Peterchens Mondfahrt, a hotel run by and for gliding enthusiasts. Dette considered the museum disappointingly small. One evening while he, Hanna, Neil Armstrong, and the president of the Wasserkuppe Association were sitting together at the hotel he suggested that there should be a bigger and better one. 'A fantastic idea,' Hanna agreed. There were two major problems: a site, and money. Hanna enlisted the support of the mayor of Gersfeld, the nearest town to the Wasserkuppe, and later of a colonel with whose assistance a small strip of land belonging to the air force was eventually released: 'Hey, Colonel, we both have to fight to get this land,' she told him, grabbing his tie in her enthusiasm.

It was her idea to raise funds through a glider mail flight to Fulda, a few miles from the Wasserkuppe. A stamp company near Stuttgart agreed to pay five marks each for 2000 postcards, provided Hanna Reitsch signed them all. It took her the best part of a week, and afterwards she said she never wanted to write her own name again. She helped to swell the funds further by handing round a hat at her lectures, which brought in two or three hundred marks at a time, and by donating the profit from the sale of signed copies of her books at a later Wasserkuppe meeting. It was, however, not until 1987 that the new museum was opened.

In 1971, Hanna, Jacqueline Cochran, and Jacqueline Auriol (the latter two being the first women to break the sound barrier) were invited to become honorary members of the exclusive Society of Experimental Test Pilots (SETP) in America. Women had never before joined the SETP élite. Hanna had to turn the invitation down as it clashed with a prior commitment in Germany, to the first international helicopter championships. Hanna was to fly a helicopter belonging to the firm of an old friend, Otto Rietdorf, and did not feel she could let him down by withdrawing.

She had decided that her self-imposed ban on flying in Germany did not apply to helicopters, and had willingly availed herself of an offer by Clever and Rietdorf to fly their helicopters free of charge. This had enabled her to make up her hours on helicopters to a hundred, sometimes taking a friend with her for a joy-ride above the Rhine: her passengers included Gertrud Heuberger, the composer Wagner's English daughter-in-law Winifred, and Carlos Ritter, a film director.

At the international helicopter championships at Bückeburg, she was one of only six women among competitors from fifteen countries. Eric Brown flew for England. Hanna and her co-pilot won the women's section, came sixth overall, and were second in a helicopter slalom devised by Rietdorf. While the other competitors went off for lunch, Hanna worked out her strategy, bending her knees and moving her hands and feet as she practised each manœuvre in her mind—her old technique of mental training.

When Hanna did not reappear at subsequent helicopter competitions, Eric Brown suspected that it was because she wanted to avoid him or did not feel competent to compete against the more experienced male pilots. The reason was simpler: Rietdorf had sold his company, and although she occasionally flew helicopters afterwards she had neither the time nor the money for the necessary training flights.

She was able to take up the invitation to America a year late, and in 1972 became not only an honorary member of SETP, but also Pilot of the Year in Arizona, where she received the International Award of Characters, for which she was given the name Supersonic Sue.

There were 2000 people at the Beverly Hilton in California for the SETP award dinner. Hanna could scarcely believe that in such august company and surroundings she was considered the high point of the evening. The society's president outlined her flying career and then, to her amazement, introduced a film showing her with the Deutschlandhalle helicopter, the Me 163, and the manned V1, compiled from material confiscated by the Americans after the war.

Her neighbour at dinner was Barron Hilton, 'owner of all the Hilton hotels' as Hanna commented in awe. He in turn was so bowled over by her 'charm and grace', and even more by her descriptions of the thrill of soaring over the Alps on rising currents of air, that next day he told his chief pilot: 'Go buy a sailplane'. For thirty years he had held a pilot's licence, but although he owned a ranch with perfect conditions for gliding he had flown only powered aircraft.

In 1980, Barron Hilton offered ten days of 'friendly non-competitive soaring at the Flying M Ranch as first prize in an international cross-country gliding competition. He had thought of the perfect name for the event—the Hanna Reitsch Cup—because Hanna had introduced him to gliding and typified 'the unique spirit of camaraderie and sportsmanship among the world's best soaring pilots'. Hanna would have been delighted with the compliment, but Hilton gave way reluctantly to commercial pressures and it became instead the Barron Hilton Cup.

Hanna returned from America more convinced than ever that flying linked people of all nations and transcended the boundaries of language and geographical divisions. She had suggested to Sikorsky, only half jokingly, that 'World peace might be much more easily attained if all the heads of state were pilots.' At last, after the honours showered upon her as a German, she felt that she could forget the divisions of the past. It was ironic that only a few months later a film starring Alec Guinness as Hitler should once again cast her in the role of a Nazi, one of the ladies in brown of the bunker.

The film claimed to give an authentic picture of Hitler's last days based on the published eyewitness account of Gerhard Boldt; but it also drew once again on Trevor-Roper's book, although he had not been consulted. No one had thought of contacting Hanna. The actress portraying her did a good enough job with the script, but the Hanna Reitsch of the film bore no relation to the Hanna Reitsch who was still living. It made no difference that the film was not universally well received: it was seen by millions. Hanna protested in a long article in *die Welt* about both the insult to herself and the general inaccuracy of ihe film: the atmosphere in the bunker had, she again insisted, been 'deeply oppressive, almost unreal and as silent as in a grave', she had been there purely in the line of duty, and she had never sat talking to Hitler and Eva Braun.

She had become so obsessed over the years with the constant slurs on her honour and distortions of the truth that she could not distinguish a genuine grievance from one which deserved only to be ignored. When a skit was published in a newspaper—it was a mock interview with a Mr Hundewart Zuckmoisl, describing how Hanna Reitsch had flown the offspring of a union between Hitler's Alsatian and Bormann's dachshund out of Berlin—she wrote a solemn denial: Hitler would never have thought of having dogs flown out, she would never have agreed to do it, and there had never been any such puppies.

Her more serious allegation was that the crimes of other countries, both in the Second World War and in subsequent less widespread conflicts, were ignored, while Germany was constantly accused of crimes which had often not been proved, but had become accepted as fact. 'No upstanding German will wish to deny that on our side too atrocities were committed,' she admitted; but she considered it unjust that Germans, and only Germans, should still, thirty years after the war, be made to feel a collective guilt, particularly when the Russians had been responsible for more deaths than they had.

Her campaign against injustice included giving her support to people still imprisoned for German war crimes: this seemed to her in itself a crime against humanity. She had in the years after the war frequently written letters protesting the innocence of friends awaiting trial, such as von Krosigk and Dr Theodor Benzinger. In the 1970s, she became involved with a psychological support group for long-term German prisoners of war in Italy.

Through Yvonne Pagniez she joined another campaign, to free a Frenchman who as a young man of twenty with a German wife had joined the SS as an interpreter. She also protested, like many Germans and indeed many outside Germany, against keeping Hess in solitary confinement in Spandau Prison in Berlin.

Although Hanna insisted that only by telling the truth about, and coming to terms with, the past could peace be ensured in the future, her truth was inevitably subjective and selective. When she claimed that her country was being misjudged and ill-treated, she did not appreciate the passionate feelings which still lingered in the hearts of many of Germany's wartime opponents. That she should resent and fear the Russians seemed to her reasonable, but not that others should still feel the same way about the Germans.

An element of anti-German feeling lingered in Britain in the generation which had been involved in the war. In 1973, the British Berlin Tattoo was billed as one of the most spectacular events ever held in the Deutschlandhalle. The star attraction was to be a short flight by Major-General Scott-Barrett to prove that it was possible to fly a modern helicopter safely inside the hall. Hanna, who had done this thirty-five years earlier (a fact mentioned in all the publicity, although she was wrongly said to have flown an autogiro), was not invited. But then the British had never given her much recognition, and it was no doubt felt that Berlin was not a place where someone whose name was still closely linked with the traumas of the last days of the war was likely to be popular.

It was only in America that Hanna's achievements were recognised and where she felt that there was any genuine move towards reconciliation between the victors and the vanquished. In 1975, she was invited to talk to the Society of Experimental Test Pilots: an audience of 2000 gave her a standing ovation after listening for half an hour to her experiences with the Me 163 and the manned V1. She was nervous, not because of the size of the audience, but because her work with the projects had been undertaken while her country and that of her hosts had been at war. The warmth of her reception was, she felt, as much a tribute to Germany as to herself personally, and a token of the Americans' internationalism and spiritual generosity, qualities which she still found lacking in Europe.

Two of her wartime friends and colleagues, Karl Francke

and Karl Schieferstein, were later also made members of the Society of Experimental Test Pilots. Francke and Hanna were together in Los Angeles during the week of his inauguration. When she went with him to buy his ticket to Florida, to their mutual amusement the travel agent misunderstood, and made out tickets to 'Mr and Mrs Francke'. It became a standing joke between them to refer to each other in this way.

Hanna's life had always been too full for any serious thought of marriage. She had admired, even adored, a number of men, but in the same way that she loved her family, and she had never admitted to having been in love. For twenty-five years, the man who meant most to her was the Catholic priest Fredel Volkmar, whose death in December 1976 affected her deeply. During his last illness, she was with Father Pehl at Volkmar's bedside almost constantly, even taking a mattress into the hospital so that she could be near and ready to help at any time.

It was only a year since they had read the proofs of her third book together. *Das Unzerstörbare in meinem Leben (The Indestructible in My Life)* was a biography of the first half of her life, aimed chiefly at older readers but, Hanna felt, just as relevant for the young. The indestructible elements of her life were her love for her family, her home, music, flying, and God, all illustrated with examples and anecdotes based on her simple but sincere faith in her and God's rightness and virtue. She quoted her mother's verses and homilies, and saw a silver lining to every cloud. The key to Hanna's wealth—spiritual wealth, at least—had, she explained on the first page, been best expressed by her mother: 'Happiness is not wealth, not success,/ no, happiness is God's nearness,/ [so] that in everything that happens,/ one sees God's leadership.' It sounds better in German:

> Glück ist nicht Reichtum, nicht Erfolg,
> nein, Glück ist Gottes Nähe,
> dass man in allem was geschieht,
> die Führung Gottes sehe.

Hanna later recorded the book on tape: her voice made its simple message sound natural and even moving.

It is interesting to speculate whether Hanna's life would have taken a different course after the war if her mother had still been alive to guide her. Emy Reitsch would not have been able to prevent the adverse publicity which dogged her—'the crimson thread of Trevor-Roper', as Thilo Bode put it—but she might well have persuaded her to protest less. Hanna made regular pilgrimages to the graves of her parents, and of von Greim, and reserved Christmas for a solitary spiritual tryst with her dead which she did not feel able to share with anyone else.

Her aunt Hanna Heuberger had died while she was in Ghana, and her uncle died five years later. The loss of her substitute parents strengthened Hanna's relationship with their daughter Gertrud. It became the cousins' custom to spend the New Year together in Frankfurt. Until Volkmar too died, part of the tradition was an early New Year's Eve service at his church, followed by supper with him. The women then drove back to Hanna's flat, where each went to her own room to ponder over the past year. Just before midnight, they emerged to talk and watch fireworks from the balcony.

Between Gertrud's annual visits, which usually lasted a fortnight, they rarely communicated but made notes of things they wanted to tell each other at their next meeting. They had much in common: a shared sense of humour; a love of music; a strong sense of duty; and a lively intelligence. Both were also early risers.

The one thing they could never share was any discussion to do with politics, particularly if the war was mentioned. From time to time, Gertrud tried to start a conversation when each could put forward her own arguments: Hanna invariably became so upset that she eventually gave up the attempt. It was the one subject, apart from her own honour, on which Gertrud felt that Hanna's otherwise clear intellect always lost to her intense emotions. The conflicting wartime roles of Hanna, who had flown for the Fatherland and had supported the Führer, and the equally patriotic Heubergers, who had first supported Hitler but had then done all they could to overthrow him, had never been discussed in detail. Hanna had always had an aversion to politics, and still could not see herself as having any political view or role.

They rarely saw anyone else, except Father Volkmar, who was like a member of the family, and Father Pehl, with whom Hanna's relationship was almost as close, and of course the faithful but unobtrusive Fräulein Walter, who prepared their meals but never joined them. On her day off, they contented themselves with snacks, and when they went together to the mountain retreat in the Taunus they ate at an inn. The Opel family summer house nearby had fallen into disrepair and there was a plentiful supply of wood from its decaying timbers to heat the sauna. Hanna used it even when it meant running barefoot across frozen grass or even snow and hacking a hole in the ice before jumping into the pool. After Volkmar's death, she rarely went there: to spend the night with two priests was very different from doing so with only one, and after her chalet had been broken into several times she began to be nervous about its isolated position.

Although she could cope with fear and danger in the air, as she grew older Hanna became alarmed about the possibility of attack on the ground. The inner city of Frankfurt had become so violent that the police warned her they could not guarantee her safety. Rather than walking, she was advised to use taxis. In the early 1970s, there was a spate of demonstrations against land speculators who wished to pull down old housing and build new tower-blocks. Houses all around the one in which Hanna had a flat were occupied by the protesters.

She felt increasingly uneasy about the violence in the streets, and after an attempted break-in at her flat she took first to carrying a small pistol in her handbag and then moved in the early summer of 1973 to a quieter area. On the day that she moved, a car in front of her old flat in the Kettenhofweg was overturned and set alight. She felt safer in the larger and more luxurious flat, on the top floor of a three-storey block overlooking a large park in the Zeppelinallee: she could afford it only because the owner was an admirer and benefactor.

Black-and-white photographs of the Alps, some with a glider against the cloud-hazed peaks, lined the wall up the last flight of stairs. Several family photographs, as well as portraits of von Greim and Volkmar, were displayed in what could almost be called a shrine against one wall. A watercolour painted by Otto Fuchs in Libya hung above the piano. Books and flying trophies, and an assortment of rugs, wall-hangings, and carved figures collected on her travels, gave a general impression of cosmopolitan culture. Picture windows looked out across peaceful tree-filled gardens to a church clock tower, and from her balcony Hanna watched and fed the birds which nested in the trees and under the eaves.

It was in the flat in Zeppelinallee that she worked on her last published autobiographical book, writing it out in long-hand and giving it to Fräulein Walter, who had a room with a separate entrance, to type. A large part of it was devoted to detailed explanations of how she had been hard done by at various times, and much of the rest to enthusiastic descriptions of her many triumphs since the war. She could not at first think of a title, until she said one day to her publisher that her life since 1945 had been a series of ups and downs: 'That's it—there's your title!' he exclaimed, and so she called it *Höhen und Tiefen (Ups and Downs,* or *Heights and Depths).*

Hanna had always been temperamentally up and down, swinging rapidly between moods of elation and despair. When she was up, she was pleased with herself; but when she was down, she appeared to outsiders to be displeased only with other people—they were unaware of the inner doubts which assailed her. As a friend, she demanded admiration and sympathy, although she was always as ready to reciprocate. She attacked life in her mid-sixties with undiminished energy, pursuing her personal mission as obsessively as ever. In return, life seemed all too often to retaliate. As soon as she was up, in Austria or America or after a record flight, she was dragged back down by reminders that she had been elevated to the status of a heroine by the Nazis. Gradually the constant battle began to wear her down, but she was incapable of giving it up.

It seems extraordinary that of the people who had associated with Hitler, Hanna should repeatedly have been singled out for criticism. In April 1978, she and Hans Baur, Hitler's personal pilot, were invited as VIPs to attend a public tribute in Neu-Ulm to the German pioneering pilot Hermann Köhl. Köhl, who in 1928 flew the Atlantic from east to west and died ten years later, was banned from public speaking after a difference of opinion with Goering in 1934. The participation of both Hanna and Baur was criticised as an insult to the memory of an anti-Nazi; but Baur's professional and personal association with Hitler had been far closer.

Hanna attracted good as well as bad publicity. Over the years, a number of articles praising her appeared in newspapers and magazines, and she was interviewed on radio. In 1976, she was filmed by the BBC for a television series called *Secret War*. She was interviewed in English at her own choice. The BBC team were struck by her smart, trim appearance and by the contrast between her apparent frailty and her indomitable spirit. She wore her Iron Cross proudly, and gave the film crew the impression that she still had a great admiration for Hitler. 'She was so tiny it was impossible to imagine she'd done all those things,' the assistant cameraman, Lex Tudhope, told me: 'We were fascinated.' They were so fascinated that although only short clips of the interview were used in the series, and although she refused to allow them to make a feature film about her life, there was enough material to make a documentary about her after her death. 'It showed her as she would like to be remembered, as a fearless pilot,' Eric Brown commented when it was first shown on television in Britain.

As she refused to let bygones be bygones, she was still unable to fly in Germany, but often put in an appearance at gliding competitions. The men were pleased enough to see her: they gave her something to do or someone to look after. There were few women competing: to encourage them, Hanna had formed a group of Segelfliegerinnen (women glider pilots). One of the most enthusiastic was Waltraud Bals: she thought it wonderful that a woman like Hanna should give up her time for them. When all the women were put in the back row at a briefing, Hanna marched up to the organisers and protested: the next day, they sat in the front. In an effort to uncover other talents as well as flying, she organised a literary competition for the Segelfliegerinnen: they supported it for a couple of years to please her.

At least one man, Fred Weinholtz, was aware of the problems women had in gaining recognition among the men at gliding clubs. It was at his suggestion that a Ladies' International Contest was held at Oerlinghausen in 1977. Rika

Harwood, editor of the British gliding magazine *Sailplane*, helped him with the organisation, although she did not approve in theory of separate groups for women; but then clubs in Britain accepted them more readily as equals.

A textile firm donated a batch of assorted fabrics for the competitors: Rika distributed safety-pins and material for a light-hearted fashion show which she called Operation Safety Pin. Hanna, who was at first reluctant to dress up, appeared in a sari and enthused about how clever Rika was to think of the idea.

She had been invited as the doyenne of women glider pilots and looked after the younger ones like a mother hen. She talked through their flights, took them out to dinner, and entertained them with flying stories. Many of them, particularly the Belgians and those from Eastern bloc countries, were flattered that Hanna Reitsch was taking trouble over them and sought her advice. In spite of her seniority, she was on friendly and informal terms with them, and even went to wake them up in the mornings. Her supportive non-flying participation helped to create a good atmosphere, and she enjoyed the occasion as much as did the competitors.

If she was going to set an example for younger pilots, Hanna felt that she had to prove herself by continuing to break records. At the beginning of June 1978, after several weeks of bad weather in the Alps had made flying almost impossible, she fitted two long-distance flights between storms. The second, of 715 km—ten hours in the air—was a women's world record. As usual, Hanna's letters to her friends expressed her delight at her achievement. Later in the year, she was made an honorary citizen of the area which included Timmersdorf, where she had started and ended her flight.

Fred Weinholtz, who was president of the Gliding Board of the West German Aero Club, wrote to congratulate her not only on her latest record, but on everything she had done for gliding: at sixty-six, she had been making and breaking records for forty-six years. She answered him gratefully: the younger generation had made up for the behaviour of its predecessors and there need no longer be a shadow over her relationship with the German gliding community. The twenty-year war of wills was over at last, although as no one had given in, no one had won. For a few months, Hanna was at peace with the world.

Because of her vitality as a public speaker, she was much in demand, but could not accept every invitation. She had on several occasions turned down a request from a Mr Hans Hertel to speak to the Bremen group of Stahlhelm, a right-wing organisation of old soldiers. All she knew about it was that its members had a nationalist outlook: she approved of nationalism, but preferred to call it patriotism.

Hertel was persistent, and eventually she gave in after he had congratulated her fulsomely on her world record. They agreed that he would arrange a date between 1 and 11 November. Hanna asked him to ensure that he booked a sufficiently large hall and to invite various flying and refugee groups in the area. She clearly envisaged a large audience.

In August, Hertel wrote that he was worried that if the lecture were to be held in a hall large enough to seat 1500 to 2000 people, as planned, it would mean advertising it rather than issuing private invitations and that this might cause problems. He warned her that Bremen was a 'red' town, with a 'bright red' university: it had, he told her, been known for '3000 to 5000 howling Communists' to heckle national meetings. Hanna was surprised: she assumed that she was considered a possible danger, but could not see why, as she had been giving lectures for twenty-seven years without any disruption, and had had a rapturous reception with the astronaut Neil Armstrong in Bremen in 1970. Nevertheless, early in September she agreed to a smaller venue with entry by invitation only, and left the details to Hertel, assuming that he would co-operate with the local flying clubs.

She forgot all about her November engagement in Bremen while she went again to Los Angeles and Washington. An annual visit to America was becoming as much a tradition as was spending several weeks each year in Austria. It boosted her morale as much as flying and singing in the Alps rested and relaxed her. A day or two before she left Washington, early in October, four representatives of the National Air and Space Museum at the Smithsonian Institution recorded a long interview with her in Jean Ross Howard's apartment: to her annoyance, she felt that they were concentrating on her experiences in the bunker, rather than on what she wanted to tell them about her flying achievements. Even in America, where she was used to appreciation, it seemed that she could not escape the repercussions of that one flight into Berlin. Wary of the use to which the tape might be put, she refused to assign the copyright to the Smithsonian.

As soon as she returned to Germany, Hanna contacted Hertel to find out what plans had been made for the Bremen lecture. In spite of his earlier fears, he had booked the biggest hall in the city, for 8 November. Three thousand invitations had been sent to twenty-five different organisations: she was irritated, but not alarmed, that they had been issued in the name of Stahlhelm. About fifty people were expected at a private meeting for Stahlhelm members only on the following day, as she had agreed.

It had unfortunately escaped Hanna's attention that 8 November was the eve of the fortieth anniversary of Kristallnacht. On 28 October, a number of newspaper articles appeared with headlines such as 'Protests against Stahlhelm evening' and 'Indignation over planned function': the mayor of Bremen, as well as the federation of trade unions, the local youth organisation, and various other groups were, it was reported, indignant that Stahlhelm Youth intended to hold a meeting on the eve of Kristallnacht with the woman pilot Hanna Reitsch as chief speaker. The mayor considered the timing of the meeting provocative, and feared that it would have an adverse effect on the reputation of Bremen. For the first time Hanna became aware that Stahlhelm's nationalism was considered to have fascist implications, and that Stahlhelm Youth—which was mentioned for the first time—was thought to be reminiscent of the Hitler Youth movement.

The instigator of the public attack on Hanna and Stahlhelm was Gunther Ruholl, the vicar of the suburban evangelical church of Bremen-Vahr. His comments had first been published in the church magazine, and were then repeated in the public press, in which he was quoted as having said: 'Should the planned event have the effect of glorifying Nazi belief, and in particular of exonerating the persecution of the Jews in the Third Reich, we would see it as an unacceptable provocation.'

'Stahlhelm Youth is in the tradition of Stahlhelm, which with the NSDAP, SA, and SS brought about the end of the Weimar Republic,' one newspaper stated. 'Hanna Reitsch is known as an incorrigible "war heroine" of the fascists and as Hitler's darling. She is still actively committed to the dissemination of Nazi belief.' In another report, Stahlhelm was described as a 'right-wing combat alliance for Europe', and Hanna as 'the woman, who in her book *Fliegen mein Leben* described the extermination of the Jews in gas chambers as "enemy propaganda" '. Hanna's reaction to the allegations was not reported, as no one had sought it.

She was appalled, and immediately cancelled her engagement. 'After our telephone conversation today and the discovery that my lecture cannot take place as planned before flyers, refugees, and former soldiers in the Congress Hall with the approval and agreement of the council, but only outside Bremen and clearly without the support of the senate, I must unfortunately cancel my appearance,' she wrote to Hertel. 'In addition to the above-mentioned reasons, I have the impression that my lecture about flying was, contrary to my previous assumption, being used as a political issue. You know that I have always and only been a pilot and that politics, of whatever sort, are not my thing.'

The Stahlhelm organisers had already reacted to the attack by offering to postpone the meeting, and announced its cancellation in the press on 31 October. For Hanna, the adverse publicity and the personal insults were a bombshell. All she had wanted to do was to give one of her talks about the joys of flying and to share her experiences and inspiration with a new audience. Even if she had connected the date with Kristallnacht, it would not have occurred to her that her lecture could be construed as a political act, even less as an attack on the Jews. She had after all put herself at risk by condemning the Kristallnacht attacks on the Jews.

Hanna fled to Salzburg, to commune with the souls of her parents, to lick her wounds, and to write long letters about the damage that Hertel had done to her mission and to the sales of her book: she had intended to sell signed copies at the meeting in Bremen, and to give the profit to the Wasserkuppe museum fund. 'Now Hertel has set my work—my reputation—

back years,' she complained, 'he has harmed me and my mission, the one and only reason I stayed in Germany and stayed alive, more than I can put into words.'

It was not, however, against Hertel, who had exonerated himself by cancelling the meeting, but against the mayor and the evangelical priest that she went into action. Nothing less than a public apology, and a retraction of the accusations published in the press would satisfy her. She insisted that she had never been 'Hitler's darling', had never actively or even passively disseminated or subscribed to Nazi or any other political beliefs, and had never dismissed the persecution of the Jews as 'enemy propaganda', although she had used the expression in the context of a wartime conversation with Peter Riedel.

Once again, her friends rushed into print and wrote letters on her behalf: Father Pehl, one of those who did so, was convinced that had Volkmar still been alive he would have prevented Hanna from falling into a political trap. The State Secretary, Heinrich Kohl, wrote a four-page letter to the mayor of Bremen and sent him Hanna's books to prove that the accusations made against her were libellous. Yvonne Pagniez and Lotte Schiffler wrote to Gunther Ruholl.

Waltraud Bals drafted a petition for the reinstatement of Hanna's honour which she confidently expected other women pilots to sign: 'The authors of these cruel lies are pursuing one aim, to harm Hanna spiritually and financially. They must not be allowed to succeed. Our gratitude for the help and support that we have experienced through Hanna could certainly hardly find a better expression than our joint effort to reinstate her reputation.' To her dismay, none of the Segelfliegerinnen would support her: sport and politics should, they felt, not be mixed, and the question was contentious.

# 15

# Death of
# a Patriot

Hanna's last Christmas and New Year greeting to her friends was a quotation attributed to St Francis of Assisi: 'Lord, make me an instrument of thy peace; where there is hatred, let me sow love; where there is injury, pardon; where there is doubt, faith; where there is despair, hope; where there is darkness, light; where there is sadness, joy.'

Lotte Schiffler received a three-page reply from Ruholl based on his interpretation of *Fliegen mein Leben,* which he considered a dangerous political book. He accused Hanna of extolling the virtues of the Third Reich and its leaders without pointing out their evils; she had, he maintained, described 'with unbelievable naïvety' her wish to help her homeland up to the last hour, but had not used hindsight to judge the Third Reich. Ruholl believed that Hanna represented an unacceptable viewpoint as strongly as she believed that she did not.

She was, as he said, undeniably politically naïve and trusting to the point of gullibility, but not dishonest. Even retrospectively, she was neither prepared nor able to deny the truth as she had known it, and with it her honour and that of her country. She did not feel qualified to make a political judgement and could not understand how her life could be seen in a political context. As far as she was concerned, her book was based on personal experience and fact.

That she had not written it with hindsight was deliberate: she would have considered it dishonest to bring post-war knowledge to bear on description of wartime feelings and experiences. Her sense of personal and national honour had compelled her to give her version of the truth about the past without making judgements. She disapproved of those who had adapted their views retrospectively and who had therefore become acceptable by 'distancing' themselves from the war: 'Not another who is wise after the event,' she had said to an ex-Luftwaffe pilot who had reminded her that he had foreseen the outcome of the war.

'When I imagine that I might have read this book as a boy with a passion for flying, I would not only have learnt about flying,' Ruholl wrote to Lotte Schiffler, 'but would also certainly have gained the impression that it was not so bad after all in the Third Reich.' That was precisely part of what Hanna had intended to achieve. She had been no different from many others: she had seen the good and had accepted it at face value and with relief. It had indeed, initially and for some time, not been 'so bad'—for some—under the Third Reich, which was why Hitler had been able to gain so much power. To acknowledge this was not, in her opinion, to set the Nazi regime up as an example, nor was it a statement of a post-war political attitude.

Ruholl's most serious accusation was that of anti-Semitism, based on Hanna's account of her confrontations with Riedel and Himmler. In the first edition of *Fliegen miein Leben*, she had included one sentence written with hindsight: 'Only after 1945 would I discover, to my intense consternation, how greatly Himmler had misled me, and that this terrible thing was after all true.' The admission was omitted in subsequent editions: the publisher felt that it was stating the obvious and that hindsight was irrelevant in a wartime narrative.

It was only in the wartime context that she had used the expression 'enemy propaganda' about the gas chambers, and many others had also initially assumed that the Holocaust was an invention of the enemy. Joachim Küttner told me that he had had difficulty in believing after the war that Germans had committed atrocities of which even he as a half-Jew had been unaware at the time.

At no point either in the book or elsewhere had Hanna stated that she still believed what she had assumed to be the truth in 1944, nor had she written or said anything else which might be construed as anti-Semitic. That the Holocaust had happened was a truth with which she, like many others, inevitably found it painful to come to terms. It was not something she talked about. If there had been any alternative to believing that fellow Germans had undertaken the systematic extermination of the Jews, Hanna would have welcomed it; but there was not, and she knew that there was not.

As Ruholl had accused her, in public, of anti-Semitism, Hanna felt that she had no choice but to take legal proceedings against him and his church for defamation of character. In the New Year, a civil action found in favour of Hanna against the evangelical church as represented by Ruholl. Legal costs were to be shared, with Hanna paying one-third and Ruholl's church two-thirds.

Ruholl appealed against the decision: once again, the court came down on Hanna's side and reallocated the costs so that she had only to pay a quarter. He refused to publish an apology unless Hanna reinstated the missing sentence. Hanna was equally intransigent: she had never said what he claimed she had, and would not compromise her honour by making it appear as if she was giving in.

Press statements about the judgement brought renewed publicity, in which the allegations made about Hanna, of course, gained as much attention as the fact that she had been exonerated from any expression of anti-Semitism. Her lawyer, and most of her friends, advised Hanna to let the matter drop. She would gladly have settled it out of court, but her opponents insisted on taking the case to a higher court as she would not make any of the concessions they demanded.

At the beginning and the end of February, she was treated for physical and mental symptoms of depression. She was under so much pressure that she was beginning to feel tired and old. Even this seemed less important than her battle for the truth and for her honour, which she considered inseparable.

In March, she again went to America, where she was able to throw off her depression and work on her fifth book. She stayed at the home of a young couple she had met the previous year at the international gliding competitions in France. It was a private visit: she became Karl and Suzanne Striedeck's Aunt Martha. As Karl's father had been born and brought up in Germany, it was usually an easy fiction to maintain, although when she unwittingly introduced herself to his brother Walter as his aunt from Germany it caused some hilarity.

Hanna spent several weeks in Pennsylvania with the Striedecks, whose 265-acre property, complete with an air-field, was an ideal retreat. At mealtimes, she had a new audience: Karl told me that he was enthralled by her accounts of flying adventure and disaster. Suzanne, who was the age that Hanna had been at the end of the war, tried to imagine herself alone as suddenly and as brutally: she found it remark-able that in spite of the tragedies in Hanna's life she was always happy and cheerful, as well as emotional and dramatic.

During the day, Hanna was usually alone except for two cats, and by the time she left she had completed nearly 400 handwritten pages of a book about her experiences as a test pilot. She had a list of eighty-six questions for her former colleagues: once they were answered the book would be almost ready for her publisher.

Joachim Küttner had told her about the joys of ridge-lying in the Appalachians. After a few flights she decided, egged on by Karl Striedeck, to make an attempt at a record before she left. Karl woke her early in the morning: 'Come on, Hanna. it's record flying weather.' It was very different from any flying she had ever done. Exhilarating and alarming, with long stretches over the forested bumps of the Appalachians where landing was impossible, it demanded concentration and physical fitness.

The flight was supervised in accordance with FAI proce-dures, and Karl was the official observer. As he and two other pilots flew alongside watching her the whole time, they were able to confirm in spite of a malfunctioning barograph that she did indeed break the women's world out-and-return record, with a distance of 805 km.

It seemed that whatever she did, Hanna was destined to be dogged by controversy: the validity of her record was contested. An American, Doris Groves, had also made a record attempt on the same day but had achieved a shorter flight. It was claimed on her behalf that Hanna's flight had not been correctly monitored and registered. Months later, letters were still going backwards and forwards arguing about which woman should be considered to hold the world record. Officially or not, Hanna had, just before her sixty-seventh birthday, made a longer flight in a glider than any other woman in the world.

More than 300 letters of congratulation were waiting for her on her return: her own letters had frequently referred to 'mountains of post', and this was one of the biggest mountains yet. She lost no time in writing enthusiastic accounts of her American long-distance flight to friends, and sending round her list of technical questions to former colleagues so that she could finish her book.

Her optimism gradually waned as the replies either came in or in some cases were refused: old rivalries and arguments were resurrected, it was impossible to make one person's version tally with another's, and doubts were cast on the accuracy of her account which made her wonder if her memory was indeed at fault. It was depressing, and Hanna began to think of abandoning the project and preparing instead a book about her mother, based on Emy Reitsch's verses and letters.

In the middle of May, Hanna set off for Austria, towing her glider. Although she made a number of flights, she did not manage anything approaching a record. The weather was unhelpful, and she was tired: although she would not admit it, the American flight had exhausted her, and she had still not recovered from the stress of the Bremen affair.

In Frankfurt, she was soon plunged into deepening depression by her problems over her new book, by the continuing cloud cast by the battle for her honour in Bremen, and by a letter from Louis de Lange accusing her in considerable detail of having misrepresented his participation in the Polish affair in *Höhen und Tiefen*. She was beginning to mistrust her own memory, and to feel that whatever she did was bound to go wrong.

She was neither eating nor sleeping well. She burst into tears over the telephone and with friends, and spent sleepless nights brooding over her honour. At a meeting of the Alte Adler, several people who knew her well thought that she looked ill and miserable. On 11 August, Kurt and Helma called to see her. They had planned to stay only for a few hours, but were so worried about her health that they stayed two days. She was supposed to be going to a meeting at Darmstadt, and felt that she both must and could not face it.

Kurt was unsympathetic: either she was ill and should admit it, or she was well and should carry out her duty. Afterwards he felt that he had perhaps been harsh with her. Before he and Helma left, they made Hanna promise to visit them in a fortnight and undergo medical tests in Hamburg: she was to telephone on the morning of 24 August to tell them whether she was fit enough to drive or would travel by train or plane.

On 22 August, Hanna told Gisela Holzrichter over the phone that she had pains in her heart. The next day, Joachim Küttner was passing through Frankfurt. He telephoned to ask her to drive out to the airport as she had often done before when he was there for an hour or two between flights. 'I really have a problem—I need you—I need your help,' she told him: 'But I don't think I can come—you come here.' Time was so short that he decided against it, and said that he would see her next time.

That evening Karl Pehl had supper with her at her flat. She seemed tired: he felt that her long and strenuous flight in America had exhausted her more than she admitted. 'My God, how long can she keep this up?' he wondered.

Hanna died in her bed that night. She was discovered early the next morning by Fräulein Walter, who had become worried when she was still not up some time after she usually did her exercises. Distraught, Fräulein Walter telephoned Father Pehl: 'Come quickly! Hanna is dead . . .'

It was Pehl who called the doctor, and then at eight o'clock telephoned Kurt, who was expecting Hanna to ring to tell him when and how she would arrive in Hamburg. He and Helma set out immediately. Although they had been worried about her, neither they nor anyone else had anticipated Hanna's death: she had always had so much vitality that it was impossible to believe that she could have died quietly and suddenly in her sleep. The doctor diagnosed the cause of death as a massive heart attack.

As Hanna had always said that she wanted to be buried 'in aller Stille,' *'very quietly')*, Kurt decided to postpone the announcement of her death until after the funeral. He managed to keep the arrangements secret, including the removal of her body to Salzburg. Hanna was at last to join her parents in the family grave. The only people who knew of her death and attended her funeral, apart from Kurt and Helma, Fräulein Walter, and Father Pehl, who conducted the funeral service, were the three Heuberger cousins and Hanna's friend Landa.

Landa told her choir, including some of the women who had serenaded Hanna across the water at Schloss Leopoldskron, that they were to meet her at the cemetery, but not why. At the graveside they sang an old part-song: 'Good night, good night, O world! . . .'

At Kurt's request, an old naval friend who worked for North German Radio arranged for Hanna's death to be announced two hours after she had been buried. This gave Kurt and Helma time to telephone a few friends and relatives first. Ironically, Kurt's concern to carry out his sister's wishes and to avoid publicity had the reverse effect: the secrecy gave rise to rumours. Many people were convinced she had committed suicide. Some even stated categorically that she had finally used her poison capsule. Others claimed imaginatively that because she was so controversial the German government had attempted to hush up her death for political reasons.

The suicide rumour was widespread, especially in German flying circles. Her brother was adamant that she had died of a heart attack. Karl Pehl, the last person apart from Fräulein Walter to see her alive, was equally certain that she did not commit suicide. Fräulein Walter was as loyal after Hanna's death as she had been during her life, and was certainly not prepared to entertain a suspicion which might cast a slur on Hanna's honour.

Among her closest friends, the majority refused to consider the suggestion that she might have taken her own life: it would, they said, have been totally contrary to her character. But others were equally convinced that she had at last expiated the guilt at her broken promise to von Greim. For many among them some of her oldest friends, the question remained open: Hanna had been near enough to suicide in the past, and depressed enough during the weeks preceding her death, for it to seem a possibility. There was, moreover, the precedent of her own family: she had seen the choice made by her father, and by von Greim, as honourable.

A small pistol was found among her belongings, but it appeared never to have been used. One mystery remains: what happened to the phial containing cyanide given to her in the bunker? Gretl Böss had returned it after Hanna's release from prison. Although several people have told me that they had seen it at various times, and were convinced that she still had it, there was no sign of it among her possessions after her death. She had neither shown it nor spoken of it to her brother.

Although suicide might seem a suitably dramatic end to a dramatic life, the truth is more prosaic. There was enough evidence of general exhaustion, increasingly poor health, and depression to make a heart attack a possibility, and Hanna had had recurrent mild heart trouble ever since the end of the war. She had made plans for the autumn and winter, including a reunion of old schoolfriends and the inaugural meeting of a Federation of European Women Pilots.

If Hanna had decided to make a final gesture, she would surely not have done so without making certain that everyone knew about it. She had fought her battle for the truth and for her own honour in public, and vociferously, and had always felt that she was in the right: if she had committed suicide, she would have wanted it known that she, Hanna Reitsch, pilot and patriot, had died honourably.

I am certain that Hanna did not intend to die; but I believe that she was afraid that she might die without completing her mission, and with her reputation still under threat, and that that fear contributed to her depression and exhaustion. She was, quite simply—as she had often claimed in the past—at the end of her strength.

Hanna's obsession with truth, or the truth as she saw it, had made her many enemies. Through her attempts to reinstate the honourable aspects of the past she had been for some a symbol of all that was best in Germany; but because of her refusal to condemn the past, she had become for others as much a symbol of Nazi Germany after the war as her devotion to duty had made her a heroine during the Nazi era. For this, she had, she was convinced, been deliberately made to suffer. Hanna Reitsch, who had been called the Joan of Arc of modern Germany, was psychologically burned at the stake.

After her death, she remained controversial. Her relatives and friends mourned her deeply. Almost everyone else who knew her either admired her uncritically, or persisted in remembering her as a symbol of everything that Germany wanted to forget. On one thing only was there agreement: her ability and courage as a pilot. For forty-seven years she had repeatedly proved herself in her chosen field, whether it was as a test pilot during the war or as a glider pilot in peacetime.

Even her obituaries were divided. There was almost universal praise for her courage and flying ability, and several eulogies about her as a person. Wilfred von Oven called her an 'example as a flyer, as a person, and as a German' whose 'big, warm heart' could not bear 'the worry about her Germany, our Germany'. But there were also a number of vitriolic political and personal condemnations in which the convention of not speaking ill of the recently dead was ignored. *Der Spiegel* called her the embodiment of 'the German national schizophrenia between . . . personal decency and collective barbarity'. *Die Zeit,* which summed her up as 'an excellent pilot and a naïve patriot', considered her misguided and blinkered, but grudgingly concluded that whatever she thought, she thought it honestly.

The most insulting article of all was written by Georg Salmony for the *Süddeutsche Zeitung*. It suggested that her courage and instinct in the air were opportunistic and put on for show. The danger of the yearning for heights shared in an extreme form by pilots and mountaineers was, Salmony wrote, that it was accompanied by 'temptations and seductions which can all too easily lead to the degradation of a noble sporting passion—as in the case of Hanna Reitsch'. He was equally scathing of her post-war life: 'It was not easy to create an image of a once proud, now badly damaged figurehead striving desperately for a place on the pedestal of world history out of this maze of fantasy, truth, delusion, obstinacy, and distorted idealism.' Salmony's vituperation provoked letters from angry readers: she was not as he had portrayed her, and it was her misfortune, not her fault, that she had been presented as an ideal of

German womanhood during the twelve years of the Hitler regime.

It was not only in the press that opinions were divided. In Baden-Baden a few weeks after her death, at the first meeting of the Federation of European Women Pilots, the British pioneering pilot Sheila Scott proposed a toast to Hanna Reitsch, who was to have been a founder member. 'It was', she told me, 'as if the room split in half, into pro-Hanna and anti-Hanna.' That even a proportion of the German women pilots persisted in seeing Hanna as a political symbol would not have surprised her, although she would have been hurt by their attitude.

The Bremen case was withdrawn: the evangelical church dropped its appeal against the judgement in favour of Hanna, and Kurt Reitsch decided that as this had vindicated her honour there was no need to carry on through another court. The press coverage given to the affair had magnified it and had cast a shadow over the last few months of Hanna's life, undoubtedly contributing indirectly to her death.

The argument over Hanna's last record was abandoned to allow her to rest in peace: the following March, Doris Groves created a new women's world record, of 1000 km. The German vice-president of the Whirly Girls, Irene Teutloff, raised 8000 marks for a Hanna Reitsch Memorial Trophy to be presented annually to the year's most outstanding woman helicopter pilot.

The tribute which Hanna would most have appreciated was a gathering of singers at an Austrian mountainside inn in November. This became an annual event, the Hanna Reitsch-Gedächtnis-Singen (Hanna Reitsch Remembrance Singing): the Saturday evening concert to an audience of Hanna's friends and admirers was followed by a Sunday morning ecumenical memorial service in the Catholic church.

Two years after her death, the eighty-year-old German writer Friedrich Franz von Unruh cited Hanna as an example in a slim book entitled *Ermutigung: Ein Appell on die Deutschen (Encouragement: An Appeal to the Germans)*. Von Unruh had fought and had been wounded in the First World War, and as a journalist in the 1930s had written warnings about another war and about the anti-Semitism of the new Nazi regime.

His contention after the Second World War was much the same as Hanna's: that the German people were unfairly made to suffer an unhealthy collective guilt, and needed a sense of the respectable aspects of their past and a belief in the future of their country. He put it better than Hanna had been able to: he was more politically aware, and was by profession a writer rather than a pilot, although he shared her mystical attitude towards flying, and held her up as a symbolic figure.

Like the Mother of Pondicherry, he called her 'a flyer in the higher sense', as well as 'the sister of Icarus' and 'a daughter of Heaven': Hanna Reitsch, whom he described as a tiny but energetic and inspiring figure, had by talking of flying shared with everyone who heard her a vision of international peace and brotherly understanding.

Until June 1987, Hanna's flat in Frankfurt remained exactly as it was when she died. Each year her brother Kurt and his wife spent several weeks meticulously sorting and filing her papers, helped by Fräulein Walter and Ernst Paulsen, a retired general and lawyer and the husband of Helma's cousin Carola. Kurt and Helma displayed a wartime phtograph of Hanna in pride of place on a small table.

They offered her flying-suit to the first woman helicopter pilot to fly with the German army's medical service. Her trophies and some of her books were given to flying friends, among them Waltraud Bals. Other books were presented to the Deutsches Museum in Munich and the Transport Museum in Berlin. The watercolour painted by Otto Fuchs in Libya was returned to him. Much of Hanna's furniture is now in Haus Schlesien, a museum and meeting-place for Silesian refugees, and forty files of letters and documents are in the Deutsches Museum in Munich.

Hanna's grave in the Salzburg cemetery has become a shrine for German and Austrian glider pilots. There are always lighted candles and fresh flowers under the rugged marble headstone designed by Hanna several years after the war. Her name, with the title of Flugkapitän of which she was so proud and the insignia of the Alte Adler, and the dates of her birth and death have been added to those of the rest of her family.

The closing words of one of her kinder obituaries, which called her 'a politically naïve patriot who believed that she had only served her Fatherland', seems a suitable epitaph: 'Loved by many, abused by many, Hanna Reitsch will not be forgotten.'

# Appendix 1

*Extracts from a letter by Hanna Reitsch in
June 1946 to her brother Kurt*

Whether fate will ever allow us, the sole surviving members of our family, to see each other again, only the good Lord knows . . .I hope that this letter will reach you somehow, somewhere. It will give you a truthful picture of the last historic days as I experienced them in the Führer's bunker in the Chancellery, and will describe what I felt then, not how I see it now from a greater distance. You must have been deeply upset and horrified by the ignoble, untrue, and tendentious stories invented by the enemy which have appeared in the press as 'apparent accounts' by me and have been published as falsified 'Eye-witness accounts of Hanna Reitsch' . . . I hope . . . that the honour of our family will not be affected.

*In Berlin:*

I had torn a sleeve off my blouse and wrapped it tightly round his [von Greim's] leg to stop the bleeding from the wound in his foot . . . Dr Stumpfegger . . . treated the wound . . . Herr von Greim had again regained consciousness, but looked dreadfully pale . . . I was there during the medical treatment and helped quietly when I could.

The Führer's bunker lay three floors beneath the ground: half-way down the stairs Frau Goebbels met us. I had never seen her in my life, but we recognised each other from pictures. In her pleasure at our arrival she hugged me and accompanied us down to the lowest part of the bunker (the so-called Führer-Bunker), where the Führer came towards us in his simple grey soldier's outfit. He was leaning forwards slightly, both his arms were trembling ceaselessly, and his eyes did not seem to belong to the present. In a surprisingly quiet voice he greeted us, visibly moved to see that Herr von Greim was wounded. In answer to his question, Herr von Greim reported on our flight and told him that I had saved his life. Thereupon the Führer looked at me and said in a firm but low voice: 'Brave woman, there is still truth and honour in the world.'

Then Herr von Greim learnt why he had been ordered to Berlin: 'Goering has betrayed and forsaken me,' said the Führer, and showed Herr von Greim the radio signal he had received from Goering. 'I have had him arrested and have removed all his duties.'

The Führer appointed Herr von Greim commander of the Luftwaffe and at the same time promoted him to field marshal.

It was clear from Herr von Greim's expression what inner torment such an appointment caused him, right at the end of the collapse [of Germany]. It was in his opinion Goering's moral duty to be there, at the side of the Führer. Goering had, until the moment of his arrest, not wanted to relinquish the responsibility and leadership of the Luftwaffe, and was determined to keep his position of trust with the Führer. Now, when the catastrophe was taking its unavoidable course, he should have been ready to bear defeat and its consequences beside the Führer.

German flyers were devoting their lives in the bravest, most honourable way, courageously ready to face death, in the hope that they might save their Fatherland, and with trust in the leader and pride in their air force and its chief. Leadership may be right or wrong—it is not for me to judge—but if one is responsible to this leadership, one must be ready to go down with it. There is a concept of 'soldier's honour' everywhere in the world. For that reason the newly appointed field marshal decided, for the honour of his flyers and of the air force for which he had been made responsible, to stay in the place where Goering should have been. It made no difference whether this would mean his life or his death. So he stayed in the bunker, and I with him.

The Führer asked me to take on the care of the wounded man. So it came about that suddenly I found myself for the first time in my life in the closest proximity to the Führer . . .

Everyone stayed dressed ready for an alarm [during the night]. So that I could occasionally get some rest, my sleeping place was the stretcher on which Herr von Greim had been carried down. My profession had changed completely—I was no more and no less than a nurse . . . What could have been more satisfying, in spite of our position, than to be allowed to help in this way? Is it then any wonder that the other inhabitants of the bunker only saw me as cheerful? What does one's own life matter when set against the catastrophe in which countless others are giving their lives—on one's own side, as well as on that of the enemy? Each one strengthened by the same conviction, spurred on or misled by his side's propaganda to fight for his country, for justice, and for freedom.

In the meantime I met the other inhabitants of the bunker . . . The behaviour of all, from my experience, was amazingly controlled and calm. But I saw and felt much in silence which I would have preferred never to have known. I wrote all my most personal impressions to our parents, so that I could have conversations with them in my mind. I brought these letters with me out of the bunker . . . They are hidden, where no one will find them. I often wished in the bunker that I had never been born!

As I was devoting myself exclusively to the care of Herr von Greim and to keeping the children of Dr Goebbels occupied, I had little contact with the other inhabitants . . . I taught them [the children] part-songs and was delighted at how musical they were. The thought that this was perhaps one of the last hours of their lives seemed not only to catch in one's throat, but almost to take away one's reason.

As situation reports came in the tension increased hourly

. . . In the single short conversation which I myself had with the Führer, I heard the reason for his decision to stay in Berlin and heard of the last, the only, hope, which he put into words, but which he can himself in his inner thoughts scarcely have believed: the relief of Berlin by General Wenck . . . For a layman, who had come from outside, these thought processes were incomprehensible, as they in no way corresponded with reality. If Wenck did not succeed, the Führer told me, he, together with Eva Braun, would take their own lives, so that as leader of the country he would not fall into Russian hands . . .

Among my most dreadful memories is the news which went from mouth to mouth in the bunker during 27 April: SS-Gruppenführer Fegelein was supposed to have tried secretly to escape from the bunker and to have been caught in civilian clothing by the Wehrmacht on the west side of the city and was to be shot by order of the Führer. Hitler's brother-in-law—Himmler's trusted friend—the link-man between the two—who was against whom, who was betraying whom?—was the tormented question which burned in my mind—Herr von Greim and I became lonelier from hour to hour.

During 27 April a Ju 52 landed on the East–West Axis. It had been commissioned to take Herr von Greim and me out. I heard von Greim's heated telephone conversation when he heard of it. He had not ordered a rescue attempt, and he did not want anyone's life put in danger on his behalf as he had decided to stay where he was. If the Führer had had the slightest intention of saving himself by getting out, Adolf Hitler could easily have seized the opportunity which this presented. It would be a total mis-interpretation of Hitler even to suspect this, as it was completely opposed to his method, his attitude, and his character.

. . . It is difficult to describe the feelings one has while fate slowly, inexorably takes its course until one is crushed by it. I was racked by the thought of what appalling torment each hour must be bringing outside to the people of Berlin . . . Nothing is more terrible than to be condemned to inactivity . . .

A rumour brought the news that the Russians had reached the end of the Wilhelmstrasse and had moreover got as far as the Potsdamer Platz. At about one in the morning the Führer arrived in our room; even paler, even more bent, his voice even duller and his expression even more distant than when I had first seen him on our arrival . . . 'Now Himmler has betrayed me too,' he said shortly. Through a Reuters news flash he had heard from San Francisco that Himmler had tried through Count Bernadotte of Sweden to offer capitulation behind his back. The ground seemed to disappear beneath my feet. What was treason, what betrayal, where were truth and honour—what was true, what false? 'You must leave the bunker as fast as possible,' the Führer continued, 'we have heard that during the afternoon the Russians plan to storm the Chancellery. If it is possible to bomb their preparations with a swift attack on the streets leading to the Chancellery, we can gain at least 24 hours, maybe even 48, and enable General Wenck to reach here in time.' The radio balloon had been shot down during the night and the Russians must have had the key to the radio. So no news could be sent out of the bunker without it being known to the Russians . . .

Herr von Greim himself had to take charge of issuing the order so that—or so the Führer believed—he and Berlin could be relieved. An Arado 96, which had landed safely on the East–West Axis . . . could be used. I was inwardly beside myself: how could one have the slightest belief in a rescue operation by General Wenck and for that reason send the wounded field marshal out into this hell? My strong suggestion that this would neither save the others nor change their situation was rejected with horror in the bunker.

Within 30 minutes we had left the bunker: it was about half past one in the morning. We couldn't say goodbye to the others, only briefly take our leave from the Führer and our two friends, Ambassador Hevel and General von Below, from Frau Goebbels and a few others who happened to be standing around. How hard is such a leave-taking, in which one leaves the others to their certain death, it is beyond human power to express . . .

# Appendix 2

## Extracts from 'The Last Days in Hitler's Air Raid Shelter' Interrogation Summary

*The interrogation summary entitled 'The Last Days in Hitler's Air Raid Shelter' and held in the US National Archives, Washington, DC, is dated 8 October 1945: although Hanna Reitsch did not see the summary, which was based on conversations with Captian Work, she objected strongly to certain parts of it as they were quoted in books and articles. The text is given with the original spelling. Hanna's main objections are given in italics and are enclosed in square brackets.*

1. *Source*
   Name: Fraulein Hanna Reitsch
   Rank: Flugkapiten (Captain of the Air—Honorary title given for outstanding aeronautical achievement).
   Date of birth: 29 March 1912.
   Marital Status: Single.
   Occupation: Test-pilot and aeronautical research expert.
   Citizenship: German.
   Address: Leopolds Krone Castle, Salzburg, Austria.
   Political Status: Non-party member.
   Decorations: Iron Cross first class.

2. *Introduction:* This report is the story of the last days of the War as they were experienced by Hanna Reitsch,

the well-known German test-pilot and aeronautical expert. Her story does not pretend to add any sensational details to what is already known of those days; it is rather an eyewitness account of what actually happened in the highest places during the last moments of the War. Her account of the flight into Berlin to report to Hitler and of her stay in the Fuehrer's bunker is probably as accurate a one as will be obtained of those last days . . .

3. Her story is remarkable only in that she played a small part in the events of the War's end and that she had personal contact with the top-bracket Nazis as that end descended upon them. It is also of interest as it is likely that Reitsch is one of the last, if not the very last person who got out of the shelter alive. Her information is evaluated as reliable and it is possible that her story may throw some light or perhaps serve as an aid to a fuller knowledge of what happened during the last days of Berlin and of the War.

5. It will be noted that much of the report concerns itself with the Nazi and German interpretation of 'honor'. Reitsch herself, in answering queries, carefully weighs the 'honor' aspects of every remark and then gives her answers carefully but truthfully. The use of the word amounts practically to a fetish complex with the source and is almost an incongruous embodiment of her entire philosophy. Her constant repetition of the word is by no means as obvious to her as it is to the interrogator, nor is the meaning the same, nor does she recognise the incongruous use she makes of the word. Therefore, each time 'honor' appears it is apologetically submitted in quotations.

6. She tells her story in conversational form, and although it is, in part, reproduced in that manner here, no pretense is made that the quotations are in all cases exact; they are simply given as she remembers them. [*In many cases she later disclaimed ever having used anything approximating to the words quoted.*] . . .

7. *The Trip to Berlin:* Hitler had sent a telegram to Munich on the 24th April to Lieutenant General Ritter von

Greim, instructing him to report to the Reichschancellery on a highly urgent matter. The problem of getting into Berlin was by then a very precarious one, as the Russians had practically encircled the city. Greim, however, decided that by availing himself of Hanna Reitsch as pilot, the entrance might be accomplished by means of an autogiro [*helicopter*], which could land on the streets or in the gardens of the Reichschancellery.

9. Forty fighters were taken to fly cover. Almost immediately upon take-off they were engaged by Russian aircraft. A running, hedgehopping flight got them to the Gatow airfield, the only Berlin field still in German hands. Their own craft got through with nothing more than a few wing shots but the cost was heavy to the supporting fighters [*denied by HR*].

12. *Arrival at Hitler's Shelter:* Greim and Reitsch arrived in the bunker between 6 and 7 o'clock on the evening of the 26th of April. First to meet them was Frau Goebbels, who fell upon Reitsch with tears and kisses, expressing her astonishment that anyone still possessed the courage and loyalty to come to the Fuehrer, in stark contrast to all those who had deserted him. Greim was immediately taken to the operation room where Hitler's physician tended the injured foot.

13. Hitler came into the sick room, according to Reitsch, with his face showing deep gratitude over Greim's coming. He remarked something to the effect that even a soldier has the right to disobey an order when everything indicates that to carry it out would be futile and useless. Greim then reported his presence in the official manner.

14. *Hitler's Denunciation of Goering:*
   Hitler: 'Do you know why I have called you?'
   Greim: 'No, mein Fuehrer.'
   Hitler: 'Because Hermann Goering has betrayed and deserted me and his Fatherland. Behind my back he has established contacts with the enemy. His action was a mark of cowardice. And against my orders he has gone to save himself at Berchtesgaden. From there he sent me a disre-

spectful telegram. He said that I had once named him as my successor and that now, as I was no longer able to rule from Berlin, he was prepared to rule from Berchtesgaden in my place. He closes the wire by stating that if he had no answer from me by nine-thirty on the date of the wire he would assume my answer to be in the affirmative.'

15. The scene Reitsch describes as 'touchingly dramatic,' that there were tears in the Fuehrer's eyes as he told them of Goering's treachery, that his head sagged, that his face was deathly pallid, and that the uncontrollable shaking of his hands made the message flutter wildly as he handed it to Greim.

16. The Fuehrer's face remained deathly earnest as Greim read. Then every muscle in it began to twitch and his breath came in explosive puffs; only with effort did he gain sufficient control to actually shout:

17. 'An ultimatum! A crass ultimatum!! Now nothing remains. Nothing is spared me. No allegiances are kept, no "honor" lived up to, no disappointments that I have not had, no betrayals that I have not experienced, and now this above all else. Nothing remains. Every wrong has already been done me.'

18. As Reitsch explains it, the scene was in the typical 'et tu Brute' manner, full of remorse and self-pity. It was long before he could gather enough self-control to continue. [*HR later claimed that although description and conversation were exaggerated they were approximately accurate in tone.*]

19. With eyes hard and half-closed and in a voice unusually low he went on: 'I immediately had Goering arrested as a traitor to the Reich, took from him all his offices, and removed him from all organizations. That is why I have called you to me. I hereby declare you Goering's successor as Oberbefehlshaber der Luftwaffe. In the name of the German people I give you my hand.'

20. *'To die for the "Honor" of the Luftwaffe':* Greim and Reitsch were deeply stunned with the news of Goering's

betrayal. As with one mind they grasped Hitler's hands and begged to be allowed to remain in the bunker, and with their own lives atone for the great wrong that Goering had perpetrated against the Fuehrer, against the German people, and against the Luftwaffe itself. To save the 'honor' of the flyers who had died, to reestablish the 'honor' of the Luftwaffe that Goering had destroyed, and to guarantee the 'honor' of their land in the eyes of the world, they begged to remain. Hitler agreed to all of this and told them they might stay and told them too that their decision would long be remembered by the Luftwaffe. It had been previously arranged with operations at Rechlin that an aircraft was to come in the next day to take Greim and Reitsch out of Berlin. Now that they decided to stay it was impossible to get the information out. Rechlin, in the meantime, was sending plane after plane, each shot down in turn by the Russians. Finally on the 27th a Ju 52, loaded with SS guards and ammunition, managed to land on the East—West traffic axis, but because Reitsch and Greim had intended to stay, was sent back empty. [*This was the only aircraft mentioned elsewhere by HR.*] (The order cashiering Goering was released from the underground headquarters sometime on the 23rd of April.)

21. *Hitler Sees the Cause As Lost:* Later that first evening Hitler called Reitsch to him in his room. She remembers that his face was deeply lined and that there was a constant film of moisture in his eyes. In a very small voice he said, 'Hanna, you belong to those who will die with me. Each of us has a vial of poison such as this,' with which he handed her one for herself and one for Greim. 'I do not wish that one of us falls to the Russians alive, nor do I wish our bodies to be found by them. Each person is responsible for destroying his body so that nothing recognizable remains. Eva and I will have our bodies burned. You will devise your own method [*not mentioned elsewhere by HR*]. Will you please inform von Greim?'

22. Reitsch sank to a chair in tears, not, she claims, over the certainty of her own end but because for the first time she knew that the Fuehrer saw the cause as lost.

Through the sobs she said, 'Mein Fuehrer, why do you stay? Why do you deprive Germany of your life? When the news was released that you would remain in Berlin to the last, the people were amazed with horror. "The Fuehrer must live so that Germany can live," the people said. Save yourself, mein Fuehrer, that is the will of every German.'

23. 'No Hanna, if I die it is for the "honor" of our country, it is because as a soldier I must obey my own command that I would defend Berlin to the last. My dear girl, I did not intend it so, I believed firmly that Berlin would be saved at the banks of the Oder. [*HR objected that Hitler never either used her first name, nor called her his dear girl, but addressed her formally as was suitable.*] Everything we had was moved to hold that position. You may believe that when our best efforts failed, I was the most horror-struck of all. Then when the encirclement of the city began the knowledge that there were three million of my country-men still in Berlin made it necessary that I stay to defend them. By staying I believed that all the troops of the land would take example through my act and come to the rescue of the city. I hoped that they would rise to superhuman efforts to save me and thereby save my three million country-men. But, my Hanna, I still have hope. The army of General Wenck's is moving up from the south. He must and will drive the Russians back long enough to save our people. Then we will fall back to hold again.'

24. It appeared almost as if he believed this himself and as the conversation closed, he was walking about the room with quick, stumbling strides, his hands clasped behind him and his head bobbing up and down as he walked. Although his words spoke of hope, Hanna claims that his face showed that the War was over.

25. Hanna returned to Greim's bedside, handed him the poison, and then decided with him, should the end really come, that they would quickly drink the contents of the vial and then each pull the pin from a heavy grenade and

hold it tightly to their bodies. [*Grenades are mentioned only in the interrogation report.*]

26. Late in the night of 26th to 27th April the first heavy barrage bracketed the Chancellery. The splattering of heavy shells and the crashing of falling buildings directly above the air-raid shelter tightened the nervous strain of everyone so that here and there deep sobbing came through the doors [*denied*]. Hanna spent the night tending Greim, who was in great pain, and in getting grenades ready in the event that the Russians should enter the Chancellery grounds before morning.

27. *Hitler's Guests in the Shelter:* The next morning she was introduced to the other occupants and learned for the first time the identity of all those who were facing the end with the Fuehrer. Present in the elaborate shelter on the 27th of April were Goebbels and his wife with their six children; State Secretary Neaman [*sic*]: Hitler's right hand, Reichsleiter Martin Bormann; Hevel from Ribbentrop's office; Admiral Vosz [*sic*] as representative from Doenitz; General Krebs of the infantry and his adjutant Burgdorf; Hitler's personal pilot, Hansel Bauer; another pilot Baetz; Eva Braun; SS Obergruppenfuehrer Fegelein as liaison between Himmler and Hitler and husband of Eva Braun's sister; Hitler's personal Physician, Dr Stumpfecker [*sic*]; Oberst von Below, Hitler's Luftwaffe Adjutant; Dr Lorenz representing Reichspresse chief Dr Dietrich for the German press; two of Hitler's secretaries, a Frau Christian, wife of the General der Flieger Christian and a Fräulein Kreuger; and various SS orderlies and messengers. Reitsch claims that these composed the entire assembly.

28. A regular visitor during the last days was Reichsjugendfuehrer Axman who was commanding a Hitlerjugend division committed to the defense of the city. From Axman came current information as to the ground situation against the Russians which was well mirrored by the increasingly despondent manner of each visit.

29. *Another Betrayal:* Late in the afternoon of the 27th Obergruppenfuehrer Fegelein disappeared. Shortly there-

after it was rumoured that he had been captured on the outskirts of Berlin disguised in civilian clothes, claiming to be a refugee. The news of his capture was immediately brought to Hitler who instantly ordered him shot. The rest of the evening Fegelein's betrayal weighed heavily on the Fuehrer and in conversation he indicated a half-way doubt as to Himmler's position, fearing that Fegelein's desertion might have been known and even condoned by the SS leader.

30.  *Observations on Shelter Occupants:* Reitsch had little contact with most of the people in the shelter, being mostly occupied in nursing von Greim, but she did have the opportunity to speak to many of them and observe their reactions under the trying conditions of the last days in the bunker . . .

31.  *Doctor Goebbels:* She describes Goebbels as being insanely incensed over Goering's treachery. He strode about his small, luxurious quarters like an animal, muttering vile accusations concerning the Luftwaffe leader and what he had done. The precarious military situation of the moment was Goering's fault. Their present plight was Goering's fault. Should the war be lost, as it certainly now seemed it would be, that too would be Goering's fault.

32.  'That swine,' Goebbels said, 'who has always set himself up as the Fuehrer's greatest support now does not have the couarge to stand beside him. As if that were not enough, he wants to replace the Fuehrer as head of the State. He, an incessant incompetent, who has destroyed the Fatherland with his mishandling and stupidity, now wants to lead the entire nation. By this alone he proves that he was never truly one of us, that at heart he was always weak and a traitor.'

33.  All this, as Hanna saw it, was in the best theatrical manner, with much hand waving and fine gestures, made even more grotesque by the jerky up-and-down hobbling as he strode about the room. When he wasn't railing about Goering he spoke to the world about the example those in the bunker were setting for history. As on a platform and gripping a chair-back like a rostrum he said:

34. 'We are teaching the world how men die for their "honor." Our deaths shall be an eternal example to all Germans, to all friends and enemies alike. One day the world will acknowledge that we did right, that we sought to protect the world against Bolshevism with our lives. One day it will be set down in the history of all time.'

35. It appears that Goebbels exercised his greatest ability to the very last. The rooms of Goebbels and Reitsch adjoined each other and doors were usually open. [*HR dismissed this as 'nonsense'.*] Through them the Goebbels oratory would sound out at any hour of day or night [*also 'nonsense'.*] And always the talk was of 'honor', of 'how to die,' of 'standing true to the Fuehrer to the last,' of 'setting an example that would long blaze as a holy thing from the pages of history.'

36. One of the last things Reitsch remembers hearing from the lips of the propaganda master was: 'We shall go down for the glory of the Reich, so that the name of Germany will live forever.' Even Reitsch was moved to conclude that the Goebbels display, in spite of the tenseness of the situation, was a bit over-drawn and out-and-out theatrical. She claims that in her opinion Goebbels, then as he always had, performed as if he were speaking to a legion of historians who were avidly awaiting and recording every word. She adds that her own dubious opinions regarding Goebbels' mannerisms, his superficiality, and studied oratory, were well substantiated by these outbursts. She claims, too, that after listening to these tirades she and von Greim often asked each other, with a sad, head-shaking attitude, 'Are these the people who ruled our country?'

37. *Frau Goebbels:* Frau Goebbels she described as a very brave woman, whose control, which was at most times strong, did break down now and then to pitiful spasms of weeping. Her main concern was her children, and in their presence her manner was always delightful and cheery. Much of her day was occupied in keeping the children's clothes clean and tidy [*more 'nonsense'*] and as

they had only the clothes they wore this kept Frau Goebbels occupied. Often she would quickly retire to her room to hide the tears. It appears from Hanna's description that Frau Goebbels probably represented the epitome of nazi indoctrination.

38. If the Third Reich could not live she preferred to die with it, nor would she allow her children to outlive it. In recognition of the example she embodied of true German womanhood, Hitler, in the presence of all the occupants of the bunker, presented her with his personal gold party insignia [*before HR's arrival: Frau G told her about it*]. 'A staunch pillar of the "honor" on which National Socialism was built and the German Fatherland founded,' was his approximate remark as he pinned it to her dress.

39. Frau Goebbels often thanked God that she was alive so that she could kill her children to save them from whatever 'evil' would follow the collapse. To Reitsch she said, 'My dear Hanna, when the end comes you must help me if I become weak about the children. You must help me to help them out of this life. They belong to the Third Reich and to the Fuehrer and if those two things cease to exist there can be no further place for them. But you must help me. My greatest fear is that at the last moment I will be too weak.'

40. It is Hanna's belief that in the last moment she was not weak.

42. *The Goebbels children:* The Goebbels children numbered six. Their names and approximate ages were: Hela, 12; Hilda, 11; Helmut, 9; Holde, 7; Hedda, 5; Heide, 3. They were the one bright spot of relief in the stark death-shadowed life of the bunker. Reitsch taught them songs which they sang for the Fuehrer and for the injured von Greim. Their talk was full of being in 'the cave' with their 'Uncle Fuehrer' and in spite of the fact that there were bombs outside, nothing could really harm them as long as they were with him. And anyway 'Uncle Fuehrer' had said that soon the soldiers would come and drive the Russians away, and then tomorrow they could all go back to play in

their garden. Everyone in the bunker entered into the game of making time as pleasant as possible for them. Frau Goebbels repeatedly thanked Reitsch for making their last days enjoyable, as Reitsch often gathered them about her and told them long stories of her flying and of the places she had been and the countries she had seen.

43. *Eva Braun:* It seems to Reitsch that Hitler's 'girl friend' remained studiously true to her position as the 'show-piece' in the Fuehrer's circle. Most of her time was occupied in finger nail polishing, changing of clothes for each hour of the day, and all the other little feminine tasks of grooming, combing, and polishing. [*HR denied ever having said any of this.*] She seemed to take the prospect of dying with the Fuehrer as quite matter of fact, with an attitude that seemed to say: '* * * had not the relationship been of 12 long years duration and had she not seriously threatened suicide when Hitler once wanted to be rid of her. This would be a much easier way to die and much more proper * * *.' Her constant remark was 'Poor, poor Adolf, deserted by everyone, betrayed by all. Better that ten thousand others die than that he be lost to Germany.' [*She also denied reporting this.*]

44. In Hitler's presence she was always charming and thoughtful of his every comfort. But only while she was with him was she completely in character, for all the while he was out of ear-shot she would rave about all the ungrateful swine who had deserted their Fuehrer and that each of them should be destroyed. All her remarks had an adolescent tinge and it appeared that the only 'good' Germans at the moment were those who were caught in the bunker and that all the others were traitors because they were not there to die with him [*all comments attributed to HR on Eva Braun denied.*] The reasons for her willingness to die with the rest were similar to those of Frau Goebbels. She was simply convinced that whatever followed the Third Reich would not be fit to live in for a true German. Often she expressed sorrow for those people who were unable to destroy themselves

as they would be forever forced to live without 'honor' and reduced instead to living as empty beings without souls.

45. Reitsch emphasises that Braun was very apparently of rather shallow mentality, but she also agrees that she was a very beautiful woman. Beyond fulfilling her purpose, Reitsch considers it highly unlikely that Braun had any control or influence over Hitler. The rumor of the last-minute marriage ceremony Reitsch considers as highly unlikely, not only because she believes that Hitler had no such intention, but also because the circumstances in the bunker in the last days would have made such a ceremony ludicrous. Certainly, up to the time Reitsch left the bunker, hardly a day before Hitler's death was announced, there had not been the slightest mention of such a ceremony. The rumor that there had been children out of the union, Reitsch quickly dismisses as fantastic.

46. *Martin Bormann:* Bormann moved about very little, kept instead very close to his writing desk. He was 'recording the momentous events in the bunker for posterity.' Every word, every action, went down on his paper. Often he would visit this person or that to scowlingly demand what the exact remark had been that passed between the Fuehrer and the person he had just had an audience with. Things that passed between other occupants of the bunker were also carefully recorded. This document was to be spirited out of the bunker at the very last moment so that, according to the modest Bormann, it could, 'take its place among the greatest chapters of German history.' [*HR denied any knowledge of Bormann's bunker activities.*]

47. *Adolf Hitler:* Throughout Hanna's stay in the bunker Hitler's manner and physical condition sunk to lower and lower depths. At first he seemed to be playing the proper part of leading the defense of Germany and Berlin. And at first this was in some manner possible as communications were still quite reliable. Messages were telephoned to a flak tower and from there were radioed out by means of a portable, balloon-suspended aerial. But each day this

was more and more difficult until late in the afternoon of the 28th and all day on the 29th communications were almost impossible . . .

48. Occasionally he still seemed to hold to the hope of General Wenck's success in breaking through from the South. He talked of little else, and all day on the 28th and 29th he was mentally planning the tactics that Wenck might use in freeing Berlin. He would stride about the shelter, waving a road map that was fast distintegrating from the sweat of his hands and planning Wenck's campaign with anyone who happened to be listening [*later denied*]. When he became overly excited he would snatch the map from where it lay, pace with a quick, nervous stride about the room, and loudly 'direct' the city's defense with armies that no longer existed (as even Wenck, unknown to the Fuehrer, had already been routed and destroyed).

49. Reitsch describes it as a pathetic thing, the picture of a man's complete disintegration. A comic-tragedy of futility and uselessness. The picture of a man running almost blindly from wall to wall in his last retreat waving papers that fluttered like leaves in his nervous, twitching hands, or sitting stooped and crumpled before his table moving buttons to represent his non-existent armies, back and forth on a sweat-stained map, like a young boy playing at war. [*HR later denied having seen or described this.*]

50. *The Possibility That Hitler Still Lives:* The possibility that Hitler might have gotten out of the bunker alive, Reitsch dismisses as completely absurd. She claims that she is convinced that the Hitler she left in the shelter was physically incapable to have gotten away. 'Had a path been cleared for him from the bunker to freedom he would not have had the strength to use it,' she says. She believes too, that at the very end he had no intention to live, that only the Wenck hope stayed his hand from putting the mass suicide plan into operation. News that Wenck could not get through, she feels, would immediately have set off

the well-rehearsed plans of destruction. [*HR later claimed that there were no rehearsals, at least while she was present.*]

51. When confronted with the rumor that Hitler might still be alive in Tyrol and that her own flight to that area, after she had left the bunker, might be more than coincidental, she appears deeply upset that such opinions are even entertained. She says only, 'Hitler is dead! The man I saw in the shelter could not have lived. He had no reason to live and the tragedy was that he knew it well, knew it perhaps better than anyone else did.'

52. *Hanna's Opinion of the Fuehrer:* It is apparent from Reitsch's conversation that she held the Fuehrer in high esteem. It is also true when she says that her 'good' opinion suffered considerably during the closing stages of the war. She is emphatic when she describes the apparent mismanagement she observed and learned of in the bunker . . .

53. Hanna claims that Hitler the idealist died, and his country with him, because of the incompetence of Hitler the soldier and Hitler the statesman. She concludes, still with a faint touch of allegiance, that no one who knew him would deny his idealistically motivated intentions nor could they deny that he was simply infinitely incompetent to rule his country, that one of his great faults was proper character analysis in the people about him which led to the selection of persons equally incompetent to fill important positions. (Most important example: Goering.)

54. She repeatedly remarked that never again must such a person be allowed to gain control of Germany or of any country. But strangely enough she does not appear to hold him personally responsible for many of the wrongs and evils that she recognises completely and is quick to point out. She says rather, 'A great part of the fault lies with those who led him, lured him, criminally misdirected him, and informed him falsely. But that he himself selected the men who led him can never be forgiven.'

55. *A Criminal Against the World:* 'Hitler ended his life as a criminal against the world,' but she is quick to add, 'he did not begin it that way. At first his thoughts were only of how to make Germany healthy again, how to give his people a life free from economic insufficiencies and social maladjustments. To do this he gambled much, with a stake that no man has the right to jeopardise—the lives of his people. This was the first great wrong, his first great failure. But once the first few risks had been successful, he fell into the faults of every gambler, he risked more and more, and each time that he won was more easily led to the next gamble.' According to Reitsch it all began with the occupation of the Ruhr. This was the first and most difficult gamble of all and when the world did not answer the Ruhr bluff with war every succeeding risk became progressively easier.

56. Each success made the enthusiasm of the people greater and this gave him the necessary support to take the next step. The end-result, Reitsch claims, was that Hitler himself underwent a character change that transformed him from a idealistically motivated benefactor to a grasping, scheming despot, a victim of his own delusions of grandeur. 'Never again,' she concludes, 'in the history of the world must such power be allowed to rest with one man.'

57. *Suicide Council:* On the night of the 27th to 28th the Russian bombardment of the Chancellery reached the highest pitch it had yet attained. The accuracy, to those in the shelter below, was astounding. It seemed as if each shell landed in exactly the same place as the one before, all dead-center on the Chancellery buildings. As this indicated that the Russian ground troops would over-run the area at any moment, another suicide council was called by the Fuehrer. All plans as to the destruction of the bodies of everyone in the shelter were gone over again. The decision was that as soon as the Russians reached the Chancellery grounds the mass suicide would begin. Last instructions were given as to the use of the poison vials [*there was no such council, HR later insisted*].

58. The group was hypnotized with the suicide rehearsal and a general discussion was entered into to determine in which manner the most thorough destruction of the human body could be performed [*denied.*] Then everyone made little speeches swearing allegiance again and again to the Fuehrer and to Germany. Yet, through it all, ran the faint hope that Wenck might get in the hold long enough to effect an evacuation. But even on the 27th, Reitsch claims, the others paid lip-service to the Wenck hope only to follow the lead of the Fuehrer. Almost everyone had given up all thoughts of being saved, and said so to each other whenever Hitler was not present. Closing the discussions on the destruction of the bodies there was talk that SS men would be assigned to see that no trace remained. Throughout the day of the 28th the intensity of Russian fire continued while the suicide talk kept pace with the shelling in the shelter below [*suicide talk again denied.*]

59. *The Himmler Betrayal:* Then on the 29th fell the greatest blow of all. A telegram arrived which indicated that the staunch and trusted Himmler had joined Goering on the traitor list. It was like a death blow to the entire assembly. Reitsch claims that men and women alike cried and screamed with rage, fear and desperation, all mixed into one emotional spasm. [*Their reaction was less hysterical than implied, she later claimed.*] Himmler the protector of the Reich, now a traitor was impossible. The telegram message was that Himmler had contacted the British and American authorities through Sweden to propose a capitulation to the San Francisco conference. Hitler had raged as a mad man [*denied by HR later*]. His color rose to a heated red and his face was virtually unrecognizable. Additional evidence of Himmler's 'treachery' was that he had asked not to be identified with the capitulation proposals; American authorities were said to have abided by this request, while the British did not.

60. After the lengthy out-burst Hitler sank into a stupor and for a time the entire bunker was silent.

61. Later came the anti-climactic news that the Russians would make a full force bid to over-run the Chancel-

lery on the morning of the 30th. Even then small-arms fire was beginning to sprinkle the area above the shelter. Ground reports indicated that the Russians were nearing the Potsdamer Platz and were losing thousands of men as they fanatically prepared the positions from which the attack of the next morning was to be launched.

62. Reitsch claims that everyone again looked to their poison [*denied*].

63. *Orders to leave the Shelter*: at one-thirty on the morning of the 30th of April Hitler, with chalk-white face, came to Greim's room and slumped down on the edge of the bed. 'Our only hope is Wenck,' he said, 'and to make his entry possible we must call up every available aircraft to cover his approach.' Hitler then claimed that he had just been informed that Wenck's guns were already shelling the Russians in Potsdamer Platz.

64. 'Every available plane', Hitler said, 'must be called up by daylight, therefore it is my order to you to return to Rechlin and muster your planes from there. It is the task of your aircraft to destroy the positions from which the Russians will launch their attack on the Chancellery. With Luftwaffe help Wenck may get through. That is the first reason why you must leave the shelter. The second is that Himmler must be stopped,' and immediately he mentioned the SS Fuehrer his voice became more unsteady and both his lips and hands trembled. The order to Greim was that if Himmler had actually made the reported contact, and could be found, he should immediately be arrested [*HR denied that they were to seek out Himmler*].

65. 'A traitor must never succeed me as Fuehrer! You must set out to insure that he will not.'

66. Greim and Reitsch both protested vehemently that the attempt would be futile, that it would be impossible to reach Rechlin, that they preferred to die in the shelter, that the mission could not succeed, that it was insane.

67. 'As soldiers of the Reich,' Hitler answered, 'it is our holy duty to exhaust every possibility. This is the only

chance of success that remains. It is your duty and mine to take it.'

68. Hanna was not convinced. 'No, no,' she screamed, 'what can be accomplished now, even if we should get through. Everything is lost, to try to change it now would be insane.' But Greim thought differently. 'Hanna,' he said, 'we are the only hope for those who remain here. If the chance is just the smallest, we owe it to them to take it. Not to go would rob them of the only light that remains. Maybe Wenck is there. Maybe we can help, but whether we can or not, we will go.'

69. Hanna, still convinced as to the absurdity of attempting an escape, went alone to the Fuehrer while Greim was making his preparations. [*She claimed to have had only one conversation with Hitler in the bunker.*] Through her sobbing she begged, 'Mein Fuehrer why, why don't you let us stay?' He looked at her for a moment and said only: 'God protect you.'

70. *The Leave Taking:* Preparations were quickly made and Reitsch is graphic in her description of the leave taking. Below, late Goering's liaison officer with the Fuehrer and now staunch Greim-man said, 'You must get out. It depends upon you to tell the truth to our people, to save the 'honor' of the Luftwaffe: to save the meaning of Germany to the rest of the world.' Everyone gave the departing duo some token, something to take back into the world [*denied*]. Everyone wrote quick, last minute letters for them to take along [*denied—HR claimed they took the Goebbels' and Eva Braun's letters and some official dispatches only*]. Reitsch says she and Greim destroyed all but two of the letters which were from Goebbels and his wife to their oldest son, by Frau Goebbels' first marriage who was then in an Allied prisoner of war camp. [*HR admitted to destroying only that from Eva Braun.*] These Reitsch still had. Frau Goebbels also gave her a diamond ring from her finger to wear in her memory'.

71. Thirty minutes after Hitler gave the order they left the shelter.

72. *The Flight Out of Berlin:* Outside the whole city was aflame and heavy small-arm fire was already plainly audible a short distance away. SS troops, committed to guarding Hitler to the end, were moving about. These men brought up a small armored vehicle which was to take Reitsch and Greim to where an Arado 96 was hidden near the Brandenburger Tor. The sky was filled with the thunder of shells, some of which landed so close that their vehicle was knocked out several hundred yards short of the revetment where the Arado was stationed. (Reitsch claims that she is certain that this was the last craft available. The possibility of another plane having gotten in and possibly out again with Hitler as passenger, she dismisses as highly unlikely as Greim would certainly have been informed. She knows that such a message was never delivered. She knows too, that Greim had ordered other planes in but that each craft was shot down in the attempt and as Russian troops had already solidly ringed the city, she is certain that Hitler never left Berlin.)

73. The broad street leading from Brandenburger Tor was to be used for take-off. About 400 meters of uncratered pavement was available as run-way. The take-off was made under hailing Russian fire and as the plane rose to rooftop level it was picked up by countless searchlights and at once bracketed in a barrage of shelling. Explosions tossed the craft like a feather, but only a few splinters hit the plane. Reitsch circled to about 20,000 feet from where Berlin was a sea of flames beneath her. From that altitude the magnitude of the destruction of Berlin she describes as stark and fantastic. Heading north, 50 minutes saw them in Rechlin, where the landing was again made through a screen of Russian fighter craft.

74. *The Last German Reports:* Greim at once issued the orders calling all available craft to the aid of Berlin. Having performed the first of Hitler's commands he immediately decided to fly to Ploen, near Kiel, to determine what information Doenitz might have regarding Himmler, A Bucker 181 was used and by the time they got into the air German aircraft were already arriving in compliance

with Greim's order. The entire heavens were soon a seething mass of German and Russian planes. Reitsch kept her own plane at 1 and 2 meters altitude and even with such protection against visibility she was twice unsuccessfully attacked. Landing at Lubeck still necessitated an automobile trip to Ploen, during which time they were again under constant Russian attack. On arrival they found that Doenitz knew nothing of Himmler's actions. The next move was to see Keitel in the event that a change in air tactics should be employed in helping Wenck in his entry into Berlin.

75. *The News of Wenck's Non-Existence:* Keitel was found in the early morning of the first of May and gave them the news that Wenck's army had long ago been destroyed or captured. [*HR claimed that they knew this before going to the bunker.*] And that he (Keitel) had sent word to Hitler to that effect the day before (30th of April).

76. Greim and Reitsch now knew that Hitler must surely have given up all hope and both fully expected that the well-rehearsed suicide plans had already been put into operation.

77. *The 'New' Government:* The advance of the English necessitated a retreat into Schleswig late on the first day of May. Here, the same evening, Reitsch and Greim learned that the announcement of Hitler's death had been made and that he had been succeeded by Doenitz. [*HR claimed to have heard this at midnight.*] On the 2nd of May the new government was called to Ploen. Greim and Reitsch, to receive orders from Doenitz as to immediate Luftwaffe activities, had the additional purpose of meeting Himmler and confronting him with the betrayal story. [*HR elsewhere claimed her meeting with H. was accidental.*]

78. *Himmler's Capitulation Explanation:* Himmler arrived late so that all the others were in the conference room, leaving Reitsch alone when he walked in.

'One moment Herr Reichsfuehrer, a matter of the highest importance, if you can spare the time?' Reitsch asked.

Himmler seemed almost jovial as he said, 'Of course.'

'Is it true, Herr Reichsfuehrer, that you contacted the Allies with proposals of peace without orders to do so from Hitler?'

'But, of course.'

'You betrayed your Fuehrer and your people in the very darkest hour? Such a thing is high treason, Herr Reichsfuehrer. You did that when your place was actually in the bunker with Hitler?'

'High treason? No! You'll see, history will weigh it differently. Hitler wanted to continue the fight. He was mad with his pride and his "honor". He wanted to shed more German blood when there was none left to flow. Hitler was insane. It should have been stopped long ago.'

'Insane? I came from him less than 36 hours ago. He died for the cause he believed in. He died bravely and filled with the "honor" you speak of, while you and Goering and the rest must now live as branded traitors and cowards.'

'I did what I did to save German blood, to rescue what was left of our country.'

'You speak of German blood, Herr Reichsfuehrer? You speak of it now? You should have thought of it years ago, before you became associated with the useless shedding of so much of it.'

A sudden strafing attack terminated the conversation.

79. *The Last Orders—To Hold the Russians:* Greim indicated that little had been decided at the first Doenitz war council. However everyone was in accord that at best, resistance would only be possible for a few days longer. In the meantime commanders against the Russians were to hold to the last to enable as many civilians as possible to flee from the advance . . .

[*The description of their frantic flights around Germany do not differ from HR's authorised account.*]

83. *The End at Zell am See*: . . . Just before the capitulation they left Zell am See for Kitzbuhl to place themselves under the care of a well known Doctor who had just opened his hospital there.

84. Reitsch claims that had it not been for the severe agony of Greim's foot she would not have been able to convince him to save his limb. To the last he wanted to encourage resistance against the Russians.

86. *Reporting to the Americans:* They arrived in Kitzbuhl on the morning of the 9th and reported to American Military authorities shortly thereafter. Greim was under treatment until the 23rd of May when he was taken to Salzburg, prior to being taken on to Germany as a prisoner of War. [*HR claimed he was to be taken to England.*] He committed suicide with Hitler's poison capsule in Salzburg on the night of the 24th of May. Although he was much less known than his corpulent predecessor, both in Germany and in the world, in Hanna's opinion he should have had Goering's position years ago. The fact that he disagreed with Goering on almost every count is, to her, evidence enough of his capabilities.

87. *Evaluation of Source:* It is the opinion of the interrogator [i.e. Captain Robert Work] that the above information in given with a sincere and conscientious effort to be truthful and exact. The suicide of her family, the death of her closest friend von Greim, the physical pain of Germany, and the trying nature of her experiences during the closing days of the war combined themselves to seriously tempt her to commit suicide as well. She claims that the only reason she remained alive was for the sake of the truth; to tell the truth about Goering, 'the shallow showman,' to tell the truth about Hitler 'the criminal incompetent', and to tell the German people the dangers about the form of government that the Third Reich gave them. She believes that she is fulfilling much of this mission when she speaks to the interrogator. It is therefore felt that her remarks may be considered as her deepest efforts at sincerity and honesty. At the moment she is undergoing a severe mental struggle in her efforts to reconcile her conception of 'honor' with her denunciations of Goering, of Himmler, and of Hitler himself. [*HR did not in her view denounce Hitler.*] This difficulty appears less great when she is speaking to the interrogator than it is when

she speaks to civilians, but from civilians who have led her conversation and then, unknown to her, reported the results to the interrogator it appears that she is striving to exert a progressively more democratic influence over her countrymen.

# Appendix 3

*Extracts from Trevor-Roper's Introduction to
the second edition (1950) of his book* The Last Days
*of Hitler*

It is clearly certain that Frl Reitsch was questioned; it is
clearly possible that the interrogation report did not
give a completely fair version of her statements as it
certainly did not give a temperate version of the facts; it is
clearly equally possible that Frl Reitsch, under the emotional stresses of 1945, genuinely gave her interrogators an
impression which is no longer valid. Historically it would
be improper to accept Frl Reitsch's present disclaimers as
completely cancelling the evidence of 1945, and equally
improper to ignore these disclaimers. Certainty in such a
matter is unattainable . . . To her German friends as to her
American interrogators Frl Reitsch has given a clear impression of one dominant charactertistic: a tendency to
think in abstract terms, to isolate such conceptions as
'honour', 'idealism', 'the greatness of Germany', and to
pursue them in a category distinct from the concrete facts
which they sometimes comprehend. Now this is perhaps a
German characteristic, and it clearly has not seemed eccentric to Frl Reitsch and her friends. But I am English
and my book . . . 'reflects the prevalent English outlook';
and to me such an attitude is incomprehensible. I am
incapable of conceiving of abstract ideas apart from their
practical and concrete expression and consequences. 'Loy-

alty' without an object of loyalty', 'idealism' without a positive ideal capable of expression in concrete terms, 'honour' without a limited significance—these are to me meaningless syllables; I cannot consider 'success abroad' admirable in the abstract if it entails conquest and destruction in the concrete, or 'unity at home' if it entails pogroms and concentration camps; and the idea of anyone being led by pure 'bravery and nobility' to Hitler's Bunker in besieged and battered Berlin, at the risk of death and misinterpretation, and in spite of profound disagreement with the politics of Nazism and the useless continuation of the war which it symbolised, is a conception too transcendent and metaphysical for my more factual and prosaic mind. To me it seems more natural for one who disapproved of Hitler's war and Hitler's politics to have worked for his overthrow rather than consoled his last hours with gestures of loyalty, or at least to have kept as far away from him as possible and left him to stew in his own Bunker; and for one who merely disapproved of the strategy and wished to win the war which he was obstinately losing, to have shared the sentiment of the pedestrian but sensible General Koller: 'what would happen to Germany if all those who were responsible for the conduct of affairs were to lock themselves up in bunkers?'

If this is Frl Reitsch's philosophy, then it seems to me that our divergence is understandable. Her presentation of the facts could easily have been as incomprehensible to her American interrogators (who may well have shared my Anglo-Saxon attitude) as her philosophy is to me; it is possible that they failed to represent her ideas, just as they found her incapable of recognising theirs; and it is possible that after two years Frl Reitsch herself, remembering the facts in comparative tranquillity, may have forgotten the form in which, in different circumstances, she may originally have described them. With this conclusion I have decided to rest content; I have decided to treat her report not as true, nor as false, but as suspect; on that basis I have re-read the evidence and re-phrased the deductions. The effect has not been to alter the narrative of fact, but it has altered the description of personality; and I regret that my first edition may have caused her pain and involved us both in controversy.

# Bibliography

**BOOKS:**

Baumbach, Werner, *Broken Swastika* (Robert Hale, 1974).

Bethell, Nicholas, *The War Hitler Won* (Penguin, 1972).

Bielenberg, Christabel, *The Past is Myself* (Chatto & Windus, 1968).

Bing, Geoffrey, *Reap the Whirlwind* (MacGibbon & Kee, 1968).

Birke, Ernst (ed.), *das Riesengebirge* (Gerhard Rautenberg-Leer, 1958).

Boldt, Gerhard, *Hitler's Last Days* (Arthur Barker, 1973).

Brown, Dale M. (ed.), *The Luftwaffe* (Time-Life, 1982).

Brown, Eric. *Wings on my Sleeve* (Airlife, 1978).

——*Wings of the Weird and Wonderful* (Airlife. Vol. 1 1983, Vol. 2 1985).

Bullock, Alan, *Hitler: A Study in Tyranny* (Penguin, 1962).

Calleo, David, *The German Problem Reconsidered* (Cambridge University Press, 1978).

Catchpole, Brian, *A Map History of the Modern World* (Heinemann, 1970).

Collier, Basil, *The Battle of the V-Weapons* (Elmfield Press, 1976).

Dank, Milton, *The Glider Gang* (Cassell, 1977).

Davidson, Basil, *Africa in History* (Paladin, 1984).

*Documents concerning German-Polish Relations* (HMSO, 1939).

Ernst, Fritz, *The Germans and Their Modern History*, (Columbia University Press, 1966).

Fleming, Gerald, *Hitler and the Final Solution* (Hamish Hamilton, 1985).

Fraenkel, Heinrich, and Manvell, Roger, *Hitler: The Man and the Myth* (Colling, Grafton Books, 1986).

Galland, Adolf, *The First and the Last* (Fontana, 1970).

Gilbert, James, *The World's Worst Aircraft* (Michael Joseph, 1975).

Gilbert, Martin, *The Holocaust* (Collins, 1986).

Golding, Louis, *The Jewish Problem* (Penguin, 1938).

Hart, W. E., *Hitler's Generals* (Cresset Press, 1944).

Heiss, L., *Hirth* (Rheinhold A. Mueller, 1949).

Herlin, Hans, *Udet* (Macdonald, 1960).

Hildebrand, K., *The Third Reich*, trans. P. S. Falla (Allen & Unwin, 1984).

Hirth, Wolf, *The Art of Soaring Flight* (Wolf Hirth, 1938).

Hitler, Adolf, *Mein Kampf* (Hutchinson, 1974).

Hopkinson, Tom (ed.), *Picture Post 1938–50* (Penguin, 1970).

Irving. David, *The War Path* (Macmillan, 1978).

———*Hitler's War* (Macmillan, 1983, 2 vols.).

———*The Rise and Fall of the Luftwaffe* (Weidenfeld & Nicolson, 1973).

———*The Mare's Nest* (Kimber, 1964).

Jaffe, Hosea, *A History of Africa* (Zed Books, 1985).

Jessen, Hans, *Hirschberg* (Holzner, 1959).

Jochim, B., *Flug mit der Bombe* (der Landseer Grossband, 1977).

Jones, R. V., *Most Secret War* (Hamish Hamilton, 1978).

Kalnocky, Countess/Herisko, Ilona, *The Witness House* (NEL, 1974).

Kaps, Johannes (ed.), *die Tragödie Schlesiens* (Deutsche Taschenbuch Verlag, 1962).

King-Hall, Stephen, *King-Hall Survey 1936* (Newnes, 1937).

Knoke, Heinz, *I Flew for the Fuehrer*, trans. J. Ewing (Evans Books, 1953).

Koller, Karl, *Der letzte Monat* (Norbert Wohlgemuth Verlag, 1949).

Koonz, Claudia, *Mothers in the Fatherland* (Jonathan Cape, 1987).

Krosigk, Lutz Graf Schwerin von, *Memoiren* (Seewald, 1977).

Lee, Asher, *Goering—Air Leader* (Duckworth, 1972).

Lerche, H. W., *Luftwaffe Test Pilot* (Janes, 1980).

Longmate, Norman, *The Doodlebugs* (Hutchinson, 1981).

Mann, Erica, *School for Barbarians* (Stephen Austin & Sons, 1939).

Mayer, S. L., & Masawi, Tokoi (eds.), *DerAdler* (Arms & Armour Press, 1978).

Mrazek, J., *Fighting Gliders of World War II* (Arms & Armour Press, 1977).

Munson, Kenneth, *German Aircraft of WW2* (Blandford Press. 1978).

Musmanno, Michael Angelo, *Ten Days to Die* (Doubleday, 1950; Peter Davies, 1951).

O'Donnell, James, *The Berlin Bunker* (Dent, 1979).

Okey, Robin, *Eastern Europe 1740–1980* (Hutchinson, 1982).

Pope, Ernest R., *Munich Playground* (W. H. Allen & Co., 1942).

Powell, Erica, *Private Secretary (Female) Gold Coast* (Hurst, 1984).

Prittie, Terence, *My Germans* (Oswald Wolff, 1983).

Rautenberg, Hilda, and Rommel, Mechtild, *Die koloniale Frauenschulen* (Tropenlandwirt, Beiheft Nr. 16, Witzenhausen, 1983).

Reitsch Hanna, *Fliegen mein Leben* (first published by Deutschen Verlagsanstalt, 1951: republished by J. F. Lehmanns Verlag, 1968, and Wilhelm Heyne Verlag, 1981). Translations: *Aventures en plein ciel*, trans. Yvonne Pagniez (Palantine, 1952); *The Sky My Kingdom*, trans. Lawrence Wilson (Bodley Head, 1955).

——*Ich flog für Kwame Nkrumah* (J. F. Lehmanns Verlag, 1968).

——*Das unzerstörbare in meinem Leben* (first published by J. F. Lehmanns Verlag, 1975; reprinted by Herbig Verlag, 1983).

——*Höhen und Tiefen* (first published 1978; reprinted by Herbig Verlag, 1984).

Riedel, Peter, *Start in den Wind* (Motorbuch Verlag, 1986).

——*Vom Hangwind zur Thermik* (Motorbuch Verlag, 1985).

——*Ueber sonnige Weiten* (Motorbuch Verlag, 1985).

*Rise and Fall of the German Air Force* (Arms & Armour Press, 1983).

Russell, Lord, *The Scourge of the Swastika* (Cassell, 1954).

Schwarzschild, Leopold, *World in Trance* (Hamish Hamilton, 1943).

Shirer, William L., *The Rise and Fall of the Third Reich* (Secker & Warburg, 1960).

Späte, Wolfgang, *Der streng geheime Vogel Me 163* (Verlag für Wehrwissenschaften, 1983).

————*Alles was mit F anfängt: der Flieger und die Frau* (Littmann, 1986).

Speer, Albert, *Inside the Third Reich* (Weidenfeld & Nicolson, 1970).

Taylor, A. J. P., *The Origins of the Second World War* (Penguin, 1963).

————*From Sarajevo to Potsdam* (Thames and Hudson, 1966).

————*The Course of German History* (Methuen, 1978).

————*How Wars End* (Hamish Hamilton, 1985).

Teuber, Alfons (ed.), *Silesia in Pictures* ('Christ Unterwegs', 1956).

Thomas, Hugh, *The Spanish Civil War* (Penguin, 1965).

Trevor-Roper, Hugh (ed.), *The Goebbels Diaries* (Secker & Warburg, 1977).

————*The Last Days of Hitler* (Macmillan, 1978, 5th ed.).

Udet, Ernst; Ulanoff, Stanley (ed.), *Ace of the Iron Cross* (Arco, N.Y., 1981).

Unruh, Friedrich Franz von, *Ermutigung* (Hohenstaufen, 1981).

Vara, Chad, *The Samaritans* (Constable, 1965).

von Below, Nicolaus, *Als Hitlers Adjutant, 1937–45* (v. Hase Köhler Verlag, 1980).

Welch, Ann, *Happy to Fly,* (John Murray, 1983).

————*The Story of Gliding* (John Murray, 1980).

Ziegler, Mano, *Raketenjäger Me 163* (Motorbuch Verlag, 1969); trans. *Rocket Fighter: Story of the Messerschmitt Me 163* (Arms & Armour Press, 1976).

————*Kampf um Mach 1* (Ehapa, 1965).

## NEWSPAPERS AND PERIODICALS:

*die Abendzeitung* (WG); *Aerocourier* (WG); *Aeroplane Monthly*, (GB); *Army Times* (USA); *Bergwacht* (WG); *Bremen Nachrichten* (WG); *Daily Mail* (GB); *Daily Mirror* (GB); *Daily Telegraph* (GB); *Deutsche Soldatenzeitung* (WG); *Eve-*

*ning News* (GB); *Evening Star* (USA); *Flight* (GB); *Flight International* (GB); *Frankfurt Neue Presse* (WG); *Frankfurter Allgemeine Zeitung* (WG); *Frankfurter Rundschau* (WG); *Frau im Spiegel* (WG); *Ghana Studies Bulletin; Ghana Year Book 1964; Herald Tribune* (USA); *Illustrierter Beobachter* (G); *Maine Post* (USA); *Manchester Guardian* (G); *Minneapolis Star* (USA); *Münchner Illustrierte* (WG); *National Geographic* (USA); *National-Zeitung* (WG); *New York Herald Tribune* (USA); *New York Sun* (USA); *New York Times* (USA): *New York World Telegram* (USA); *News Chronicle* (GB); *Planeur* (Holland); *Rendsburger Tagesblatt* (WG); *Schlesische Bergwacht* (WG); *Schleswig-Holsteinische Landeszeitung* (WG); *Sikorsky News* (USA); *Soaring* (USA); *Spectator* (GB); *Spiegel* (WG); *Stars and Stripes* (USA/WG); *Süddeutsche Zeitung* (WG); *Sunday Telegraph* (GB); *Sunday Times* (GB); *Thermik* (WG); *The Times* (GB); *Völkischer Beobachter* (G); *Washington Star* (USA): *die Welt* (WG); *Weser Kurier* (WG); *Wiener Illustrierte* (Austria).

## FILMS

*Operation Crossbow*, with Barbara Rütting as Hanna Reitsch, 1965.
*The Last Days*, starring Alec Guinness as Hitler, 1973.
*Test Pilot*, BBC, producer Brian Johnson, 1979.
*Flug ins Ungewisse*, German TV (Hesaen), 1987.

# Chronology

| | |
|---|---|
| 1912 | 29 March, Date of birth |
| 1931 | Abitur (school leaving examination) |
| 1931–2 | Koloniale Frauenschule, Rendsburg |
| 1931 | First gliding course, Grunau |
| 1932 | Gliding and powered flying licences; women's endurance gliding record; medical studies, Berlin and Kiel |
| 1933 | Altitude record; film *Rivalen der Luft* |
| 1934 | South American and Finland expeditions; medical studies dropped; test pilot at German Gliding Institute, Darmstadt |
| 1935 | Tests with Kranich and See Adler gliders designed by Hans Jacobs, second visit to Finland |
| 1936 | Dive-brake tests with gliders; Berlin Olympics |
| 1937 | Alpine glider crossing; promotion to civilian rank of Flukapitän; seconded to military testing station, Rechlin, for dive-brake tests on military aircraft |
| 1938 | Helicopter flight in the Deutschlandhalle; tests with transport glider; acrobatic display at Cleveland Air Races, America; protest at treatment of Jews on Kristallnacht |
| 1939–44 | Expedition to Libya; outbreak of war; troop-carrying glider tests; throughout war employed by DFS as test pilot, with secondments to Rechlin and other military testing stations and airfields; tests with Gigant, petrol-tanker glider, bed-of-ropes landing, balloon cable-cutting device, Me 163, and manned VI, |

| | |
|---|---|
| 1941 | Awarded medal and Iron Cross, Second Class; honorary citizenship of Hirschberg |
| 1942 | Me 163 test flights and accident, serious injuries; awarded Iron Cross, First Class |
| 1943 | Instigation of plans for manned VI, suicide mission. |
| 1945 | 26 April, flight into Berlin with General von Greim; 29 April, flight out of Berlin after three days in bunker; May, deaths of parents and von Greim, taken into American custody; December, so-called eyewitness accounts of bunker appear in the press, based on interrogation reports |
| 1946 | August, released by Americans; under surveillance |
| 1949 | Move to Frankfurt; voluntary social work |
| 1951 | Publication of first autobiographical book |
| 1952 | With German gliding team in Spain; bronze medal |
| 1954 | Conversion to Catholic Church; participation in world gliding championship in England banned by German government and team sent without her |
| 1955 | German gliding champion |
| 1956 | International gliding championship, France |
| 1957 | Women's altitude record |
| 1958 | Refused visa by Poles for international contest in Poland; connections with German Aero Club severed |
| 1959 | Official mission to India |
| 1961 | Received at the White House in United States; Finland |
| 1962–6 | At invitation of President Nkrumah, founded and ran National School of Gliding in Ghana; expelled after 1966 coup which deposed Nkrumah |
| 1968 | Book *Ich flog für Kwame Nkrumah* published; new edition of *Fliegen mein Leben* |
| 1969 | First international helicopter championship |
| 1970 | Women's gliding record; with Neil Armstrong at the Wasserkuppe jubilee |
| 1971 | First helicopter international, women's champion |
| 1972 | In United States, honorary membership of Society of Experimental Test Pilots, Pilot of the Year, Order of Characters |
| 1974 | Austrian citizenship |
| 1974–6 | VIP treatment in United States during visits there |
| 1975 | Publication of *Das Unzerstörbare in meinem Leben* |

1978    Publication of *Höhen und Tiefen:* women's world
        gliding record, Austria: end of feud with German
        Aero Club; adverse publicity and lawsuit in Bremen
1979    World record flight in United States; 24 August,
        death from heart attack; 29 August, announcement
        of death, after funeral in Salzburg

# A Note About
# The Bantam Air &
# Space Series

This is the era of flight—the century which has seen man soar, not only into the skies of Earth but beyond the gravity of his home planet and out into the blank void of space. An incredible accomplishment achieved in an incredibly short time.

How did it happen?

The AIR & SPACE series is dedicated to the men and women who brought this fantastic accomplishment about, often at the cost of their lives—a library of books which will tell the grand story of man's indomitable determination to seek the new, to explore the farthest frontier.

The driving theme of the series is the skill of *piloting*, for without this, not even the first step would have been possible. Like the Wright Brothers and those who, for some 35 years, followed in their erratic flight path, the early flyers had to be designer, engineer and inventor. Of necessity, they were the pilots of the crazy machines they dreamt up and strung together.

Even when the technology became slightly more sophisticated, and piloting became a separate skill, the quality of a flyer's ability remained rooted in a sound working knowledge of his machine. World War I, with its spurt of development in aircraft, made little change in the role of the flyer who remained, basically, pilot-navigator-engineer.

Various individuals, like Charles Lindbergh, risked their lives and made high drama of the new dimension they were carving in the air. But still, until 1939, flying was a romantic, devil-may-care wonder, confined to a relative handful of hardy individuals. Commercial flight on a large scale was a mere gleam in the eye of men like Howard Hughes.

It took a second major conflict, World War II, from 1939 to 1945, to provoke the imperative that required new concepts from the designers—and created the arena where hundreds of young men and women would learn the expertise demanded by high-speed, high-tech aircraft.

From the start of flight, death has taken its toll. Flying has always been a high-risk adventure. Never, since men first launched themselves into the air, has the new element given up its sacrifice of stolen lives, just as men have never given up the driving urge to go farther, higher, faster. Despite only a fifty-fifty chance of any mission succeeding, *still* the dream draws many more men and women to spaceflight than any program can accommodate. And still, in 1969, when Michael Collins, Buzz Aldrin and Neil Armstrong first took man to the Moon, the skill of piloting, sheer flying ability, was what actually landed the "Eagle" on the Moon's surface. And still, despite technological sophistication undreamed of 30 or 40 years earlier, despite demands on any flyer for levels of performance and competence and the new understanding of computer science not necessary in early aircraft, it is piloting, *human* control of the aircraft—sometimes, indeed, inspired control—that remains the major factor in getting there and back safely. From this rugged breed of individualists came the bush pilots and the astronauts of today.

After America first landed men on the Moon, the Russian space program pushed ahead with plans for eventually creating a permanent space station where men could live. And in 1982 they sent up two men—Valentin Lebedev and Anatoly Berezovoy—to live on Solyut-7 for seven months. This extraordinary feat has been recorded in the diaries of pilot Lebedev, DIARY OF A COSMONAUT: 211 DAYS IN SPACE.

The Bantam AIR & SPACE series will include several titles by or about flyers from all over the world—and about the planes they flew, including World War II, the postwar era of barnstorming and into the jet age, plus the personal histories of many of the world's greatest pilots. Man is still the most important element in flying.

# Index

Abitur, 8
Accra, 185, 186, 188, 190, 193
   Gliding Club, 185, 186, 190, 195, 196
Achgelis, Gerd, 54
Aero Club, German, 35, 171, 173–78, 179, 183, 184, 211
   of Delhi, 176
Aeronautical Research Institute, Berlin, 105
Afienya, 185, 186, 188, 190
Africa, 10, 192; see also Ghana
Ainring, 107, 142, 143
aircraft: Arado, 127, 128, 130, 251
   Bücker 181, 115, 131, 251
   Cierva autogiro, 56
   Cirrus (glider), 200
   Condor (glider), 22, 25
   DFS230 (troop-carrying glider), 73, 75–76, 77
   Dornier: Do 17, 54, 82; Do 217, 107, 119, 133
      bombers, 51, 54
      flying-boat, 35
   Fafnir (glider), 25
   Fieseler Storch, 51, 56, 84, 122, 123
   Fi 103, manned V1, see V1

Focke-Wulf: FW 61, 54–55; FW 190, 109, 110, 121
freight-carrying glider, 72
Grunau Baby (glider), 18–20, 22, 23, 25, 43, 86
Habicht (glider), 65
Heinkel: He 70 Blitz, 42; He III, 107
helicopter, 54–62, 115–16, 119, 172, 181, 202, 203, 205, 235
Junkers: Ju 52, 73, 127, 231, 237
   Ju 87 see Stuka
   Ju 188, 120
   Mammoth, 77
Ka 7 (glider), 177
Klemm, 26, 32, 50
Komet, see Me 163
Kranich (glider), 33, 70
Minimoa (glider), 50
Moazagotl (glider), 17, 23, 25
Messerschmitt: Gigant, 77–80
   Me 110, 79
   Me 163 Komet, 89–91, 98, 100, 102, 108
   Me 262, 106
   Me 328, 106, 107
Piper Super Cub, 193

aircraft *(cont.)*
  Reiher (glider), 49, 70;
    Reiher III, 61
  Rhönsperber Junior (glider),
    43
  See Adler/Sea Eagle (am-
    phibian glider), 34–35
  Slingsby T21 (glider), 188
  Spatz, 186
  Sperber (glider), 38–39
    Junior, 48–49
  Stuka, 37, 53, 57, 115
  V1 *see separate entry*
  Zugvogel III (glider), 183,
    200
Air Ministry, German, 29, 76,
    88, 91
Akaflieger, 28, 32, 70
Alabama, 182
Allahabad, 177
Allies, 117, 141, 152, 170
Alps, 48–49, 200, 203, 208,
    211, 212
Alte Adler, 175, 220, 226
American Counter Intelligence
    Corps, 138, 139, 141,
    143, 146, 154–59
  military authorities, 254
  Property Control Commis-
    sion, 141
Anglo-German Friendship Fel-
    lowship, 50
Ankrah, General, 196
Anschluss, 63
anti-Nazi, 70, 192, 210
anti-Semitism, 40, 41, 64,
    67–68, 217–18
  Appalachians, 219
Arado 96, 127, 128, 130,
    251
Argentina, 25
Arizona, 202
Armstrong, Neil, 182, 201, 212
Assisi, St Francis of, 216

Augsburg, 54, 91
Auriol, Jacqueline, 201
Austria, 1, 2, 7, 42, 48, 50,
    63, 67, 98, 103, 142,
    200, 209, 212, 220, 225
  border, 118, 159, 197
  citizenship, 200–201
  relatives, *see* Heuberger
  resistance, 95, 140
autobiographies (HR), 114,
    164–65, 166–67, 198,
    201, 206, 209, 216–17,
    220
  unpublished, 198, 218, 220
autogiro, 56, 205, 235
Auto-Union, 57
Axmann, Artur, 239

Baako, Kofi, 188, 196
Baden-Baden, 225
Bad Nauheim, 154, 155
Bad Zwischenahn, 100
Bals, Waltraud, 187, 210, 215,
    226
Baltic, 4, 24, 90
Bangalore, 177
barrage balloons, 82–83
Baumbach, Colonel, 112
Baur, Hans, 126, 209, 239
Beinhorn, Elly, 16, 59, 157, 200
Belgium, 76
Benares, 177
Benziger, Dr Theodor, 97, 104,
    204
Berchtesgaden, 105, 129, 235,
    236
Berg, Marianne, 155
Berlin, 28, 53, 82, 85, 87, 115,
    116, 119, 121, 122,
    123, 124, 137, 140, 144,
    173, 175, 178, 187,
    204, 205, 228, 234
  Aeronautical Research Insti-
    tute, 105

Berlin (*cont.*)
  bunker, 124–30, 228–32,
    234–50
  last flight into, 120–23,
    234–35; out of, 130,
    231, 251
  medical studies in, 16
  Motor Show, 57–61
  Olympics, 39
  radio, 110
  Transport Museum, 226
Bernadotte, Count, 232
Betz, 126, 239
Beverly Hilton, 202
Bialystok, 103
Bird, Captain, 141–42, 143
Blasius, Mayor of Hirschberg,
    116
Bode, Karl, 57, 59
Bode, Thilo, 165–66
Bodewig, Dr Hans, 96
Boldt, Gerhard, 203
Bolshevik/Bolshevism, 67, 72,
    117, 132
Bombay, 177
Bonn, 173, 188
  government in, 184, 188,
    192
Bormann, Martin, 127, 129,
    151, 204, 239, 244
Böss, Gretl (Margarethe), 85,
    96, 143, 144, 153,
    156–57, 162, 167–68, 223
Boxsey, F/Lt Clifford, 193
Brandenburg, 130
  Gate, 123, 130, 251
Braun, Eva, 127, 129, 130,
    142, 149, 151, 204,
    231, 237, 243–44, 250
Braunschweig, 174
Bräutigam, Otto, 42, 76, 78,
    86
Brazil, 24–25
Bredl, Fritz, 157, 159

Bremen, 54, 56, 212–14, 220,
    225
*Bremen*, 64
Bremen-Vahr, church of, 213
Breslau, 116
Breslau-Schöngarten, 96
Brie, Reginald, 51, 56
Britain, 44, 50, 66, 72, 74
  Battle of, 87
  planned invasion of, 76, 77
British, 50, 82, 109, 248
  Berlin Tattoo, 205
  Broadcasting Corporation,
    210
  in Ghana, 185, 192
  press, 50, 52, 111, 173
  royal visit to Ghana, 187
Brown, Eric, 42, 58, 91, 134,
    146, 202, 210
Bückeburg, 202
Bücker 181, 115, 131, 251
Bulgaria, 42
Bund Deutscher Mädel, 85,
    99
bunker, Hitler's in Berlin,
    124–30, 144, 149,
    228–32, 234–50, 257
Burgdorf, General, 126, 239
buzz bomb, 110

cable-cutting, 82–83
Calcutta, 177
California, 182, 202
Campbell, Nora, 8
Camphill, 50, 172–73
Camp King, 147
capitulation, 134, 136, 232,
    248
Catholic Church, 4, 8, 169
Chancellery, 85, 119, 122, 128,
    228–32, 234–50
Christian, Frau, 239
Cierva autogiro, 56
Cirrus glider, 200

Civil Airways Training School, 29–30
Cleveland Air Races, 64–65
Clever and Reitdorf, 202
Cochran, Jacqueline, 202
Cohn, Captain, 150, 151, 160, 167
colonies, 10, 59
Communism, 4–5, 22, 68, 72, 116, 159, 179
Communists, 212
concentration camps, 113
Condor glider, 22, 25
conscription, 32
coup, in Ghana, 196–97
Crete, 76
Czechoslovakia, 2, 20, 48, 50, 65, 71, 133

*Daily Mail*, 173
Danzig, 72, 74
Darmstadt, 26, 27, 28, 32, 33, 39, 49, 68, 69, 70, 72
D-Day, 109
Defence Ministry, 31
de Lange, Louis, 176, 220
Delhi, 176–77
de-Nazification, 161, 163
Dette, Helmut, 201
Deutscher Forschungsanstalt für Segelflug (DFS), *see* Gliding Research Institute
Deutscher Luftsport Verband, 28
Deutsches Museum, 226
*Deutschland*, 47
Deutschlandhalle, 57, 63, 86, 203, 205
Deutschmann, Hans, 17
DFS, *see* Gliding Research Institute
DFS 230, troop-carrying glider, 73, 75–76
Dietrich, Dr, 239

Dittmar, Edgar, 52
Dittmar, Heini, 23, 24, 28, 48, 49, 52, 88, 89–90, 91
dive brakes, 37–39, 53, 73
Dollfuss, Engelbert, 63
Dönitz, Admiral, 131, 132, 239, 251, 252, 253
Dornberger, General, 147
Dresden, 117
Dunstable, 50

East Germany, 179, 192
East-West Axis, 231, 232, 237
East-West relations, 175
Eastern Front, 87, 100–102, 103, 115
Eben Emael, 76
Edwards Test Center, 182
el Hassan, Suzanne, 196
Embassy
  German, Stockholm, 113
  West German
    in Ghana, 191
    in London, 173
    in New Delhi, 166, 177, 178
evangelical church, 213, 225

Fafnir glider, 25
FAI (Fédération d'Aviation Internationale), 175, 219
Farnborough, 91
Federation of European Women Pilots, 223, 225
Fegelein, Hermann, 127, 231, 239–40
Finland, 28–29, 35–36, 41, 181
Flinch, Bernard, 78
Flugkapitän, 47, 53, 84, 226
*Flugsport*, 22
flying bomb, *see* V1
Focke, Professor, 54

Focke-Wulf, 30, 54, 57, 134,
172
  FW 61, 54–55; FW 190,
    109, 110, 121
Foreign Office (West German),
    184, 187 (*see also*
    Embassy)
France, 7, 32, 44, 48, 66, 69,
    72, 74, 75, 76, 173, 218
Franco, 44, 48
Franco-German relations, 164
Franke, Karl, 54–55, 77, 78,
    205, 206
Frankfurt, 168, 170, 171,
    198, 200, 207, 208, 220,
    226
*Frankfurter Allgemeine Zeitung*,
    170
freemasonry, 3, 81
freight-carrying glider, 72
Freising, 147
French, 139, 140
  in Ghana, 192
Frowein, Dr Ernst, 174
Fuchs, Otto, 68, 70, 71, 78,
    81, 85, 99, 111, 116, 208,
    226
Fulda, 201

Galgenberg, 6
Gandhi, Indira, 177–79
  Rajiv, 178, 179
  Sanjay, 178
Gatow, 121, 122, 130
Gauleiter, 68
Georgii, Professor Walter, 23,
    26, 28, 38, 48, 68, 105,
    142–44
German Aero Club, *see* Aero
    Club
German/American friendship
    groups, 65
German Association of Women
    Pilots, 200
  of Women Glider Pilots, *see*
    Segelfliegerinnen
Gersfeld, 201
Gestapo, 32, 95
Ghana, 184–99, 200
Ghanaian air force, 193,
    198
Ghana government, 187, 189
  Young Pioneers, 187, 193
Gigant, 77–80
Glasenapp, Irwin, 111
glider assault unit, 75–76
gliding
  ban on, 170
  as character training, 185
  development of, 13
  lecture about, 170
  school
    Grunau, 8, 13–15
    Hornberg, 21
  in Alps, 200
  in Austria, 200
  in Finland, 28–29, 181
  in India, 176–78
  International School of,
    Ghana, 184–97
  mystical power of, 171
  post-war resumption, 172
  tests: A, B, C, 14
Gliding Research Institute
    (DFS), 26, 28, 38, 44,
    47, 61, 67, 68, 70, 72,
    73, 88
Gmunden, 143
Goebbels, Dr Joseph, 39,
    67, 69, 112, 116, 124,
    125, 126, 230, 240,
    241
  children of Joseph and
    Magda G., 149, 230, 242
  Magda, 124–26, 228, 232,
    235, 240–42
  last letters of Joseph and
    Magda G., 129, 250

Goering, Hermann, 31, 32, 40, 43, 51, 52, 53, 58, 59, 84, 85, 86–87, 95, 98, 102, 104, 124, 131, 133, 135, 143, 144, 147, 229, 235–37, 240, 246, 248, 253, 254
Gold Coast, 184
Graz, 133
Groves, Doris, 219, 225
Grunau, 8, 13–15, 17, 18, 20, 85
Grunau Baby glider, 18–20, 22, 23, 25, 43, 86
Grunewald, 122
Guernica, 48
Guinea, 197

Haase, Ernst Gunther, 175
Habicht glider, 65
Hamburg, 26, 44, 49, 188, 221
Handscomb, Frank, 186, 188, 189, 191, 198
Hardop, Gustav, 183
Harwood, Rika, 210–11
Hauptmann, Gerhart, 86
Haus Alaska, 148
Haus der Flieger, 88
Haus Schlesien, 226
Hawe, Dr Albert, 185, 189
Heinkel, Dr Ernst, 30, 37, 134
He 70 Blitz, 42
He III, 107
helicopter, 54–62, 115–16, 119, 172, 181, 202, 203, 205, 235
Herrligkoffer, Professor, 172
Hertel, Hans, 212–13
Hess, Rudolf, 205
Heuberger, family, 21, 47, 103, 140, 157, 207, 222
Gertrud, 3, 47, 202, 207
Hanna (aunt), 180–81, 207, 208

Hanna (niece), 180
Helmut, 63, 140, 172, 183
Richard, 63, 207
Wolfgang, 180
Hevel, 129, 232, 239
Hildesheim, 75, 76
Himalayas, 172
Hilton, Barron, 203
Himmler, Heinrich, 95, 99, 107, 110, 112, 114, 128, 131, 132, 138, 143, 217, 231, 232, 239, 240, 248, 249, 251, 252–53, 254
Hirschberg, 2, 5, 6, 7, 8, 9, 17, 47, 85, 87, 116, 118, 179
Hirth, Wolf, 14, 15, 17–20, 21, 23, 25, 50, 86, 157, 171, 172
Hirth, Lala, 14, 171
Hitler, Adolf, 21, 25, 31, 32, 37, 39, 41, 57, 63, 66, 68, 69, 71–72, 74, 83, 84, 85, 97, 98, 99, 100, 105, 106, 107, 110, 116, 119, 124–32, 138, 140, 141, 144, 148, 149, 150, 151, 160, 161, 167, 172, 173, 178, 204, 209, 214, 215, 225, 228–31, 233–55, 256, 257
Hitler Youth, 44, 63, 85, 98, 99, 193, 213, 239
Hofmann, 42
Holocaust, 113, 217
Holzrichter, Gisela, 10–12, 84, 180, 221
Holzrichter, Armin, 180
honour, 2, 5, 84, 87, 99, 112, 119, 125, 129, 132, 135, 138, 151, 153, 176, 183, 216, 218, 220, 223, 225, 228, 234, 236–37, 241, 242, 250, 254, 256, 257

Hornberg, 21
Hungary, 42
Huntsville, Alabama, 182
Huth, 42

Ibiza, 47
India, 176–79, 184
Indian government, 198
Indians in Ghana, 192
Innsbruck, 103, 140
intelligence, allied, 141
    American, 140–41, 170
international gliding contests, in
        England, 172–73
    Award of Characters, 202
    in France, 173, 218
    in Poland, 174–75
    in Spain, 172
    Helicopter Championships,
        202
interrogation, 144–46
    Air Force, 141
    Center, Oberursel, 147–48
    extracts from 'Last Days'
        summary, 233–55
    summaries, 145, 147, 149,
        150; quoted, 149; quoted
        in press, 150–51
invasion
    of France, 75
    planned, of Britain, 76, 77
Iron Cross, 7, 84, 85, 95, 101,
        105, 110, 210
Israel, ambassador of in Ghana,
        192
Italy, 7, 44, 48, 66, 70, 204

Jachtmann, Ernst, 41
Jacobs, Hans, 34, 37–38, 46,
        48, 49, 65, 68, 72, 73,
        75
Japan, 97
Jeschonnek, General Hans,
        58

Jews, 28, 29, 40, 41, 67, 68,
        113, 130–31, 132, 150,
        214, 215
Johl, Otto, 7, 157, 180
Juist, 187

Ka 7 glider, 177
Kamikaze, 97
Kathmandu, 177
Keitel, Field Marshal, 131, 252
Kennedy, President J. F., 181
Kensche, Heinz, 107, 173
Kesselring, General, 73, 133,
        161
Kiel, 17, 94, 144, 251
Kiel, Canal, 10
King-Hall, Commander Ste-
        phen, 41
Kitzbühel, 118, 134, 138, 139,
        140, 254
Klaus, Landa, 117, 136, 142,
        157, 222
Klemm, 26, 32, 50
Kohl, Heinrich, State Secretary,
        215
Kohl, Hermann, 209
Koller, General, 127, 133–35,
        137, 257
Koloniale Frauenschule
        (Koloschule), 10, 11, 13,
        14, 21, 142, 180
Königratz, 133
Kranich, 33, 70
Krebs, General, 126, 239
Krekel, Paul, 42
Kristallnacht, 67, 213, 214
Krönberg/Taunus, 155
Kuntz, Rolf, 174, 175
Küttner, Dr Joachim, 28–29,
        41, 69, 113, 163, 182,
        201, 217, 219, 221

Lange, Heinrich, 97, 104, 110
League of German Girls, 85, 99

Lebensraum, 52
Leonidas Squadron, 108
Leszno, 175
Libya, 70–71, 208, 226
Libyans, in Ghana, 192
Lilienthal, Otto, 171
Lindbergh, Charles, 55, 56
Lindner, Gerd, 134
Lipetsk, 31, 70
Lippisch, Alexander, 90, 91
Lisbon, 32, 33
Löhr, Täwe, 189, 190
London, 110, 179, 190, 195
Lorenz, Dr, 239
Los Angeles, 206, 212
Loyola, St Ignatius, 9
Lübeck, 132, 156, 252
Lüders, Dr, 191
Lufthansa, 31, 41, 46
*Luftsport,* 42
Luftwaffe, 31, 32, 39, 40, 42,
    43, 52, 53, 56, 61, 70, 75,
    84, 85, 86, 87, 90, 95, 98,
    102, 106, 107, 111, 112,
    124, 138, 141, 147, 157,
    158, 229, 237, 249, 251

Macholz, Gustav-Adolf, 7, 47,
    87
Madras, 177
Maginot Line, 75
Mahoney, William, 192
Majdanek, 113
Mammoth (Junkers), 77
*Manchester Guardian,* 50
medical studies, 9, 16
meditation, 190, 196
memorials: Hanna Reitsch-
    Gedächtnis-Singen, 225
  Hanna Reitsch Memorial
    Trophy, 225
Mercedes-Benz, 57
Messerschmitt, Professor Willi,
    37, 76, 77, 79, 134, 184

Messerschmitt
  factory, 91
  Gigant, 77–80
  Me 110, 79
  Me 163 (Komet), 89–91, 98,
    100, 102, 108, 111,
    146, 167, 203, 205
  Me 262 (jet fighter), 106
  Me 328 (monoplane fighter),
    106, 107
military government, 170
Milch, Erhard, 31, 32, 51, 73,
    87, 95, 96, 104, 112
mission, sense of, 139, 153,
    161, 168, 209, 214–15
Moazagotl, 17, 23, 25
Model, General Walther, 73
model aircraft, 191, 193
Molden, Fritz, 98
Molders, 58
Moosburg, 159
Motor Baby, 28
Mukerjee, Air Marshal, 178
Munich, 35, 40, 66, 118,
    120
  Deutsches Museum in, 226
Musmanno, Michael Angelo
    (*Ten Days to Die*), 160
Mussolini, 107, 131

Narvik, 81
National Air and Space Mu-
    seum, USA, 212
National Archives, US, 233
National Gliding School, Ghana,
    190–93
National Liberation Council,
    Ghana, 196
National Socialism, 66, 129,
    242
National Socialist Party, 32, 40,
    41, 63, 81
Naumann, State Secretary, 116,
    239

Nazi, 40, 41, 44, 52, 57, 65, 67, 111, 135, 158, 209, 257
  administrative district, 68
  belief, 213
  faith, 129
  flying corps, 44
  N. Germany, 1, 52, 57, 62, 65
    symbol of, 223
    heroine of, 1, 62, 95
  leaders, 99, 114, 162, 234
  loyalty, 129
  marching song, 57
  news, 72
  party, 81, 95, 146, 154, 161
  press, 48, 72
  propaganda, 58, 91
  regime, 113, 125, 217, 226
  reputation, 192
  slogans, 44
  symbol, 223
  women's and girls' organisations, 85, 99
  youth organisations, 106; see also Hitler Youth
Nehru, Jawaharlal 'Pandit', 177–78, 185
Neu-Bieberg, 120
Neuburg, 91
Neu-Ulm, 209
New York, 64
*New York Times,* 64
*News Chronicle,* 151
Ninety-Nines (99s), 200
Nkrumah, President, 184–99
Nkrumah, wife of, 186, 190
North German Radio, 222
Nuremberg, 138, 145

Oberursel, 156
  interrogation center, 148
  prison, 147
  town hall, 163

obituaries, 224
Oder, 238
Oerlinghausen, 210
Opel, 168, 208
Operation
  REICHENBERG, 107–11
  SEALION, 76, 77
  self-sacrifice, 104–13
  SKYLARK, 155–56
Opitz, Rudi, 90
Organisation of African Unity, 195
Orscha, 101
OSTIV, 176

Pagniez, Yvonne, 164, 204, 215
Pakistan, 172
Pakistanis, in Ghana, 192
Pan-American, 172
Panzer, SS P. Corps, 101
Paris, 67
Pasewaldt, Colonel Georg, 29–30, 95, 104
Patna, 177
patriotism, 1, 2, 16, 52, 81, 87, 103, 116, 138, 164, 212
Paulsen, General Ernst, 226
Paulsen, Carola, 87, 226
Peenemünde, 90, 94
Pehl, Father Karl, 168, 169, 194, 206, 208, 215, 221, 222
Pennsylvania, 219
Philp, Colonel William R., 154–59
Piper Super Cub, 193
Plön, 131, 132, 251, 252
Poland, 2, 4, 25, 49, 71, 72, 74, 100, 116, 174
Polish corridor, 72
Pondicherry, 177
  ashram, 177
  mother of, 177, 226

Poona, 177
Portugal, 32–33, 35, 44
Potsdamer Platz, 232, 249
Powell, Erica, 193, 198
press conference, 148–50
*Princeton University Quarterly Review,* 150
propaganda, 56, 58, 86, 91, 97, 112, 113, 116, 214, 217
Protestant church, 8
Prussia, 1, 2, 31

Quandt, Harald, 129, 149, 174–76

Ranganathananda, 178
Ravensbruck, 164
rearmament, 32, 52, 57, 64
Rechlin, 42, 53, 61, 82, 88, 91, 121, 130, 131, 251
records, 15, 20, 28, 49, 209, 211
   in Alps, 48–49, 211
   in USA, 219, 225
Red Cross, 140
Regensburg, 92, 94, 96, 157
Reichhold, Dr Walter, 191, 192
Reichsfrauenführerin, 85
Reiher, 49, 70
   III, 61
Reitsch
   Emy, 1–10, 16–17, 36, 39, 46, 47, 81, 87, 94, 95, 96, 116, 117, 118, 136–37, 142, 164, 169, 180, 206
   family, 136–37, 142, 180–81, 206
   Heidi, 1–10, 47, 81, 117, 118, 120, 137
   Helma, 143–44, 220–22, 226
   Kurt, 1–10, 47, 58, 81, 116, 118, 144, 155–56, 180, 194, 220, 222, 225, 226

   letter to Kurt, extracts from, 228–32
   parents, 1–10, 21, 26, 58, 81, 85, 116, 117, 118, 120
   Willy, Dr, 1–10, 47, 81, 118, 136, 137
Rendsburg, 10, 12, 21
resistance
   Austrian, 139
   French, 164
Reuters, 232
revolution in Austria, France, Germany, 7
Rheindorf, Professor, 165
Rhineland, military occupation of, 41
Rhön, soaring contests, 22, 43, 44
Rhönsperber Junior, glider, 43
ridge-flying, 219
Riedel, Helen, 88
Riedel, Peter, 22, 23, 24, 25, 27, 40, 41, 44, 64, 88, 113–15, 138, 184, 215, 217
Riesengebirge, 19, 96
Rietdorf, Otto, 202
Rio de Janeiro, 24
Ritter, Carlos, 202
rocket, A4/V2, 90
   on Gigant, 77
   Me 163, rocket plane, 90–93
   Saturn, 182
Rositten, 24
Ross Howard, Jean, 181, 212
Royal Air Force, 193
Rudel, Colonel Hans-Ulrich, 115, 127, 157
   Oberst R. Movement, 158
Ruholl, Gunther, 213, 215, 216–18
Russia, 2, 31, 44, 74, 97, 100–102

Russian fighters, 121
  front, 100–102, 104
  Revolution, 4
  troops, 119
  zone, 168
Russians, 116, 117, 118, 121,
  128, 134, 136, 141,
  232, 237, 238, 247,
  248–49, 251, 252, 253,
  254
  in Ghana, 192

*Sailplane*, 211
Salmony, Georg, 224
Salzburg, 48, 105, 117, 118,
  129, 134, 138, 143,
  144, 214, 222, 226, 254
  prison, 146–47, 157
Samaritans, 168
San Francisco, 232, 248
São Paulo, 25
Sattler, Dr, 184, 187, 190,
  198
'Saturn', 157, 159
Schantl, Hanna, 180–81
Scheel, Elisabeth, 117
Schempp-Hirth, factory, 187
Schieferstein, Karl, 206
Schiffler, Lotte, 163–64, 215,
  216, 217
Schiller, Melitta, 42, 53
Schleswig, 252
Schloss Leopoldskron, 117,
  120, 136, 141, 144,
  146, 157, 200
Schmidt, Eva, 50
Schneider, 20, 28
Schnitke, Kurt, 157
Schöner, Field Marshal, 133
Schuschnigg, Kurt von, 63
Schütz, Hans, 102
Scott, Sheila, 225
Scott-Barrett, Major-General,
  205

See Adler (Sea Eagle), amphib-
  ian glider, 34–35
*Seeadler*, 47
Segefliegerinnen, 210, 215
SETP, 202, 205
Sikorsky, Igor, 181
  factory, 181
Silesia, 1, 2, 4, 72, 74, 85–86,
  116, 117, 118, 133,
  136, 174
  Polish, 74
  Upper, 4
Silesian refugees, 226
Silver C Soaring Medal, 25
Skorzeny, Otto, 107, 172
SKYLARK, Operation, 155–56
Slingsby T21 glider, 188
Smithsonian Institution, 212
Society of Experimental Tests
  Pilots (SETP), 202, 205
Soni, Pauli, 177
South America, 23, 24–26, 70
Soviet Union, 159
Spain, 32, 44, 48, 172
Spandau prison, 205
Spanish Civil War, 44
Späte, Wolfgang, 15, 44, 49,
  70, 71, 88, 90, 91, 94,
  100, 171
Spatz glider, 186
Speer, Albert, 121
Sperber, 38–39
Sperber Junior, 48–49
*Spiegel, der*, 224
SS, 95, 124, 157, 237, 239,
  240, 248, 249, 251
Staaken, 16, 42, 56
Stahlhelm, 213, 214
Stahlhelm Youth, 213, 214
Stalingrad, 97, 98
*Stars and Stripes*, 110, 151,
  171
Steltzer, Georg, 176, 178, 192,
  193, 197

Stendal, 73
Stettin, 29, 30, 95
Stockholm, 113, 115
Storck, Rudi, 155
Striedeck, Karl & Susanne, 218–19
Stuka, 37, 53, 57, 115
Stumpfegger, Dr, 124, 127, 228, 239
*Süddeutsche Zeitung*, 224
Sudetenland, 66, 67, 72
suicide
  attacks, 97
  councils, in bunker, 130, 247–48
  mission, 97, 104–107, 111, 112, 113, 144, 147
  pledge, 106
  possibility of, 222–23
  of father, 137
  of Hitler, Eva Braun, Joseph and Magda Goebbels, 132
  of Udet, 86, 87
  of von Greim, 137–39, 254
  squadron, 143
Syria, 195
swastika, 32, 50, 57, 182
Sweden, 31, 41, 114, 115, 232, 248
Switzerland, 32, 42, 48

Taj Mahal, 178
Takoradi, 195
Tank, Kurt, 134
Taunus, 168, 173, 181
television
  BBC, 210
  German, 71
Tempelhof, 28, 42
test flights
  bed or ropes, 80
  cable cutting, 82–83, 90
  catapault launching devices, 35

DFS 230, 73, 75, 76
dive brakes, 37–39, 46, 53
Gigant, 77–79
helicopter, 55–56
Kranich, 33
pilotless flying petrol tanker, 80
manned flying bomb, *see* V1
Me 163, 89–91, 98, 100
  at Rechlin, 53, 88
See Adler, 34–35
troop-carrying glider, *see* DFS 230
V1, 97, 104, 106–11
Teutloff, Irene, 224
thermal flight, 17, 25, 70
Third Reich, 1, 39, 41, 161, 166, 213, 217, 242, 254
Tichy, Herbert, 172
Timmersdorf, 211
torpedo, 106
Traunkirchen, 143
Transport Museum, 226
Treblinka, 103
Trevor-Roper, Hugh, 146, 160, 165, 192, 203, 207, 256–57
Troika-Schlepp, 77
troop-carrying glider, 73, 75–76, 77
Tucker, James, 7
Tudhope, Lex, 210
Tyrol, 7, 8, 21

Udet, Ernst, 39, 40, 42, 43, 51, 52, 53, 54, 57–58, 64, 73, 78, 83, 86, 87, 95, 100, 144, 147
UFA, 23
Ursinus, Oskar, 22
USA, visits to, 64, 181, 202, 212, 218–19
  Forces, European Theatre (USFET), 154, 156, 158

USA, visits to (*cont.*)
  Air Force Intelligence, 145
  USAF Technical Intelligence,
    145
  government, 140
  government mission, 157
  National Archives, 233

V1, flying bomb, 90, 102, 106,
    111
  manned flying bomb, Fi 103,
    97, 104, 106–11, 141,
    147
V2, 90, 147
van Husen, Pit, 13
Velbert, gliding club of, 183
Versailles, Treaty of, 4, 10,
    13, 32, 41
Vietnam, peace mission to,
    196
Villa Glanzenbichl, 143, 145
Volkmar, Father Friedel,
    162–63, 168, 169, 194,
    206, 207, 208, 215
Volkswagen, 57, 166, 171,
    187
von Below, Nicolaus, 105,
    122, 126, 130, 131, 232,
    250
von Berg, Edelgard, 94
von Braun, Wernher, 14, 134,
    147, 181, 182
von Cochenhausen, General,
    69
von Cochenhausen, Käthe,
    94
von Gronau, Wolfgang, 35
von Greim, Ritter, 39, 73, 76,
    83, 87, 100–103, 119–35,
    137–39, 142, 147, 149,
    156, 162, 207, 222–23,
    228–32, 234–42
von Krosigk, Schwerin, 148,
    161, 204

von Oven, Wilfred, 224
von Unruh, Friedrich Franz,
    225
Voss, Admiral, 239

Wagner, Winifred, 202
Walter, Anna, 168, 208, 209,
    221, 222, 226
Warmbrunn, 117
Washington, 212, 233
Wasserkuppe, 22, 31, 43, 44,
    50, 170, 171, 201
Wehrmacht, 231
Weinholtz, Fred, 210, 211
*Welt, die,* 204
Wenck, General, 127, 231,
    232, 238, 245, 248,
    249, 250, 252
West Germany
  Aero Club, *see* Aero Club
  embassy, 173, 177; *see also*
    Embassy
  foreign office, 184
  gliding clubs, 183
  government, 184, 197, 222
West Germany, 172, 173, 174,
    175, 176, 186
Westphalia, 172
Whirly Girls, 181, 225
Wiemann, Matthias, 16,
    165
Wiesbaden, 164
Wieser, Ernst, 189, 190,
    196
Wilhelmstrasse, 232
Winter, Herr, 159
Winter Olympics, 40
Work, Captain Robert, 140–46,
    147, 155, 160, 165, 233
  intelligence summary by,
    quoted, 233–55
World War, First, 1, 4, 7, 13,
    31, 63, 85, 87, 100,
    170, 225

World War, Second, 74–133, 226

yoga, 178, 179, 190, 196
Young Pioneers, 187, 193
Ysenberg, Count, 28
Yugoslavia, 42, 50

*Zeit, die,* 224
Zellam See, 133, 134, 140, 141, 253
Zeppelin, 46
Ziegler, Mano, 100
Zugvogel III glider, 183, 200
Zurich, 51

# A Note About
# The Author

**Judy Lomax** was born in Surrey in 1939 and brought up in Southampton. She has lived in France and Germany, and is an Oxford graduate in Modern Languages. Her interests include German history and politics, and aviation.

Judy Lomax is the author of *Women of the Air* (1986) and *Walking in the Clouds: Impressions of Nepal* (1981).

# 1

IN THE REPUBLIC OF CHINA . . .
DURING THE YEAR OF THE HARE
1963

Mr. Wellington Kee was very proud of his status as one of the senior controllers at Taipei International Airport. He was also pleased with his salary, which was a great deal more than most Chinese were able to capture during these discouraging times when the aging Chiang was still ranting about reconquering mainland China. All thinking people knew this was political nonsense, but they knew better than to say so if they worked for the government.

Mr. Wellington Kee was a small round man with a face like an overripe apple. He was bald and meticulous of manner. His command of English, the international language of aviation, plus a favorable word from a distant relative in the Executive Yuan, accounted for his original hiring by the Civil Aeronautics Administration of the Chinese Republic.

Now on this humid October night Wellington Kee made a loud sucking noise as he sipped at the teacup he had placed beside his microphone. He sucked and watched the occasional spewings against the tower windows of rain which gathered into rivulets and distorted the view beyond. On clearer nights he normally enjoyed a sweeping view from his 110-foot-high perch. Beyond the perimeter and runway lights lay the city of Taipei itself, glittering in the night with promises of easily imaginable delights. At his back there was a considerable area of unlighted shadow, which would be the Keelung River and the hills to the north. Across the river and a considerable distance to the west he could see the pagodalike Grand Hotel, which was built on the side of a hill. Sometimes the hotel appeared to hang from the heavens in more ways than one, for government employees of Wellington Kee's civil status could only speculate upon the extravagant entertainments which must take place within such a splendid building. Only tourists and very great officials could afford to be at ease within its rather complex and expensive environs.

Air traffic had been sparse this night and the lack of activity had brought a nearly overwhelming sense of ennui upon Wellington Kee. There had been one flight earlier in the evening from Hong Kong, one from Guam, and two more within the past hour from Tokyo. Now until the end of his shift only one flight was scheduled. That would be Far Eastern's flight three coming north from Manila and Wellington. Kee could hardly wait for a hand-off from Approach Control once the aircraft had arrived within the control area.

Even as he yawned and stretched his arms as high above his head as he could reach and then stood on tiptoe for as long as his balance held, he heard Approach Control acknowledging flight three's arrival over Taoyuam at eleven thousand feet. That would be over a navigational aid about twenty miles southwest of the airport. As he listened to the flat tones of the squawk box reciting flight three's clearance for descent, Kee continued to stretch and calculated he had approximately five minutes before his part in the routine performance.

Every man of technical status in government service had an assistant and Wellington Kee had two. Now he nodded to the white shirts that marked their location in the gloom of the darkened tower and said in his thick Fukien dialect "Bring up the approach lights and give me a ceiling and visibility estimate. I want you to reach your estimates individually."

While he waited for their judgments, which he expected to find in at least small error (otherwise why was he in charge?), he made a considerable business of tapping the glass face of the altimeter on the console before him and reading the barometric pressure.

He sucked again at his teacup while he listened to the squawk box. He was pleased to compare his own slightly accented English with that of the approach controller, and he judged his own diction definitely superior. He heard the approach controller clear Far Eastern flight three for an automatic direction finder approach to Taipei Airport and he heard the customary advice to call Taipei tower upon passing the outer marker. He listened to the acknowledgments and clearance repetitions transmitted by flight three and decided his own English was better than that of the first officer or the flight engineer, whichever was doing the talking. The captain of course would be an American, as were all Far Eastern's, and his voice would be easily recognizable.

Wellington Kee listened more attentively while flight three reported approaching the outer marker and requested a change to tower frequency. When it was granted he put down his cup and addressed the microphone. He waited patiently. No aircraft would have to wait for a reply from Taipei tower if Kee was on duty.

"Taipei tower. . . . Far Eastern three."

"Roger, Far Eastern three," Wellington Kee said carefully. "Continue approach to runway ten. Wind zero eight zero at ten knots. Altimeter two nine five five. Report approach lights in sight."

Flight three acknowledged the advice and silence once more enwrapped the darkened tower. Kee broke it with a final slurp at his tea. Then his assistants said they were ready with their weather observations—ceiling overcast three thousand with lower scattered clouds one thousand. Light to moderate rain with visibility two to three miles. Kee grunted his approval. Their conclusions were comfortably close to his own.

Kee waited and still there was only silence. He squirmed in his chair and heard it scrape against the cement floor. He watched the anemometer climb to fifteen knots and then subside. It brought a soft yet audible lashing of raindrops against the windows.

Kee noted it was near the end of his shift, and he was momentarily annoyed that his relief had not as yet appeared. Or perhaps he was waiting in the darkness behind him?

He turned to look at the doorway. It was not only securely locked at all times but guarded by a soldier on the outside, as was every other vital facility about the airport. For, Kee reminded himself wistfully, his country was more than technically at war with Mao's communist bandits and apparently would be forever.

Disappointed at the lack of activity in the vicinity of the door, he looked out toward the west, where he now might reasonably expect to find the running lights of Far Eastern three. Had they ignored his request to report the runway approach lights in sight? If so he would consider filing a report against the American captain. Almost at once he decided against such action, since it would involve a great deal of paperwork. There was no other traffic, so the American captain could hardly be accused of creating a dangerous situation.

Once more he studied the windows to the west and saw only rain dribbling across a black sky. He turned to the white shirt on his right. "What time did you record our last transmission?"

"Eight nineteen."

Four minutes had gone by since then. Certainly flight three must have passed the outer marker? Kee cleared his throat and pressed his microphone button.

"Far Eastern three . . . Taipei tower. Have you passed the outer marker?"

Silence. Kee frowned. There was a faint note of annoyance in his voice when he spoke again, "Far Eastern three? Do you have the runway lights in sight? Say your position."

Silence.

"Far Eastern three . . . Taipei tower. If you read me show a light."

Kee decided that the Boeing must have experienced total radio failure. Given all the back-ups and redundancies in a jet airliner's electrical system, it was a situation that simply could not happen.

He pressed the switch on the squawk box and addressed his colleague in Approach Control. "Have you had any contact with Far Eastern's flight three since the hand-off?"

"Negative."

"Thanks. Please check Center and see if they've heard anything."

"Will do."

Wellington Kee was becoming increasingly uneasy. This sort of thing had never happened before. Airliners just didn't vanish in the night—especially on final approach.

"Far Eastern flight three. Do you read Taipei tower on one one eight decimal one?"

He continued calling and searching the sky for four additional minutes. Quite to his surprise he found that his heart was beating with ever-increasing tempo, and the tea he had consumed had transformed itself into a flood of perspiration.

Wellington Kee rose to take a final look into the western darkness and, seeing nothing, leaned down until his wet face was close to the squawk box. He pressed the switch reluctantly.

"Tower here. I think we have a serious problem."

Y. K. Tien enjoyed several blood connections within the government. He had two cousins in the Legislative Yuan, an uncle in Customs, and another uncle in the Ministry of Communications who had been particularly helpful. It was thanks to him that Y. K. Tien had been appointed official photographer to the Ministry, a job not overly demanding and thus well suited to Tien's mild character. He sat for days, sometimes for more than a week without any demand being made for his services, but the possibiity that he might be considered a drone had never troubled him. There were countless people employed within the various government offices who did nothing at all.

Tien was a small man with a potbelly which projected forward and hung down from his waistline like a marsupial pouch. When he was required to perform, he normally photographed the installation of new transformers, downed power lines, new type insulators or telephonic equipment and some-times special circuitry for technical reference and study. His photographs were usually in focus but not much more, since he had little interest in his profession.

Like so many Chinese, Tien was a realist and, recognizing his limitations, was content to enjoy the vicarious thrills he found in the creations of others. Perhaps that is why he was an avid philatelist and longed for a small store of his own where he could deal in beautiful stamps.

There was considerable appreciation of all beautiful things locked in Tien's most inner being, and he was deeply dis-tressed at the ugly task assigned him on an otherwise lovely morning. He had been roused from his slumbers long before dawn and transported by government car to the plateau which rose west of the city. Arriving just as the sun was melting away the mist which lay over a rice paddy, he was directed to photograph everything within range of his lens.

The perimeter of the paddy was lined with peasants who stood and pointed and squatted and spit and groaned and fell silent as they watched the revelations of disaster. Soldiers were everywhere, and it seemed to Tien they interfered more than helped with removal of bodies from the wreckage which rested in the shallow water of the paddy.

At first Tien's task was not too unbearable, although he disliked removing his shoes and rolling up his pants so he could wade through the muck and photograph the aircraft's tail section, which lay some distance from the main wreckage.

The tall tail rose at an angle toward the clear blue sky, and Tien saw how the tip of it glistened in the first of the sun. One of the men probing about its conical base recognized him and insisted he photograph the black box which he held in his muddy hands. Tien learned he was a technician from the Aeronautics Administration, and he said the box was a re-corder which contained the last communications between the aircraft and the ground in addition to whatever orders or comments the crew might have exchanged. They agreed it was a marvelous device, and Tien's mannerisms as he set about photographing the box suggested his own very impor-tant connection with it. Since he assumed all of the crew were dead, it suddenly occurred to him that the image of the black box he saw on the camera's ground glass had an eerie quality. And why not? Within that small receptacle were stored forever the voices of men who would never be heard again. He photographed it first as found, with muddy exterior, and then again after the technician had cleaned it.

Next Tien sloshed across the paddy and photographed the main wreckage from several angles. He was relieved that the firemen and military rescue teams who disappeared and reappeared within the great broken shell of metal did not find anything while his lens was pointed in their direction.

Finally he crossed the paddy to the opposite side, where he photographed a piece of wing and a single engine which had somehow broken away and was buried partway in the surrounding dike. It was here that he was discovered by his supervisor, who told him to come at once to the dike on the opposite side. It was extremely important he declared, and there must be no delay.

Tien suspected the origin of his supervisor's demand and did his best to comply. Holding his camera high lest he splash it with water, he tried to set a fast pace across the paddy. But it was like moving in a dream, so as he approached the dike and saw what he knew he would see, he moved ever more slowly. Even the angry urgings of his supervisor echoing clearly across the water failed to increase his pace.

Tien shut one eye and hid his other behind the camera's viewfinder. He tried to think of the images he observed on the ground glass as remote things, not parts of humans like himself who only a few hours before had various functions to perform. Under the direction of his supervisor he focused on nakedness askew, and ruptured spleens, and smashed heads in want of a body. These things, buzzing with flies, were arranged all along the length of the dike like broken toys on a shelf, and even as he worked Tien saw the rescue teams were bringing more.

By the time he was finished the sun was searing hot, and Tien was trembling so much that in order to avoid a fuzzy negative he was obliged to greatly increase the shutter speed of his camera. His supervisor, whose dedication to the gruesome task seemed to magnify when they were joined by an Army officer, kept fanning the flies away from each object and cautioning Tien repeatedly of the necessity for clarity and detail.

Finally they were done, and as he put away his camera Tien ventured to inquire if anyone had survived the crash.

"Yes. All but one of the crew."

"No others?"

"Yes. But how many I cannot say. They were taken away first to the hospitals."

His chief then said that if Tien was sure he had photographed everything he could go.

Tien turned his back on the scene and half ran to the end of the dike. Once there, he paused in the shade of a group of trees and tried to vomit. But he had not eaten since the evening before and his efforts produced only a dry hacking. Bending over, he stared at the dark blotches his spittle had made upon the ocher earth, and suddenly he wanted nothing more of his life than to hear the birds in the trees above him.

October 15, 1963

CIVIL AERONAUTICS ADMINISTRATION
MINISTRY OF COMMUNICATIONS

ACCIDENT
FAR EASTERN AIRWAYS BOEING 727

*CONFIDENTIAL*

(Translation)

1. Prior to accident aircraft was certified airworthy.
See log, documents, and overhaul data, 1963.

2. Weather analysis: Temperature, atmospheric pressure, and wind velocity at time of crash would dismiss any possibility of violent turbulence or other harmful meteorological phenomena. Thus accident not caused by weather factors.
See pertinent meteorology data October 5-7, 1963.

3. Two hours before and after subject accident a total of five aircraft landed at Taipei International Airport. Thus accident not due to any failure in instrument landing system.

See traffic record, Customs and Immigration forms, October 5, 1963, 1900-2300 hrs.

4. According to voice recordings, normal contacts were maintained between aircraft and Air Traffic Control. No errors were made. Thus accident not due to any fault of ATC personnel.

See pertinent recording tapes #607-42, 607-43, 1900-2300 hrs., October 5, 1963.

5. CONCLUSION: Captain Alexander Malloy, American citizen (Work Permit #87426), was in command of the flight. Captain Malloy did misjudge his approach to the outer marker and ignored available radio navigational aids. His approach to Taipei Airport was much below the required altitude and the aircraft struck the ground approximately 12 miles southwest of the runway. The accident was therefore due to pilot negligence.

DISTRIBUTION:
AACL: MGDR (via President)
SAP
SAFE
AVP
FILE (4)
CB

The apartment on the Ile de la Cité was so old the parquet floors rose and fell as if under the influence of a distant ocean, but the commanding view across the Seine toward the Left Bank made such a residence nearly priceless to those who still valued Old World Charm combined with a chic address.

Each time he flew to Paris and found an excuse to visit his friends, Captain Lew Horn made a secret wager with himself that the fragile *ascenseur* which hoisted him from ground level to the apartment would refuse its duty. Smiling fondly upon its antiquity, he often wondered if his 180 pounds plus suitcase and flight kit would not exceed its gross take-off capability.

He moved with great natural dignity, and yet any suggestion of the pompous was instantly denied by the wry amusement in his eyes. His features were devoid of excess flesh, hard-cut, and reflecting about the set of his mouth a life of special responsibility. His eyebrows, heavy twin hedges flecked with gray, plainly signaled his enjoyment of challenge.

At present Captain Horn was a very unhappy man. A divorce, he had recently discovered, was a far more traumatic experience than he had ever imagined. To his friends Geoff and Dorothy, who owned the apartment, he explained, "This is not one of my regular Paris flights. The line has given me a leave, so if you don't object, I may stay more than a night or two. Barbara and I have decided to part company while we are still friends. I suppose it was my fault because I have been away so much and there were no children to hold us together."

It was typical of Geoff and Dorothy, he thought that they would at first make no further inquiries. Instead they had inaugurated a tour of the Parisian galleries, for they knew that if there was one thing other than flying itself capable of recharging Horn's spirits, it was painting. He could become utterly lost in a good exhibition, and his own skyscapes in oil and watercolor revealed a surprising sensitivity.

"It is something I'm saving for my retirement instead of money," he had told them quietly. "I intend to become a painter, clumsy as my present work may be."

"At least you have twenty years to improve," Geoff had once commented after studying several of his North Atlantic skies.

"How do you know he won't someday hang in the Louvre?" Dorothy had asked.

"Because there isn't a tree in the whole complex big enough for the job. Thank God he doesn't fly like he paints."

These, Horn had decided, were the kind of friends he needed when what had been the good life suddenly spun out of control. Had it been only a week since Brewster had summoned him to the office from which he directed the overseas flight operations of his airline?

Brewster had closed the door, offered a cigar which was refused, and assumed his confidential pilot-to-pilot pose. "Have a good trip?"

"Thunderstorms all around Paris. Once we cleared them,

fine weather all the way. The winds forecast was wrong as usual, so we were ten minutes late.''

"Don't try to snow me. You were lost," Brewster stated with a half smile.

"How did you know?''

"I know innumerable things. They include such information as your taking three of your stewardesses for a midnight swim in the fountain beneath the Eiffel Tower. The gendarmes' report is even more explicit than the photo stories in *Figaro* and the *Paris-Soir.*'' Brewster held up a paper and shook it as if it was contaminated. "Our people in advertising spend hundreds of thousands every year to assure the traveling public our captains are supercautious, square-jawed, eagle-eyed father images. You don't make it any easier for them.''

Horn wanted to say he regretted the incident. It had been a hot and muggy night, the plaza beneath the tower was deserted, and only one of the stewardesses had disrobed completely. He decided to remain silent out of deference to his superior.

Brewster was a man pushing sixty very hard, one of the real old-timers from Douglas DC-2 days when the whole line cheered if all fourteen seats in one airplane were booked. His battered face betrayed every minute of a very hard life aloft as well as on the ground, and his always melancholy eyes seemed perpetually yearning for a return of more exciting times. Horn was convinced that soon he would accept a retirement gift watch from the company and would then, like a very old elephant, just go away to a remote place and die. Watching his tormented eyes that afternoon, Horn realized that he loved the man, as did most of Brewster's captains. He knew no hours, his job was his life, and Horn thought he must be very lonely.

"As if your recent Parisian caper were not enough,'' Brewster intoned, "I am adding to your remarkable file this further report.'' He held up another paper. "It states that on a routine test flight exactly ten days ago you executed a slow roll in the Boeing 727 which this company entrusted to your tender mercies.''

"It was an impulse. I asked the crew if they minded and they said go right ahead. We made sure everything was tied down—''

"Thumbing through your file, I am impressed by what is *not* included. I am personally aware that you have received two speeding tickets within the past few months and that you drove a formula one racing car at Mineola during the June Rally and furthermore won with an average speed of one hundred and thirty-four point five miles per hour. When your victory was announced over the public address system and in the newspapers, you were identified as a captain of this line. I again wonder how the image of a staid, reliable aircraft commander suffered in our customers' eyes."

"Would it have been better if I had come in last?"

Brewster ignored him as he ruffled through additional papers. "You own an aerobatic airplane, and on April tenth last you received a citation from the FAA for performing aerobatics at an illegal altitude in the vicinity of Farmingdale, Long Island. The altitude was stated as fifty feet. Three years ago while you were still flying first officer you were involved in a sordid tavern brawl which resulted in injury to an unidentified man.

"He was drunk and threw a glass of beer in my wife's face. What would you have done?"

Brewster doubled his freckled fists and placed them deliberately on the file before him. "What am I going to do with you, Horn? As a pilot I am willing to concede you have class. You pass your flight checks with grades no one can match. But you're a goddamned maverick and the days for mavericks in this business are long gone. There is no room for your kind in a modern airline. And another thing—" Brewster relaxed his fists and an unusual softness came to his eyes—"it is one of those things so far not in your file."

Horn sensed his discomfort when he said, "I understand you and Barbara are having a problem."

"Is there a married couple that doesn't?"

"You know as well as I do that a man with emotional problems has no business flying a hundred and eighty passengers across the ocean or anywhere else for that matter."

"I keep my ground life and my flying life separated."

"Nonsense. Certain things just won't stay on the ground.

They haunt a man no matter where he is. I don't like it and the company doesn't like it, and because I don't want a hassle with your union I am going to make a mandatory suggestion upon which I expect you to act as the sensible man I wish you were."

The history of man in flight....

# THE BANTAM AIR AND SPACE SERIES

The Bantam Air and Space Series is dedicated to the men and women who brought about this, the era of flight -- the century in which mankind not only learned to soar the skies, but has journeyed out into the blank void of space.

# THE STORY OF AN AMERICAN HERO

☐ YEAGER: An Autobiography  25674-2/$5.95

The story of Chuck Yeager who rose from rural boyhood to become the one man who, more than any other, led America into space.  From his humble West Virginia roots to his adventures as a World War II fighter pilot; from the man who escaped from German-occupied France to the test pilot who first broke the sound barrier: this is the real story of the man with the RIGHT STUFF.

☐ YEAGER:  AN AUTOBIOGRAPHY is now on
  audiocassette!  45012-3/$7.95

This exclusive 60-minute audio adaptation of the bestselling autobiography, YEAGER: AN AUTOBIOGRAPHY, features General Chuck Yeager telling in his own words the amazing story of his life and exploits.

☐ PRESS ON! Further Adventures in the Good Life
  by Chuck Yeager  28216-6/$4.95

PRESS ON! is a remarkable portrait of a remarkable individual—it completely captures Yeager's head-on approach to living the good life. Using extensive examples and stories from all the times of his life, Chuck Yeager makes it clear that he always did—and always will—live the way he wants to.

Look for both these books at your bookstore or use this page to order:

Bantam Books, Dept. YE2, 414 East Golf Road, Des Plaines, IL  60016

Please send me the items I have checked above.  I am enclosing $_____
(please add $2.00 to cover postage and handling).  Send check or money
order, no cash or C.O.D.s please.  (Tape offer good in USA only.)

Mr/Ms _____

Address _____

City/State_____ Zip_____

YE2–11/90

Please allow four to six weeks for deliver
Prices and availability subject to change without notice.

# William L. Shirer

## A Memoir of a Life and the Times Vol. 1 & 2

☐ 34204-5   TWENTIETH CENTURY JOURNEY,
               The Start 1904-1930                    $12.95

☐ 34179-0   THE NIGHTMARE YEARS,
               1930-1940                              $14.95

In Volume 1, Shirer recounts American/European history as seen through his eyes. In Volume 2, he provides an intensely personal vision of the crucible out of which the Nazi monster appeared.

---

# Charles B. MacDonald

☐ 34226-6   A TIME FOR TRUMPETS          $14.95
The untold story of the Battle of the Bulge.